Strategic Management and Core Competencies

Strategic Management and Core Competencies

Theory and Application

Anders Drejer

Q

QUORUM BOOKS
Westport, Connecticut • London

Library of Congress Cataloging-in-Publication Data

Drejer, Anders, 1969–
    Strategic management and core competencies : theory and application /
    Anders Drejer.
       p. cm.
    Includes bibliographical references and index.
    ISBN 1-56720-508-9 (alk. paper)
      1. Strategic planning. 2. Core competencies. I. Title.
    HD30.28 .D735 2002
    658.4′012—dc21   2001058938

British Library Cataloguing in Publication Data is available.

Library of Congress Catalog Card Number: 2001058938
ISBN: 1-56720-508-9

First published in 2002

Quorum Books, 88 Post Road West, Westport, CT 06881
An imprint of Greenwood Publishing Group, Inc.
www.quorumbooks.com

Printed in the United States of America

The paper used in this book complies with the
Permanent Paper Standard issued by the National
Information Standards Organization (Z39.48-1984).

10 9 8 7 6 5 4 3 2 1

To Pia

Contents

Illustrations

TABLES

Preface

A specter is haunting strategic management these days—it is the specter of competencies. This is a book on strategy and competencies, the latter being a relatively new concept that can serve to enlighten and improve theory and application of strategic management. Many firms and managers today are forced to recognize that the way things used to be done is no longer adequate to the external and internal dynamics of organizations of today and tomorrow. Strategic management has always been about matching the internal knowledge and work of the organization to the external challenges posed by its environment, as Peter Drucker pointed out almost 50 years ago (Drucker, 1958). However, today external dynamics are much greater than 50 years ago—at least it seems as if we live in a very turbulent age. Furthermore, internally, new kinds of employees demand new forms of management and work to achieve personal satisfaction from work. So the challenges are there for those of us who research, teach, and/or practice strategic management. Recently the notion of core competencies and competencies has emerged as a means of explaining competitive advantage and its creation much better than we used to.

The basis of this book is that we can use the notion of competencies to explain why some firms are more competitive than other firms with greater precision and relevance than we could before. That, of course, is one great advantage, but it is not quite enough for managers who want to create competitive advantage ahead of their competitors. Luckily, by adding a structural viewpoint to the current body of theory on competencies, we are actually able to help managers in the latter respect. We can, so to speak, open up competencies and see how they are designed. This enables us to propose models and means for how managers can proactively identify, design, and develop core competencies of their firm. This is the main contribution of this book.

The origin of the book lies in my feeling that a book of this kind has not yet been written. Several books call attention to the notion of core competencies and competence-based strategy, Hamel and Prahalad's 1994 book being the seminal example—as well as several books consisting of compilations of articles (usually from conferences) pushing the limits of research on competencies (for example, Sanchez et al., 1996). But a comprehensive overview of the area of competencies and its relationship to strategic management in general *and* a discussion of how managers can practice competence-based strategy has not been written. This book aims at being such a book.

It is important for me that the book is not "merely" a how-to book on competence-based strategy. As important as that may seem—and is!—I find it equally important to discuss and determine the fundamentals of competencies and competence-based strategy. We should not only be interested in the "how to" of competence-based strategy but also in the "why" and "what" of the subject. That is why I have attempted to treat the theoretical background of competencies and competence-based strategy with equal emphasis as the subject of how managers can formulate and implement a competence-based strategy. From this follows another important point—this book draws on the work of many others. Let there be no doubt that I am standing on the shoulders of the giants of the strategy field as well as of the emerging field of competence-based strategy. I find it extremely important to cover the existing body of knowledge and use what is already known. In fact, I find that my own personal contribution mainly lies in the collection and discussion of existing and seminal knowledge and only secondarily lies in a few original ideas about competence-based strategy. Not that this is a problem. We all stand on the shoulders of giants.

In light of the aims of the book, its intended readership includes managers, students, and researchers with an interest in strategy and competencies. All three parties should have an interest in the background of competence-based strategy, the relationship between strategic management and competence-based strategy, and the application of competence-based strategy to praxis, albeit probably with different emphasis. I also hope that all three parties can appreciate the style of this book. After having written quite a few articles and five books, I seem to have developed or found a style that gives the reader several different perspectives and a discussion, but still forces the reader to make up his or her own mind about the subjects at hand. This is not because I am indecisive. Rather I am convinced that every firm and situation in some respect is unique and that the idea of a generally applicable theory of, say, strategic management is a fallacy. Instead what I can do is to offer many perspectives to my readership, perhaps order the perspectives a bit, and leave it to the reader to decide what is applicable in his or her situation. As for the personal style of writing—the use of "I" instead of "the author"—this is not typical for scientific texts. I grant that to those who dislike that part of my "style." However, this book is intended as something other than a scientific text; it is intended to be a text for managers and practitioners who do not need the impersonal style of a scientific text. Furthermore, the personal style, I believe, goes well with the presentation of different arguments and points to the reader, who in turn is inclined to make up his or her own mind about things.

No man is an island—not even a writer. I have relied heavily on the insights of other people who have taken the time and trouble to share their thoughts, questions, experiences, and opinions with me over the past 10 years. This book has benefited greatly from my collaboration with practitioners such as Henning Vestergaard, Tommi Sørensen, Gert Spender-Andersen, Niels Spender-Andersen, Seamus Grannell, Thorkild Stokholm, Andreas Bürger, Peter Busch, Ellen Salomonsen, Frank Stenzhorn, Thorkild Vorm, and many others. As for researchers I am particularly indebted to my mentor Jens Ove Riis, John Johansen, Louis Prinz, David Bennett, Chris Voss, Ron Sanchez, Dominique Jolly, Steen Hildebrandt, Lars Mathiassen, Harry Boer, Mogens Myrup Andreasen, and Camilla de Witt. I have learned a great deal from the students at our Master's in Management of Technology program at Aalborg University over the years; they have sharpened the discussion and theories. And finally I am, as always, grateful to have a wonderful wife in Pia, the most important person in my life, who incidentally wishes to disassociate herself from the linguistic errors and weirdness of the book. This reminds me to note that as much as I am grateful for the help of the many people mentioned here, the responsibility for interpreting their help as well as all other responsibility is mine and mine alone.

Introduction

Organizations change and organizations compete for the same resources, competencies, and customers. These are the cruel realities of management that cannot be neglected. This also means that the notion of strategy and strategic management cannot be neglected as an integral part of what managers do. Strategy is about affecting the overall activities of an organization in ways to make the organization a winner. Strategy is about survival in fierce competition, and this book is about strategy.

In this section, I investigate the notion of strategy and strategic management. I also discuss some of the challenges, whether internal or external to the organization, that push the limits of strategy. Finally, I define the key concepts for this book and describe the rest of the book for the reader.

STRATEGY AND STRATEGIC DECISIONS

What does strategy mean? This is a difficult question to answer, as the notion of strategy is used in so many contexts these days that strategy seems to mean everything. When this happens, I for one always wonder whether strategy then means anything at all. Taking a quick look at the applications of the word *strategy* reveals that it has become one of those words that has even made it into our everyday language. Today, people can claim to have a strategy for getting a job or a date! More seriously, strategy can apply to the firm as a whole (corporate strategy), to parts of the firm (as in R&D strategy), and even to specific, cross-functional or not, activities within the firm (e.g., quality strategy,

Computer Integrated Manufacturing (CIM) strategy, and so on). In other words, strategy no longer has one area of application and means so many things that its concrete meaning has become blurred. There are so many different concepts at play in the strategy world today that one must wonder how all these concepts are related to each other and what they mean. I will attempt to provide some answers in this chapter of the book.

Strategy—A Seminal Definition

In his 1970 book, Russel L. Ackoff discusses the characteristics of strategy. He describes three characteristics that define the concept of strategy:

- Strategy deals with concerns that are central to the livelihood and survival of the entire corporation and usually involve a large portion of the organization's resources.
- Strategy represents new activities or areas of concern and typically addresses issues that are unusual for the organization rather than issues that lend themselves to routine decision making.
- Strategy has repercussions for the way other, lower-level decisions in the organization are made.

Even though these characteristics certainly may be open for interpretation, there is almost universal agreement on them in the strategy literature to this day. For instance, Robert Grant defines almost similar characteristics of strategy in his 1995 book.

This is not to say that there is universal agreement on the process and content of strategic management. With minor outbursts in earlier times, the 1980s saw growing differences of opinion between different authors regarding strategy. We shall focus on two debates: one related to the process of strategy and the other to the content of strategy.

The Process and Content of Strategic Management

Strategic management has a content and a process side to it. Content is about the issues that are dealt with by those who are responsible for strategy, whereas process is about how decisions are arrived at.

The Process of Strategy: From Planning to Crafting
Two people, H. Igor Ansoff and Henry Mintzberg, have been at the center of the debate on the process of strategy, mainly because their debate has become personal and fierce. Let us take a look at their discussion.

In the 1960s and before, matters were relatively simple. Strategy was synonymous with strategic planning based on the SWOT notion. In other words, strategy was a plan to link opportunities and threats with strengths and weaknesses (see Andrews, 1971). As we shall see in Chapter 2, Ansoff was one of many to contribute to this understanding (Ansoff, 1965) with his work on strategic analysis of external and internal factors relevant to strategy. In the words of Mintzberg: ". . . So-called strategic planning arrived on the scene in the mid-1960s with a vengeance, boosted by the popularity of Igor Ansoff's book *Corporate Strategy* . . ." (Mintzberg, 1994, p. 12). Even though there were many others to contribute to the strategic planning notion, Mintzberg is right in his basic point: In the 1960s, strategy became a popular concept among researchers and managers, and Ansoff was one of those to make that happen.

Throughout the 1980s and 1990s, however, Henry Mintzberg and others became the devil's advocate in strategy theory, claiming that the planning notion is theoretically unsound; that is, human beings are not capable of understanding, analyzing, or comprehending the complex task of strategic decisions. Hence, strategies should be formulated as intuitive, synthesis processes. Again in the words of Mintzberg: ". . . Strategic planning, as it has been practiced, has really been strategic programming, the articulation and elaboration of strategies, or visions, that already exist. When companies understand the difference between planning and strategic thinking, they can go back to what the strategy-making process should be: capturing what the manager learns from all sources . . . and then synthesizing that learning into a vision of the direction that the business should pursue . . ." (Mintzberg, 1994, p. 107).

Very little has been said about what the content of strategic decisions is supposed to be; focus is mainly on *how* strategic decisions should be made. Nonetheless, Mintzberg's argument is that planners should not create strategies—that is the task of the entrepreneurial manager—but planners can supply data, help managers to think strategically, and later program their visions into plans. By arguing so, Mintzberg is in line with authors such as C. West Churchman and Peter Checkland, who on a more general level divide (managerial) problems into "open" and "closed" problems (Churchman, 1968; Checkland, 1981). The latter type of problems can be solved by quantitative, analytical means, mainly because the problem itself can be expressed before the problem-solving effort, criteria can be formulated (in quantitative terms), solutions can be found and evaluated (in quantitative terms), and the "optimal" solution can be chosen. The former kind, "open" problems, have the opposite characteristics; that is, the problem itself must be part of the problem-solving efforts, criteria may change throughout the process, and no optimal solution can be found. Remembering the characteristics of strategic decisions outlined previously, it is not surprising that Mintzberg sees strategic decisions as such.

What are the counterarguments? For one, Ansoff has made quite a few arguments in favor of strategic planning both in 1990 and in 1991. It appears that Ansoff's arguments, apart from those rather personally insulting Mintzberg, fall in two categories: (1) Mintzberg's arguments are not logical and factually wrong and (2) the practice of strategic planning has led to much more elaborate versions of strategic planning than proposed in the 1960s. The former argument is based on the fact that in his 1980 articles, Mintzberg built his arguments on the work of just one author (in one article it is Kenneth Andrews) and hence fails to "prove" much. From a logical standpoint, this may be true even though Mintzberg's 1994 book takes into account quite a few of the authors related to the strategic planning school. Still, this argument fails to consider the content of Mintzberg's work.

This leads us to the second counterargument. In Ansoff's work, as well as in that of many others, planning has been developed into a highly complex art compared to the normative proposals of the 1960s (Ansoff & McDonnel, 1990) or others. In Ansoff's own words: ". . . In practical reality, making strategic planning flexible has been a central theme in the transmutation of strategic planning into its present variety . . ." (Ansoff, 1991, p. 31). As we shall see, this is basically true, and hence it seems to be rather unfair to attack the work of the 1960s for not having developed. However, most authors contributing with new work on strategic planning still have the same basic assumptions, most notably about whether planning strategies is possible, as did Ansoff and others in the 1960s. In other words, most new approaches have failed to question their own basic assumptions, a natural consequence of being firmly within one perception or paradigm of strategy; however, this does very little to convince Mintzberg and others who share different assumptions regarding the strategy process.

The Content of Strategic Management: From Product-market Strategy to Competencies

As with the process of strategic management, there are different viewpoints regarding the content of strategic management. I have chosen to focus on two viewpoints: product-market and competence.

The dominant line of research is that of product-market focused strategic management, most prominently represented by Michael Porter, who concentrates on maintaining market positions within a given industry. According to Porter, competition within an industry can be described by means of five forces—the famous five-forces model—and the individual firm is seen essentially as a black box. Consequently, competitive advantage stems from building entry barriers to the firm's market-segment, and sustainability is secured by managing a balanced portfolio of product/market segments. This view is the *product-market view,* so called because managing products and markets is "business" to most people.

Over the years it has become evident that the competitive power of the products in the marketplace is not synonymous with sustainable competitive advantage. Michael Porter himself has admitted this (Porter, 1991). Furthermore, in practice it may be difficult to "translate" the selection of a selected product/market strategy into organizational action. This has led a number of recent authors to propose another view of the corporation: the competence view (Prahalad & Hamel, 1990; Prahalad, 1993; Grant, 1991). Within this view the level of analysis is taken to be the company, and differences in competitive power is explained in terms of company-specific core competencies. Aaker summarizes the arguments of this line of thought:

> . . . competing the right way in the right arena can be extremely profitable, but only for a limited time. The . . . [core competencies] of the corporation, which are the basis of competition, provide the foundation of a sustainable competitive advantage . . . and long term performance. Unless there is an advantage over competitors that is not easily duplicated or countered, long term performance is likely to be elusive . . . (Aaker, 1989, p. 91).

Strategy theory based on core competencies—or technology, since these two words are not clearly defined as mutually exclusive conceptions— has become an alternative approach to strategy making. For obvious reasons, this approach has been called *the competence view* of strategy theory.

The two alternative approaches to strategic management cannot deal with the entire task of strategy alone. Aaker's argument regarding the profitability of competing the right way in the right arena can be reversed. You may have world-class competencies in may areas, but if this does not correspond to what the customers want or is offered to the wrong customers, long-term performance is, indeed, likely to be elusive. For instance, what competencies contribute to a given product line and what are the demands for competence development resulting from expanding this product line? On the other hand, which possibilities result from the development of a new core competence (e.g., high-speed manufacturing)? These questions illustrate that while product-market strategy cannot explain sustainable competitive advantage, competence development does not automatically lead to the creation of business. Thus there is a need for an integration of the two approaches to strategic management to secure sustainable competitive advantage.

The Role of Strategic Management

In light of the discussion so far, I feel that it is fair to assert that the role of strategic management is to make sure that the organization at all times is in line with the demands of its environment. We could say that strategic management is about *balancing the customer and the competencies of the organization,* and there is, indeed, some truth in that. The customers make up one of the main stakeholders in any organization and providing value to the customers certainly should be a guiding principle in any organization's work with its competencies. However, strategic management is far from that simple. As illustrated in Figure I-1, the environment is much more complex than just the customers of the organization. There are many other stakeholders in an organization. There are the shareholders—owners—of the organization, legislative bodies, financial institutions, suppliers, competitors, and many others. Thus, there are many different interests to fulfill in a complex interplay between many stakeholders and their political power over the organization.

What we can say, then, is that *the role of strategic management is to link the organization to its environment and make the proper adjustments to the organization.* This is, in fact, even more complex than "just" dealing with the many different external stakeholders of the organization. There are other important forces at play in the environment of an organization. Demographics, legislation, financial climate, and technological changes are major forces for any organization and too often forces that the organization can do little more about than adapt to them. These forces are on the left in the figure to indicate that they push the strategic management of a firm, whereas customers and other stakeholders (on the right) pull the strategic management of the firm.

What is it, then, that is to be adjusted as a result of these external forces pushing and pulling the organization? I would say that it is the competencies of the organization that need to be adjusted. Thus, when

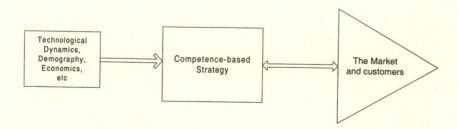

Figure I-1. The role of strategic management.

the formal structure of an organization is adjusted or new technology is implemented, this is a means for improving the competencies of the firm rather than an end in itself. We all know that technologies are nothing but means to justify certain ends and, as we shall see, the notion of a competence is an excellent means for discussing what those ends are. Competencies are, as we will discuss in great detail in Chapter 3, systems of people, technology, organizational structure, and culture that together work to create value for the customers and other stakeholders of the organization. Furthermore, each individual competence rarely functions in a vacuum; the competencies of the firm work together in yet another systemic relationship so that the changes in one competence will most likely affect the other competencies as well. This makes the internal adjustment part of strategic management no less complex than the external handling of stakeholders. This, in turn, calls for specific attention to the former, in the form of a competence-based strategy, and serves as a justification for this book.

In summary, the role of strategic management is to serve as a link between the forces of the organization's environment and its internal system of competencies and to achieve a balance between the two.

A NEW COMPETITIVE LANDSCAPE

Now that we have some feeling about the role of strategic management as well as its content and process, it is useful to take a look at some of the developments in the general business landscape that seriously challenge the way we have come to see strategic management in the 1980s and 1990s.

External Pressure: Innovate or Die!

Many authors seem to agree that the external dynamics of industrial firms has increased over the last decade or so. Some speak of increased competition and the need for more market-focused organizations, whereas others discuss technological pressures on firms. Regarding the former idea, it seems to have become accepted that whereas firms in the 1960s and before could rely on stable (expanding) market conditions and customer-emphasis on price alone, markets today are less than stable and emphasis is on price, quality, delivery, innovation, and so on (Womack et al., 1992; Ansoff & McDonell, 1990). Ansoff writes: ". . . From the mid-1950s accelerating and cumulating events began to change the boundaries, the structure, and the dynamics of the business environment. Firms were increasingly confronted with novel and unexpected challenges which were so far reaching that Peter Drucker called the new era an 'age of discontinuity' . . ." (p. 5). Hammer and

Champy, in their 1993 book on Business Process Reengineering (BPR), write of a crisis that will not go away: "... In short, in place of the expanding mass markets of the 1950s, 1960s, and 1970s, companies today have customers ... who know what they want, what they want to pay for, and how to get it on the terms they demand..." (p. 21). Furthermore, others place emphasis on the increased global competition from first Japanese firms, later Korean, and other so-called Tiger economies, and their possible replacements in China and in Eastern Europe (Quinn, 1992; Kiernan, 1995).

In general, there seems to be agreement that an entirely new competitive situation has arisen. This is nicely summarized by D'Aveni under the concept of "hyper competition" (1994). According to D'Aveni, hyper competition is a competitive situation where the key competitive success factor is the ability to constantly develop new products, processes, or services that provide the customer with increased functionality and performance. In a hyper competitive environment, firms cannot count on a sustainable competitive advantage, but must continuously develop themselves in new directions.

Furthermore, there are also increased technological pressures on firms. It has become accepted that technological life cycles in some industries seem to be decreasing (Dussage et al., 1991; Foster, 1986), thereby putting pressure on firms to constantly innovate (Kiernan, 1995). Much of this thinking stems from the electronics industry; for instance, the new generation of SEGA video games that your six-year-old plays with contains as much computing power as the Cray super-computers of the mid-70s (Kiernan, 1995). Even though this situation does not have to be equally dynamic in other industries (indeed, some questions have been raised concerning that issue) (Bayus, 1994), it seems as if the belief in the technology dynamics creed is so strong that firms simply follow that creed, thereby inflicting the dynamics on themselves unnecessarily (Noori, 1990). Either way, many authors agree on the need for firms to move technology up on the corporate agenda (Clark, 1989) and make it a strategic issue (Bhalla, 1987; Betz, 1989; Drejer, 1996a).

These trends, of course, cannot be kept separate. New technologies have a strong competitive impact in general (Tushman & Anderson, 1986), and hence the technological dynamics also influence the competitive dynamics of firms. Bettis and Hitt writes on this issue that: "... technology is rapidly altering the nature of competition in the late twentieth century..." (Bettis & Hitt, 1995) and, in fact, guest-edit an issue of the *Strategic Management Journal* entirely devoted to discussing how technology will change the nature of competition and strategy in the future. Bettis and Hitt refer to the situation as "the new competitive landscape." This new competitive landscape is responsible for a trend in management theory that creates the need for theory-building on the selection and evaluation of subsuppliers, and the establishment of proper integrative measures to work with suppliers along a firm's value chain.

In summary, seems fair to say that the pressure for innovation and reinventing the firm is greater than ever. The corresponding need for strategic changes and organizational adjustment challenges several established notions of strategic management, not the least of which is the idea of rational planning and implementation.

Internal Challenges

These days the traditional ways to organize and work in industrial firms seem to become rapidly obsolete. First and foremost, there is a lot of talk these days about "the new economy," an economy where tangible, technological assets are no longer the primary foundation for competition and/or building a firm. In recent years the notion of intellectual capital has begun to rise in management circles, both among researchers of management and practitioners of it. A stream of articles, conferences, seminars, and lately books (Stewart, 1997; Edvinson & Malone, 1997; Kaplan & Norton, 1996) show that "intellectual capital" is an alternative way of viewing the assets and value creation of the firm.

This coincides with the emergence of "knowledge intensive firms", that is, firms that base their activities, products/services, and value on knowledge of their employees and external partners. Charles Handy quotes a McKinsey report concluding that in 2000, 70% of all jobs will be knowledge-based rather than based on manual labor (Handy, 1995); 50 years ago the situation was the oppposite.

Furthermore, new (information) technologies are arising every day that make possible entirely new ways of working and organizing. For instance, Savage (1990) spoke of the possibility of "Fifth Generation Organization" based on ideas of networking, virtuality, and so on. Using the same ideas, Martin (1996) discussed the notion of "cybercorp" as an entirely new way of managing and organizing firms. This seems to be a kind of organization where traditional boundaries of time, space, and communication no longer exist because of information and communication technologies. This, in turn, challenges traditional ideas of leadership and management, again in a much more dynamic way. It also emphasizes the role of the employees of the organization.

Regarding the latter, it also seems that a new breed of corporate people are coming to the work market these days. In most Western countries, at least, a small percentage of youngsters born in the 1970s, being brought up with a lot of information technology and family support, now find their way into work. These youngsters cannot be

managed in the same manner as we have been used to. David
Coupland's book about the first wave of these people—Generation
X—challenges many of the ideas we have about people in organizations
(Coupland, 1995). Several books with the overall theme "how to manage people from generation X" have since emerged, emphasizing the
challenges to managers and strategic management. Furthermore, new
generations of people are on their way. I have the feeling that Generation Disney will be no less difficult to manage by traditional means than
is Generation X.

These trends and many others point toward the idea that organizations need to address a lot of managerial issues in new ways. This means
that strategic management needs to consider the people of the organization much more than ever before. Not only do workers of today hold
much of the critical knowledge of the organization and play a crucial
role in developing the competencies, they are also looking for identity
and a sense of mission in their work and life. I believe that a competence-based strategy is one of the important means for giving employees that difficult sense of mission and personal satisfaction.

THE BASIC CONCEPTS OF THE BOOK

In light of the challenges outlined as well as the more general context
of the development of the strategy concept over the past 20 years, I
conclude that the notion of strategy needs to evolve even further than
it has so far. New organizational forms, pressure from new kinds of
employees, fierce competition, and discontinuous technological
changes are just some of the forces that are pushing strategy to evolve.
Hence, it is relevant to define the basic concepts of strategy before
embarking on the journey of this book.

A New Definition of Competition to Account for the
Competitive Landscape

In general, the new competitive situation has important ramifications
on how firms operate and are managed, as the many *different* fads on
management theory all offered with a rationalization in competition
show (Shapiro, 1996). In the new competitive situation as discussed
previously, there seems to be near universal agreement among theorists
that the focus on product-market competition (as advocated by Michael
Porter and others in the 1980s (Porter, 1980, 1985)) no longer suffices
(Barney, 1991; Grant, 1991; Kiernan, 1995). Product-market competition
needs to be supplemented with other forms of competition (Drejer,
1996a) with different time horizons and characteristics in order to cope
with the hypercompetitive dynamics of the new competitive landscape

(Hamel & Prahalad, 1994). What are those "other forms of competition"? Hamel & Prahalad (1994) have been among the few to discuss this explicitly in some detail. They propose that competition has three sides to it: product-market competition, competition to foreshorten migration paths, and competition on industry leadership (Hamel & Prahalad, 1994). The two "new" kinds of competition are:

- *Competition for industry foresight and intellectual leadership.* This is competition to gain a deeper understanding than others on the factors (be they technology, demography, lifestyle, or others) that could be used to transform current product-market competition by, for instance, creating new opportunities, new products, or new ways of viewing customer needs. This kind of competition has a long time horizon compared with the others.
- *Competition to foreshorten migration paths.* In between the battle for intellectual leadership and the battle for market share is competition to influence the direction of industry development, that is, a race to accumulate the necessary competencies, to test and prove out alternate product and service concepts, to attract coalition partners with critical complementary resources, and many other things. This kind of competition has a middle time horizon compared with the others, leaving product-market strategy as the competition with the lowest time horizon.

In short, the work of Hamel and Prahalad offers an expanded view of competition, where the well-known product-market competition is supplemented with two other forms of competition with longer time horizons and different contents.

Besides offering a more elaborate view of competition as a concept, the message of this way of thinking is that in a dynamic competitive situation continuous innovation must be achieved by an ability to exploit core competencies, technologies, and knowledge to a wide-ranging number of purposes to continually create and recreate competitive advantage. In other words, for firms competing in a hypercompetitive environment, competitive advantage must be based on what has been termed *technological platforms* (Kim & Kogut, 1996) or *core competencies* (Prahalad & Hamel, 1990).

Defining Strategic Management

In light of this definition of competition, what is strategic management? This section provides some answers. I define strategic management by means of its role, the characteristics of successful strategies, the process of strategic management, and the issues of strategic management.

The Role of Strategic Management

Strategic management is concerned with the overall direction of the firm and with those issues that require a substantial proportion of the organization's resources to deal with and play themselves out over a long time. Strategic management is also about ensuring the success and survival of the organization by adapting the organization to changes in its environment and making sure that the organization is competitive. Therefore, we can say that strategy is the link between the organization and its environment and that the task of strategic management is to determine how the organization should deploy its resources in the environment and adapt the organization to satisfy the long-term objectives of the firm.

It is important to note that strategic management deals with several time spans. The organization needs to be more than just competitive here-and-now. The competition for industry leadership is just as crucial to firms as is the competition for developing the right competencies in the right time. Thus, strategic management is also about integrating time horizons and activities related to all three kinds of competition. This often means finding those issues that should be kept invariant for the time being and adjusting other activities and issues accordingly. For instance, a company could choose to maintain its current customer base and then develop new products and competencies to account for changes in the demands of the customers. Alternatively, the firm could choose to stick to its current product portfolio and find new markets and customers for that portfolio.

As opposed to strategic management, operational management is about the short-term operation of the activities in the organization within the context of strategic management. In operational management, strategic decisions are executed and short-term results created, but this happens within the confinements of the current strategy of the firm. This also implies that strategic management plays an innovative role in firms. Innovation, in short, breaks with the assumptions of how things are currently done and, hence, always points toward the reformulation of the strategies of a firm. Therefore, strategic management is also about innovation.

In summary, strategic management's role is:

- To guide the organization in the long term.
- To provide context for the operational management and daily activities of the firm.
- To balance the three forms of competition by choosing what is to be kept invariant.
- To secure innovation in the activities, markets, products, or competencies of the firm.

Characteristics of Successful Strategies

In light of the discussions in this chapter, it is possible to formulate the following set of characteristics of successful strategies:

- A clear understanding of the external environment and the competitive situation that the firm faces
- Appreciation of the organization's internal strengths and weaknesses
- Involvement of key stakeholders to secure effective implementation
- Consistency with the values and goals of the organization

Please note that two of the characteristics are content directed, whereas the other two are process directed. The discussion of content and process in strategic management cannot be separated, nor can one side of the discussion be selected in favor of the other.

I will return to the content side of the discussion many times throughout this book. Let me devote some time now to the process side of the discussion. In formulating strategies, I assume that the main responsibility of a firm is to secure its success and survival by being profitable. At the same time, however, every company possesses broader organizational values and goals—the culture of the organization—that are crucial to the organization's sense of purpose and identity. These values and goals are determining for the way activities are done in the firm and for many kinds of decisions, including strategic ones, sometimes to a larger extent than the fundamental requirement of profitability. Therefore, strategic management needs to take into account and even support and strengthen the values and goals of the organization without sacrificing the long-term objective of being profitable and competitive. An important role of a mission statement, as a part of the strategic management of the firm, is to articulate the linkage between the underlying values of the firm and its current strategic decisions.

The main reason why a sense of mission is important in strategic management is that some employees—some even say most employees—are motivated more by the pursuit of meaning in their lives than by just material rewards and profitability. Hence, those organizations that can install a sense of purpose within their employees will prevail over those firms that cannot do so. This seems especially relevant in the future as employees belonging to Generation X or the Disney Generation will constitute the bulk of the members of our organizations. Therefore, employee involvement and mission management are paramount to developing successful strategies now and in the future.

The Process of Strategic Management

The discussion of the process of strategic management will be an underlying theme of this book. Therefore, let me conclude by describing how I believe strategic decisions should be arrived at.

The scope of strategic management is inherently greater than that of operational management. With long time spans and complex organizational-environmental links, it is often impossible to determine the causes of a particular success or failure. Hence, it is difficult, if not impossible, to learn or foresee whether a certain strategic decision is good or bad for the firm. Furthermore, strategic management is concerned with nonroutine issues and innovation at the organizational level; thus, strategic management is complex and ambiguous.

As already mentioned, complex and ambiguous problems require different approaches than simple and straightforward ones. In other words, managers who are used to managing day-to-day operations and solving the problems there may find it a challenge to be part of strategic management. A typical symptom is that of educational projection: accountants tend to view all problems in financial terms, marketing people in sales terms, and so on. Strategic management, in constrast, is the whole of all these areas; it is a holistic problem that requires a holistic approach to decision making.

For one thing this approach implies that strategic analysis, choice, and implementation cannot be kept separate. In the real world of strategic management, implementation begins at the moment it is decided to undertake a strategic analysis; and activities such as analysis, choice, and implementation are concurrent and feed off each other. Another way of saying this is that strategic management is closely related to the notion of organizational change (rather than the old-fashioned term *implementation*). In line with the latest developments within the field of organizational change, the change process is seen as a combination of dealing with the political realities of the organization at the microlevel and of analyzing and designing factual models and theories (see Kotter, 1997 for an excellent example of this kind of thinking).

This idea of the process of strategic management underlies the rest of this book, especially in Chapter 2, when I discuss competence-based strategy.

Issues of Strategic Management

In synthesis of discussions so far, strategic management may be viewed from three perspectives:

- Product-market strategy
- Competence-based strategy

- Integration of the first two by means of the mission and vision of the firm

The product-market strategy perspective views the firm as a collection of product/market combinations (i.e., a portfolio). This view sees strategy as a matter of positioning the firm in its environment, either by selecting the optimal mix of product/market combinations or by positioning in relation to stakeholders.

Instead of viewing the firm as a collection of product/markets, it is also possible/feasible to view an organization as a collection of resources or competencies. This view starts in opposite perspective from that of the traditional product-market. It assumes that a firm cannot be defined by the changing nature of its products and/or markets, but rather by its core competencies, which may be less likely to change in the long run. The rationale, then, is to generate competitive advantage by means of internal factors (i.e., technologies or core competencies). As I will argue in the next chapter, *core competencies* may be a more appropriate term for describing what generates competitive advantage for a firm.

These two views appear to be a duality. On the one hand, they appear to be rather incompatible, but on the other hand, they are still two sides to the same coin: the organization that must survive and prosper. This corresponds to the third view, which is a holistic view in the sense that it sees both product-markets and core competencies and attempts to integrate them for the benefit of the firm.

The considerations so far make it possible to propose a division of strategic management into three subdecision areas: product-market strategy, competence-based strategy, and integration of the other two decision areas.

In my experience, a set of issues that management needs to deal with in arriving at, say, a product-market strategy is a good way of communicating what strategic management is about.

Issues of Product-market Strategy

Product-market strategy deals with competition on the product/market level. Important references on the questions related to business strategy include the following: Ansoff (1965, 1990), Andrews (1971), Porter (1980, 1985), and Hofer and Schendel (1978). Important issues raised by these publications are:

- What needs does the firm attempt to fulfill with its products?
- How can these needs be met in terms of product functionalities?
- Which products should the firm produce?
- On which markets should the firm sell its products?

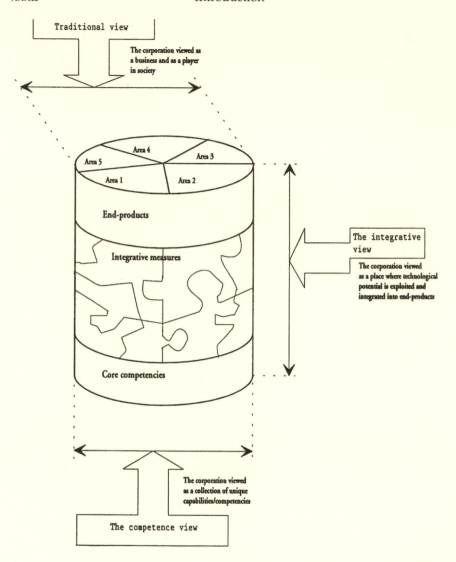

Figure I-2. Three different views of a firm and its strategy.

- How should the company compete with its products: on low cost, on differentiation from other products, or on focusing on a few customers and their needs?
- How can the company ensure that cash generated from older, mature products get reinvested in newer and cash-demanding products to maintain a steady income for the company?

- What kinds of new products and/or markets can the company diversify into without moving away from its mission?

Please note that this definition of product-market strategy also includes issues that in some of the strategy literature is attributed to "corporate strategy" and "competitive strategy." To avoid too much confusion, I have chosen to label these *product-market strategy* as a unifying concept.

Issues of Competence-based Strategy

Competence-based strategy deals with competition at competence level. Important issues include:

- Which core competencies are needed to fulfil the needs of the customers?
- Which core competencies are needed to produce and sell the current portfolio of products?
- Which core competencies should the company base its competitive strength on (e.g., innovation, service in sales, manufacturing at high speed, high quality)?
- What is needed to maintain the core competencies for the future?
- Which support competencies are needed to produce and sell the products of the company with the current set of core competencies?
- When should core competence areas be abolished to new areas?
- What are the risks/rewards related to the development of new core competencies?

Seminal references on competencies and competence-based strategy include the following: Prahalad and Hamel (1990), Prahalad (1993), Hamel and Prahalad (1994), Hayes and Pisano (1994), Chester (1994), and Eriksen (1993a).

Integrating Product-Market Strategy and Competence-Based Strategy

It is evident that the division of strategic management into two distinct decision areas—product-market strategy and competence-based strategy—should be followed by strong emphasis on their subsequent integration. Hence this third area.

The *Oxford English Dictionary* defines integration as: *the making up of a whole by adding together or combining separate parts or elements; a making of a whole or entire.* The *whole* to be the result of integration is, in this context, strategic management, and the definition seems to correspond to the definition of integration of product-market strategy and competence-based strategy as integration of two separate elements (decision areas). Consequently, it can be said that strategic management will be integrated when product-market strategy decisions and competence-based strategy decisions are joined to a larger whole.

Such an integration can come about in several ways. In some firms, the decisions manifest themselves in a formal plan for product-market strategy and a formal plan for competence-based strategy. In other firms, the decisions are "emergent," that is, not formalized in explicit plans, but still existing. At any rate, integration of product-market strategy and competence-based strategy means formulating or altering one or both in such a manner that decisions are integrated. One important means for doing that is by choosing the invariant elements of the firm's strategy, whether products, markets, customers, competencies or something else, and using that as a yardstick for integrating product-market strategy and competence-based strategy. This is where the mission and vision of the firm also come into play, as apart from giving employees a sense of identity, they essentially serve as the formulation of what is to be kept invariant in the firm's strategic management.

Defining the Basic Elements of Strategic Management

I am now able to formulate the basic elements of strategic management as they will play themselves out in the rest of this book. This will serve as a basic vocabulary for the book as well.

- **Mission of the firm:** The mission of the firm is a formulation of what is held as the most basic and invariant in that particular firm. The mission, therefore, is also close to a formulation of the identity of the firm in question and provides a sense of identity and mission for the employees of the firm.
- **Vision of the firm:** The vision of the firm is a formulation of where the firm wants to be ultimately and what it wants to achieve. A vision is a clear stretch of current achievements and position and challenges the people of the firm to reach further and higher than they would have otherwise. At the same time, the vision is in line with the mission of the firm to avoid corporate schizophrenia.
- **Product-market strategy:** Product-market strategy is the subset of strategic management that deals with competition at the product-market level and is concerned with selecting and marketing the right products at the right markets to give customers what they want.
- **Competence-based strategy:** Competence-based strategy is the subset of strategic management that deals with competition at the competence level and is concerned with identifying, selecting, and

developing the right competencies to support the current and future product-market strategy of the firm.

The Starting Point: Competencies as the Key to Competitive Advantage

The definitions in the preceding section lead us to the last part of this introduction: competencies as the key to competitive advantage. Work on this subject seems to be based on two observations. First, several authors express growing dissatisfaction with the static, equilibrium framework of much of the product-market strategy literature (Wernerfelt, 1984; Barney, 1991). This seems to be a logical stance to take in light of the preceding discussions on the new competitive situation. The second inspirational source of work is the increasingly persuasive case examples of successful organizations, such as 3M, Honda, and Canon, that appear to have developed strategy around their existing and future competencies rather than simply market and competitor analysis (Prahalad & Hamel, 1990; Meyer & Utterback, 1992).

For all practical purposes, "core competencies" seem to be the same concept as "critical capabilities," "resources," and the other possible fads since they all advocate the building of competitive advantage based on "something" internal to the firm. At least, Dorothy Leonard-Barton (1995) claims so and even quotes Gary Hamel as saying the same thing. This also applies to at least some of the perceptions of technology within work on Management of Technology (Drejer, 1996b). For instance, Zeleny's definition of technology as software, hardware, brainware, and technology support-net (including organizational structure, culture, etc.) (Zeleny, 1981) seems to be the same as core competence. Thus, the work discussed in this book stems from several different sources that share emphasis on some intrafirm element to generate competitive advantage. I will adopt the term *core competencies* within this context, but acknowledge that I draw on many (other) sources.

Typically, a core competence is defined in relation to the competitive impact of its output; that is, a core competence provides the firm with (sustainable) competitive advantage via the way it is executed (Prahalad & Hamel, 1990; Grant, 1991) or via its attributes; for example, a core competence is firm-specific and hence difficult to imitate (Barney, 1991; Grant, 1991). However useful these definitions are in terms of competition and strategy, they are not very operational (Leonard-Barton, 1995), creating some serious difficulties in identifying and developing the core competencies of a firm (Drejer & Riis, 2000).

Fortunately, some recent work has moved us toward a more operational perception of core competencies—a supplementary definition of competencies based on their structural characteristics. First, Leonard-Barton (1995) defined a core competence as a system with the elements: physical hardware, knowledge, organization, and culture and proposed that much of the effects of core competencies are generated via the relations between the elements, hence the systemic nature of competencies. I will use this as a starting point for the discussions on competence-based strategy later in this book. For now it is important to know that competitive advantage can be achieved by means of competencies of the firm.

OUTLINE OF THE BOOK

Based on my objective for the book formulated in the preface—to discuss how managers should go about competence-based strategy and to discuss and determine the fundamentals of competencies and competence-based strategy—the reader should not be surprised that the book is in two parts. This first part is dedicated to theory about competence-based strategy (and strategic management in general); the second part is dedicated to the application of those theories. To begin, I include a contextual and conceptual section.

The contextual part consists of Chapters 1 and 2. Chapter 1 will describe how the concept of strategic management has evolved over time and provides the context for the ideas and concepts discussed in this book. Chapter 2 continues this discussion in a modern context and attempts to position competence-based strategy among some of the current management fads that are popular today.

The theoretical part consists of Chapters 3 to 5. Chapter 3 discusses several strands of research that together shaped competence-based strategy. Among those strands are the resource-based view of the firm, capabilities, and technology management. Chapter 4 discusses the work on competence-based strategy, and Chapter 5 moves us from a functional perception of competencies to a structural one. This sets the scene for the last part of the book.

In the last part of the book—the application part—Chapter 6 provides a framework for competence-based strategy that I have formulated and worked on during the last four years. Chapter 7 presents a thorough discussion of the identification and selection of important competencies that is the first part of competence-based strategy. Chapter 8 contains a similar discussion on the subject of developing the competencies of the firm.

1

The History of Strategic Management

No one should grow up without a sense of history. History contains many clues to why things are the way they are today. This chapter is concerned with the history of strategic management as a theoretical and practical discipline and is an important prelude to the contents of this book.

SCHOOLS OF THOUGHT ABOUT STRATEGY

There is a rule of thumb from psychology that a person can think about seven-plus-minus-two things at any one given moment in time. In fact, Henry Mintzberg (1999) makes a point of making clear to his readers that he, a strategist, can think about *ten* schools of thought about strategic management. I am aware of my shortcomings when I assert that strategic management is divided into *four* schools of thought when viewed in a historical light.

- The school of long-range planning that originated after World War II as army officers returned from war to corporate life and took their military concepts with them.
- The school of strategic planning that originated in the 1960s as the field of strategic management became academic and filled with models and theories.
- The school of product-market strategy that originated in the 1970s as the oil crisis of those days signaled the need for a more dynamic notion of strategy.
- The latest school of complex strategic management that originated in the late 1980s as a general feeling grew that product-market

strategy does not accurately reflect the realities of competitive advantage and strategy.

I begin by describing the first three schools, which are related in many ways. Then I discuss the differences between the second and third schools and summarize the notion of strategic management before the emergence of the fourth school. The latter is somewhat in its emergence, but I try to describe its background and contents.

CONTENTS OF THE FIRST THREE SCHOOLS OF THOUGHT

Origin of Strategic Management

As early as 1916, Henry Fayol suggested that planning should be used as a technique to improve the effectiveness of a corporation's performance. Fayol stated: "Management means looking ahead . . . if foresight is not the whole of management, at least it is an essential part of it. To foresee in this context means both to assess the future and make provisions for it" (Fayol, 1916, quoted in Bhalla, 1987, p. 6).

School 1: Long-range Planning

Little attention was however paid to more formal processes of business-planning or strategic management until the end of World War II. The term *strategic management* is originated in Greek (*stratego*), where the word means *the art of a general*. A *strategist* is the leader of an army (Mintzberg & Quinn, 1991). As the word suggests, long-range planning was introduced to the work of top managers by former American army officers after World War II. Throughout their military career, the officers had been taught to consider many apparently independent decisions in one framework, and this way of working found a natural place in the corporations of the 1950s (Bakka & Fivelsdahl, 1992). Planning systems originated in this period within the corporations to deal with its businesses by predicting the future of each business and providing the economic resources required in an orderly fashion. This was done by planning on financial issues, making budgets and programs to go with these. As the reader might have guessed, the work of this school is mainly directed inside the corporation focusing on integrating the efforts of the functional units within the organization. Because of the relative stable, expanding economic development of the time in which this school originated, the planning systems may be referred to as *long-range planning* or *comprehensive planning*. Others seem to prefer the label *business policy*.

School 2: Strategic Planning

With the publication of Drucker's *The Practice of Management* in 1958, Chandler's *Strategy and Structure* in 1962, and Ansoff's *Corporate Strategy* in 1965, the field of strategic management began to become more formalized and academic. The second school in the development of the strategic concept is that of *strategic business planning* or *strategic planning*, which emphasizes directing the corporation's resources into the most promising areas, taking into consideration the present environment and anticipated future. In other words, this school saw the first signs of the SWOT template for strategy, that is, strengths, weaknesses, opportunities, and threats.

This development was the result of the more dynamic economy of the 1960s, where the future was no longer stable but rather changing and (still) growing. Thus, resources were limited, but changes in the socio-economic environment were still perceived as predictable. After World War II and until the early 1970s, the world economy had been stable and in growth. More important, consumer demand was directed primarily by price. As a result, firms could sell everything they could produce. This situation is also witnessed by the academic contributions of this school. An example is Ansoff's famous matrix for selecting product/market strategy based on whether products and markets were present or new (Ansoff, 1965). Little attention was paid to competitors and relative competitive strength of the firm. This was mainly due to the perception of the environment as relatively simple and stable; however, this environmental situation could not last forever.

After the oil crises of 1973, the world economy virtually collapsed with both inflation and stagnation at the same time. This led consumer demands to change to high quality, low-delivery-time, and more service, which in turn led to fierce international competition. The world of the corporations had become competition-led.

School 3: Product-Market Strategy

This trend in the socioeconomic environment was unfortunately to continue into the 1980s where Eastern corporations—mainly from Japan—proved capable of combining high performance in areas of productivity, timeliness, and quality with a high degree of motivation and commitment from their employees. Western corporations could only look as their Japanese counterparts attacked the world markets. These developments furthermore resulted in both technological and economic discontinuous changes that were difficult to predict with the common forecasting methods. The third school is, thus, that of *product-market strategy*, further emphasizing the dynamics of competition. In this school, techniques to explain product/market cost behavior and the dynamics of international business competition were developed and refined. Among these techniques are the concepts of product life cycle and the experience curve, which in turn led to the development of portfolio-planning methods.

THE DIFFERENCE BETWEEN SCHOOLS 2 AND 3

Before discussing the fourth school—complex strategic management—I would like to briefly describe some of the underlying concepts of the school of strategic planning and product-market strategy. The development from strategic planning to product-market strategy runs along two paths:
- Refinement of methods
- Strategic control

Some of the dominating authors of the era of product-market focused strategic management are Michael E. Porter (Porter, 1980, 1985) and H. Igor Ansoff (Ansoff & Hayes, 1976), who have evolved along with the strategic management concept. Other typical examples include Goold and Quinn (1992), Yavitz and Newmann (1982), and Yoshibara (1976).

Refinement of Methods in Strategic Management

A number of models and methods from strategic planning were refined to cope with the more complex environment of product market-focused strategic management. This section describes a few of the most important refined models.

The Experience Curve

The term *experience curve* was invented in the Boston Consulting Group (BCG) in 1968. The initial work—a number of analyses in the chemical and electronic industries—was done in 1965 and 1966. The work was originally used to explain the price and competitive behavior of the fast-growing market segments in these industries. BCG consultants observed that the cost of a product goes down as the firm's experience in production and marketing increases. The name chosen by BCG was selected to distinguish it from the well-known learning-curve effect, which relates to direct labor cost required to perform a given task, implying that cost decreases as people performing the task becomes familiar with it. The experience curve effect, on the other hand, includes other cost in addition to direct labor costs.

According to Bhalla (1987), three main factors are responsible for the existence of the experience curve: learning, economies of scale, and technology. The learning factor explains the phenomenon that as experience is gained in the field of production, marketing, and sales, efficiency increases, which is reflected in lower cost of the product. Improvements in technology yield reductions of both fixed and variable costs and overall result in lower manufacturing costs. Technology might also improve productivity among white-collar workers, further reducing costs. The economies of scale effect applies to a majority of manufacturing processes, as an increase in capacity seldom requires an equivalent increase in other cost such as capital, operating cost, inventory cost, or overhead cost.

BCG observed that costs decrease by 22% to 30% for every doubling in experience as measured by cumulative production volume; this has great strategic importance. The greatest importance lies in the relationship between the experience curve and the growth of the product. If a product is not growing, the production volume stays constant, and the rate of annual cost decline gradually slows down and approaches zero. However, in a growth industry, market share is very important. With decreased market share, according to the experience curve, come decreased costs, which in turn provide high profit margins. This phenomenon has been demonstrated firmly by Japanese corporations in high growth industries (see for example Abegglen and Stalk, 1985). In the strategic management of product lines, the experience curve has strong implications for the importance of growth rate and market share. It implies that mature products will have a low return on investment, whereas products with a high growth rate, despite a negative or low initial return on investment, will generate high profits as the result of increased market share and a decrease in cost due to gained experience.

The Product Life Cycle

Product life cycle is another well-known model. According to Bhalla (1987), it was first discussed in the 1960s and then was tested and refined in the 1970s. According to the product life cycle model, a product goes through different stages of development: conception, market acceptance, growth, maturity (where supply and demand are balanced), and decline (the final state, which occurs as new, more cost-effective products are developed, gain consumer acceptance, and replace the original product). If accumulated sales volume is plotted against time, the resulting image will be an S-shaped curve.

The product life cycle concept was initially used to explain the behavior of international competitive position of different products, vis-à-vis their position in the life cycle. It was postulated that when a new product is introduced in the international market, the originating country has a distinct advantage resulting from technology barriers, such as patent protection. This advantage disappears as the technology becomes standardized and the world market increases. The competing countries take advantage of economy of scale, raw material, positioning, and cheap labor. As a result, the innovating country loses its advantage, and its market share decreases. Eventually, the country where the product originated may even lose its domestic market to imports from other countries.

New products originate primarily in developed countries and have superior technological capabilities. In the past, the United States has been the prime innovator of new products and has successfully exploited this strength by using large domestic markets to reduce the cost of innovation since only a fraction of the ultimate market is necessary for success. During the 1980s, however, Japan successfully penetrated the U.S. market by introducing new and innovative products based on U.S. market needs (Ohmae, 1988). The industrialized countries consider product life cycle to be a dynamic process in which markets are lost in some areas and new ones are generated in others. The developed countries maintain and enhance market lead either by process or product innovations using their technological base (Dussage et al., 1991). In recent years, fast technological developments have decreased the life cycle of new products, and advantages from innovators are more likely to be short term than long term. Hence, a strong effort in deploying technology in the market is a must for continuing success in the present global competitive environment.

Portfolio Planning Methods

Portfolio methods are the most distinguishing factor in the era of strategic management compared with earlier phases. According to Bhalla (1987), up until to 1979, an estimated 53% of the diversified companies in the Fortune 500 ranking used portfolio planning techniques. As Bhalla noted in 1987, the number of companies using these techniques was probably much higher.

One of the most influential academic contributions to portfolio planning methods is Michael Porter's work on structural analysis of industry and competitive position. The starting point for portfolio methods is that strategic management-formulation is seen ". . . as attaining the ultimate objective of business success as measured by superior return on investment and cash-flow . . ." (Bhalla, 1987, p. 29). Furthermore, the approach is based on the assumption that a company consists of a number of product-market combinations (businesses). Each one of these is required to contribute toward overall corporate objectives and should be managed accordingly. The practical application of portfolio methods consist of the following four steps (Haspeslaugh, 1983):

1. Reexamination of various businesses within a corporation for strategic formulation by considering products/markets. The re-

sulting units may or may not coincide with the existing operating units and are given the name of Strategic Business Units (SBUs).
2. Classifying the businesses in some sort of "portfolio matrix" according to industry attractiveness and business strength.
3. Assigning each SBU a strategic mission depending on its growth and profit potential.
4. Allocating resources to each product-market combination based on the preceding evaluations.

The portfolio methods rely on the fact that cash generation and management within a corporation, where management expertise in deploying and controlling cash is better, is more efficient than obtaining cash from external capital markets. Thus, since the growth businesses may not be able to raise capital required and mature businesses have excess cash, a balancing of cash flow is necessary between businesses.

It must be emphasized here that two areas of major importance within a firm are not addressed in portfolio planning. The areas are (1) the management of interdependencies across various businesses, important in exploiting synergistic effects of markets and technologies, and (2) future growth by internal development, another important part of managing technology. Thus, portfolio planning must be only a part of strategic management, since it does not address two major areas that are vital to the long-term viability of the corporation.

For practical purpose all *portfolio matrices* are the same and their application requires considerable judgment as written in Phillip Haspeslaugh's Ph.D. dissertation (1983). I will therefore only present one such matrix. This matrix was designed by the BCG based on the experience curve as a four box matrix illustrated in Figure 1-1.

In the matrix, market share is defined as a ratio of the company's share in a product line to the share of the strongest competitor in the industry. BCG furthermore uses a (somewhat arbitrary) dividing line for a relative market share of 1 and a real growth rate of 10%, which results in a 2×2 matrix. According to the experience curve effect, market growth essentially portrays cash use, and market share signifies cash generation. Furthermore, the matrix is based on the philosophy that cash flow follows the same cycle as product life cycle. As long as the growth rate of a product exceeds the return on investment, the business will have a negative cash flow. Eventually when the product reaches maturity, the need for added capital diminishes and, if the business is profitable, cash flow will be positive.

Each SBU is analyzed for its growth rate and relative market share. Depending on the values of these factors, the business is assigned a position in the matrix. Each of the four boxes in the matrix has certain

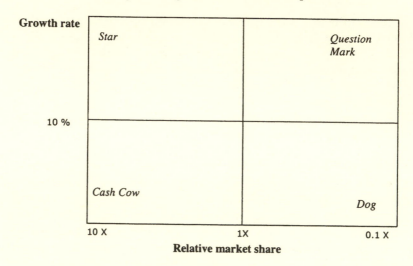

Figure 1-1. BCGs growth/share matrix.

characteristics and a recommended strategic management for management. The rationale behind the BCG matrix is that the excess cash of cash cows should be used to fund selected question marks or on research and development to create stars, which as their markets mature will generate more cash and continue the funding cycle. A number of other such matrices could be mentioned, for example:

- Industry life cycle strategic analysis by the A. D. Little Group.
- Profit improvement market strategic management by the Strategic Planning Institute.
- General Electric's business screen.

Since these methods all are based on the same rationale, I have chosen not to include them in this chapter. Descriptions can be found in the relevant literature.

Selection of Product-Market Strategy
    In the section describing the second school of strategy, *the selection of product/market strategy* within this school was illustrated using Ansoff's matrix from 1965. The difference between school 2 and school 3 can be shown by using Porter's matrix for selecting product/market strategic management from 1980, which is done in Figure 1-2. As Porter's famous generic strategies reveal, the emphasis in the school of product-market strategy is much more on competition and competitive advantage, a sign of the changed perception of the strategic management formulation fit to deal with the strategic management task.

Regarding competitive position (Porter, 1985), competition within an industry is controlled by just five elements:

1. Threat of new entry, which limits profit margins.
2. Threat of substitution, which limits prices.
3. The relative bargaining power of suppliers.
4. The relative bargaining power of customers.
5. The intensity of rivalry among competitors.

This has led to the proposal of Porter's famous five-forces model of competition. Furthermore, Porter has contributed with a perception of how to achieve competitive advantage that has been enormously influential over the years. The idea is simply that firms can try to achieve either achieve cost leadership or some sort of differentiation and at the same time focus on a portion of the market or the entire market. This gives four (actually three) basic choices for the achievement of competitive advantage. Porter's basic assumption—that firms cannot attempt to do more than one thing at a time and hence will be stuck in the middle if not one path of the generic choices is followed—has, however, not stood the test of time. Today many firms demonstrate that it is possible to find luck in the middle, whereas other firms—and Porter himself—demonstrate that it is not possible to focus on differentiation (or cost advantage for that matter) without being cost effective at the same time.

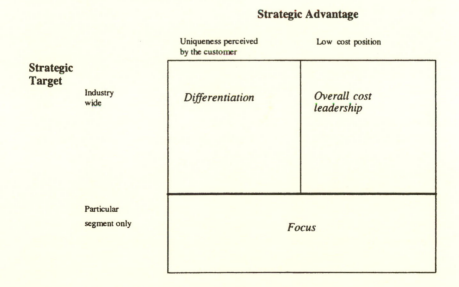

Figure 1-2. Porter's matrix for selecting product/market strategy.

Strategic Control

Strategic control evolved as another reaction to the changed perception of the socioeconomic environment in the 1970s and onwards, that is, more and more surprising and discontinuous changes. Strategic control thus emphasizes the dynamics of strategic management as opposed to strategic planning. According to Peter Lorange (1986), the school of strategic planning is fit to deal with strategic momentum control, which is called "peacetime control," while strategic control (in the product-market strategy school) is adjusted to deal with strategic leap control or "wartime control." The contents of strategic control can be described by the concepts of strategic adaptation and strategic surveillance systems.

Strategic Adaptation

(Proactive) *strategic adaptation* is, together with strategic issue management, an expansion of the issues addressed in strategic management. Adaptation recognizes the more dynamic aspects of strategic management, that is, as a process, since strategic adaptation is directed primarily at implementing strategic plans and adjusting the operating and administrative systems of the corporation according to the plans. According to Ansoff (Ansoff & Hayes, 1976), strategic adaptation thus includes three main steps :

- Formulation of new strategic plan—essentially the contents of the school of strategic planning
- Development of operating system for the new strategic plan
- Adjustment of the old administrative system

An example of strategic adaptation is diversification, where promising possibilities in the environment were coupled with the corporation's strengths and weaknesses. Thus, analyses of company capabilities became essential in the strategic work. On the basis of these analyses, decisions could be made regarding how to develop the operating system in order to exploit the possibilities/avoid the threats (e.g. acquisition, internal development, and joint venture). When this was decided, it was possible to adjust the old administrative system to cope with the new operating system.

Strategic Surveillance

Strategic surveillance systems can be defined as "Management systems with the purpose of making a corporation capable of reacting quickly and competently to changes in its environment" (inspired by Olsen, 1993). Thus, we are dealing with a more or less continuous surveillance of important factors in the socioeconomic environment. No matter how a strategic surveillance system is structured, it must have the following five main functions:

- Identification of signal sources
- Collection of signals
- Judgment of signals and their importance
- Identification of important signals—strategic discontinuities
- Effective decision makers with knowledge of these signals

Of course, the number of proposals, regarding how these five functions are to be fulfilled, is nearly as large as the number of authors in the field. However, Ansoff's management stands out as the first of the kind.

In an ever changing socioeconomic climate (as Ansoff saw the 1980s), it became increasingly clear that some issues could not be dealt with within the normal planning mode of strategic work, nor justified through normal financial procedures. To cope with issues such as less predictable changes, for example, consumer protests or environmental legislation, the notation of *strategic issue management* was developed. Strategic issue management is mainly a recognition of the fact that as predictability becomes poorer, it becomes necessary to make multiple plans: a basic plan preparing the firm for the most probable future plus contingency plans for less probable events and futures in which the basic plan would become invalid. As environmental turbulence increased further, firms began to use real-time systems as a system completely outside the planning part of the strategic management system. According to Ansoff, strategic issue management consists of the following steps (Ansoff & McDonnell, 1990):

- Environmental, business, technological, economic, and political trends are continuously monitored.
- The impact and urgency of these trends are estimated and presented to top management at frequent meetings and whenever a new major threat or opportunity is perceived.
- Together with the planning staff, top management then sorts issues into categories according to their urgency and potential impact.
- The most urgent issues of far-reaching effect are assigned for study and resolution, either to existing organizational units or to special task forces (when rapid cross-organizational response is essential).
- The resolution of issues is monitored by top management for both strategic and tactical implications.

The list of the issues and their priorities is kept up to date through periodic review by top management and used in the normal strategic planning.

STATUS 1985—THE TRADITIONAL APPROACHES TO STRATEGIC MANAGEMENT

Traditional approaches to strategic management have prevailed in the literature and academic attention throughout the 1980s, but it may be questioned whether they are realistic and/or relevant for strategic management in the 21st century. This discusses traditional approaches to strategy in light of three issues: strategic challenges, rationality of strategic managers, and sustainable competitive advantage.

Status of the Strategy Concept: After the First Three Schools

We have learned that the traditional schools of thought about strategy seem to consist of one relatively coherent whole. This section summarizes those schools. Despite the differences in definitions, the following definition seems to capture the essence of the strategy concept in the traditional schools:

> Corporate strategy is the pattern of decisions in a firm that determines and reveals its objectives, purposes, or goals; produces its principal policies and plans for achieving these ends; and defines the range of business the firm is to pursue, the kind of economic and human organization it is or intends to be, and the nature of the economic and noneconomic contribution it intends to make to its shareholders, employees, customers, and communities.

This definition is inspired by Andrews (1971), Ansoff (1965), and Drucker (1958) among others. As I have already shown, many more meanings exist concerning how this definition should be interpreted.

Elements of Corporate Strategy

Figure 1-3 describes the strategic process.

One of the distinct features of the strategy concept is the effort devoted to planning and control, so that all activities of an organization can and will work toward a common set of objectives against which their performance can be measured. The process of strategic management involves the systematic examination of a number of interrelated elements, which results in an explicit statement of company objectives and how they are to be achieved. Despite a lack of universally accepted definitions for such terms as *objectives*, *aims*, *goals*, *strategy*, and *policy*, there seems to be a certain agreement concerning the content of the elements involved in the process.

The Strategy Process

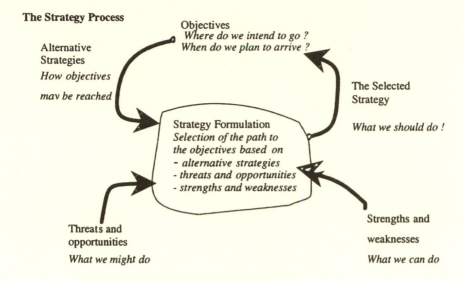

Figure 1-3. The traditional concept of strategy.

Objectives

In this context the word *objectives* is used to define medium- to long-term specific aims of the whole organization. A clear distinction is made between general objectives, sometimes referred to as the purpose or domain of the business, and specific objectives. In this sense objectives define the endpoint to be achieved (*where*) in a specified time (*when*).

Strategy

There are a number of paths by which any set of objectives can be reached. These paths are called strategies. As we have seen, a number of possible strategies exist (not necessarily mutually exclusive), since they give rise to a large number of possible combinations or alternative strategies, one of which must be selected as the most promising. The selection of which path is to be followed is referred to as strategy formulation—the *how* of the process.

The Business Environment

Strategic decisions are directed toward the future, a future in which conditions may be very different from those at the time when the strategic plan is formulated. If the objectives are to be met, they must be realistic in relation to the business environment existing at some time in the future. The same is true for strategy. Thus, a conscious view of the future, however imprecise, must be built into the strategy process.

Forecasts are needed for all important environmental factors. It is not necessary, however, to examine forecasting techniques to see that a study of the future is of great value if it enables the identification of environmental trends, which may present either a threat to existing business or an opportunity for new business and consequently lead to the consideration of possible strategies. This is the *what the company might do* of the strategic process.

Analysis of Company Strengths and Weaknesses

Of course strategy can not be formulated without considering the business itself. There is no reason, apart from difficulties in forecasting, why several different companies in the same industry should not identify the same threats, opportunities, and possible strategies. The ability of the business to meet the threats or exploit the opportunities depends on a variety of factors unique to the particular company. Thus, two companies in the same industry will choose different strategies, which are matched to their own capabilities. To do this it is necessary to carry out a critical evaluation of the company's strengths and weaknesses. By comparing the environmental analysis—*what the company might do*—with an analysis of its capabilities—*what the company can do*—it is possible to make the final choice of strategy—*what the company should do*.

The Strategic Formulation Process

In *Many Best Ways to Make Strategy*, Michael Goold and Andrew Campbell describe three successful ways to formulate strategy: strategic planning, financial control, and strategic control. This summarizes the idea of the strategy process in traditional schools of strategy. These styles are differentiated by the difference in the relationship between executives in a central office and those who run business units or divisions.

Strategic Planning Style

In many companies headquarters are deeply involved in strategy. This is characterized by unit managers formulating proposals, while headquarters reserves the right to have the final say.

Financial Control Style

The financial control style is almost the reverse image of the strategic planning style. Responsibility for strategy development rests squarely on the shoulders of business unit managers. Headquarters does not formally review strategic plans; instead, it exerts influence through short-term budgetary control.

Strategic Control Style
Companies that follow this style try to achieve a compromise between the two other styles. At best, a strategic control system accommodates the need both to build a business and maximize financial performance. Responsibility for strategy rests with the business and division managers. But strategies must be approved by headquarters. For this purpose there is an elaborate planning process that includes planning reviews among other steps.

As Campbell and Gould remark, there is no best way to make strategy (and there may just be more than three ways to make it). "The answer depends on the very things top management knows best—the characteristics of its business and the people who make them work" (Mintzberg & Quinn, 1991, p. 644).

Levels of Strategic Decisions

According to, for example, Hax & Majluf (1991), Bhalla (1987), and Ackoff (1970), strategic responsibility can be described using the following three levels of decisions.

Corporate Level
The corporate level deals with choosing the domain in which the corporation intends to do business. This includes selecting businesses; allocating resources to them, setting overall objectives for each business; formulating policies for employees, stockholders, etc; and finally organizing the overall management structure of the corporation.

Business Level
The business level deals with how to compete within a given business. This includes industry assessment, competitor assessment, business strength analysis, product analysis, and resource allocation to the functional level.

Functional Level
The functional level deals with how resources are used within a given function, for example, the manufacturing function. This includes determination of the basis on which functions will support the business and corporate strategies, and the integration of different functional plans to ensure synergism and optimum support.

Strategic Challenges of the 1980s as a Reason for Changing Strategy Theory

Why did the concept of strategy have to evolve even further? What is the background to the evolution into the fourth school of strategic management? In this section I attempt to provide an answer to these questions. Please note that this is a view of the external pressures of the 1980s and not—as in the introduction—of the future.

Categories of Strategic Challenges Perceived in the Mid 1980s
Bhalla (1987) cites a series of interviews with 18 chief executives of U.S. corporations, undertaken in 1984. Each one of these CEOs emphasized the need for a more flexible and participating management to develop strategic leadership, which had become essential for short- and long-term corporate viability. According to Bhalla, their key concerns about competition were:

- Technology, for example, communication technology, becoming available on a global basis, impacting all aspects of business
- Fierce global competition as faced by U.S. corporations
- Active participation of governments, which are concerned about the socioeconomic needs of their countries and thus changing the nature and boundaries of competition
- Changing socioeconomic and demographic factors, which have created a strong need for new goods and services while many conventional markets are declining

These concerns emphasize the need for a further evolution in the strategy concept. But two questions are still unanswered: Why is this evolution required? What is important to deal with in the future? To answer these questions, three main trends can be identified in the socioeconomic climate in the 1980s that influenced the concept of strategy: an increased importance of technology, internationalization, and a greening of consumer demands.

Increased Importance of Technology
Technology has become important for a number of reasons. First, it should be noted that the Japanese corporations during the 1970s used manufacturing technology to achieve low through-put times, higher quality, and flexibility. This was undertaken by first "cleaning up" their plants by using concepts such as kaizen, quality circles, and Just In Time and later automating heavily. This resulted in an increased importance of manufacturing in strategy in the West. In the 1980s the speed of new product development also increased, decreasing product life cycles and yielding competitive advantage to innovative firms. These two factors were supported by the emergence of new information technology, which enhanced the possibilities for communication, and by new technologies replacing old ones, for example, composites, suggesting that a number of conventional technologies had reached maturity and would

be replaced sometime in the near future. Looking at these factors, it is not surprising that manufacturing, R&D, and integration were subjects of great discussion during the 1980s and early 1990s.

According to Michael Porter (1985), technology can be used to create competitive advantages in the following way:

- It can create barriers to entry by altering economies of scale and creating capital requirements.
- It can change the bargaining relationship with buyers through product differentiation and switching costs.
- It can change the bargaining relationship with suppliers.
- It can create opportunities for product substitution.
- It can change the basis of rivalry among competitors by altering costs structures and restructuring industry boundaries.

In this way technology can alter industry structure and competitive position. The perceived importance of technology can be illustrated by a steady increase in R&D funds during the 1980s, where U.S. corporations on average spent 6.5% more per year from 1980 to 1985, while Japanese corporations spent 11.6% more on average. Compared to these figures, the EEC's increase of 4.8% on average is small, but still important (Dussage et al., 1991).

This growth in R&D expenditure can be seen both as a reaction from firms faced with the quickening pace of competition and as a process of producing innovation, which in turn is a source of more rapid and technical progress. The growing importance of technology and the increase in R&D spending are therefore linked in a chicken and egg relationship. But why, one still asks, is technology so important?

First, some authors have emphasized the fact that the length of time between the discovery of a fundamental process and its application has become progressively shorter. However, this theory is questionable since many current technologies are complex combinations of science and techniques, which makes the actual "source" of the first innovation difficult to trace. It seems clear, however, that to maintain a constant rate of innovation, R&D expenditures must be increased exponentially over time, since it becomes ever more difficult to improve or invent something new.

The growing globalization of trade and competition forms the basis of a second hypothesis, which may account for the increased importance of technology and the growth in R&D spending. According to this hypothesis, firms from developed nations are increasingly faced with challenges posed by firms from newly industrialized countries. Thus, the Japanese steel and shipbuilding industries, the American and European textile industries, and others are at a disadvantage when competing with Korean and Hong Kong firms. Furthermore Japanese corporations are imposing a tremendous pressure on European and American corporations in other industries because they are less dependent on low wages, for example. Japanese corporations are concentrating their activities in areas, where they can benefit from their strong technological capabilities. This move has amplified the importance of technological factors for firms in developed countries, which appear to be engaged in a "technology-race."

The third and final hypothesis is closely connected to the second trend in the socioeconomic climate—namely the so-called "greening" of the world. According to the crisis hypothesis, the current economic crisis, which was set off by the rise in oil prices in the 1970s, corresponds to the end of the "petrochemical" technical system, which operated during the 30 years of growth after World War II. This means that we must change the nature of our technology in accordance with the problems encountered in resources, economy, etc. We are, thus, at a turning point in history, passing from one technical system to another. This transition is reflected in a greater effort to promote the emergence of the technologies essential to the new technical system.

The Greening of Consumer Demands and Legislation

In the early 1990, it became apparent that corporations had to address increasing public concern for the environment and awareness of limited resources. The shortness of resources and increased effects of pollution (e.g., holes in the ozone layer) has perhaps made some think about the future. This may not be as theatrical as the crisis hypothesis mentioned previously, but it is almost certain that consumer demands as well as government regulations have changed in the last decade.

Companies are now faced with demands for recyclability and environmentally friendly products from customers, and it is clear that an image as a "green" corporation can yield competitive advantage in the future. Along with the growing importance of environmental movements, in some countries political parties have formed with environmental issues as a message. Corporations must also expect government regulations in areas of recyclability of both product and packing, as well as in pollution and environmental issues in general.

Even though technology has not been mentioned in this connection, it is clear that the greening effect is closely related to technology. Even if we are, in fact, not at the end of the petrochemical technical system, new and improved technologies are still required to solve the problems described in this area. The talk about green technology and the new commercials with the theme "we invent for you," to mention but a few, illustrate this point. It is also clear that government regulations will be directed toward technology (see for example, Ansoff & McDonnell, 1990), which in turn will require new strategic management methods.

It is important to note that environmental issues also were important in the 1970s because of the oil crises. But in the 1970s this problem was dealt with by making it possible for the stakeholders of the corporations to participate in the strategic management. This solution is no longer viable. In the 1990s the stakeholders forced politicians to make legislation and furthermore "put their money where their mouths are," that is, buy environmentally friendly products and services.

Internationalization

The third trend is not new. Growing international competition already occurred in the 1970s and has kept on growing ever since. According to Ansoff (Ansoff & McDonnell, 1990), this can be described in the stages of export, international, and multinational offering of products. While export and international offering are not new, multinational companies emerged in the 1980s. Thus, I have included internationalization as a trend in this context because the size of internationalism can no longer be ignored.

The number and strength of international competitors have grown to such an extent that every company now must include them in their strategic considerations, which is reflected by, for example, the work on lean production (Womack et al., 1990). This trend was started by the Japanese in the 1970s and has continued since. Now the Japanese are being replaced in "low-wage" areas such as shipbuilding and steel making by, for example Koreans, while the Japanese themselves move into other areas such as electronics and biotechnology. Japanese companies use internationalization as a means to become stronger than their competitors, a strategy that Western corporations started to adopt in the 1980s.

This trend is also connected with the technology trend, since the Japanese have sustained competitive advantage by the use of technology since the early 1970s. Then they relied on manufacturing technology, such as Just In Time, robotics, etc., to produce products at lower costs and in higher quality than those of their Western counterparts. In the 1980s and early 1990s the Japanese yielded competitive advantage through an increased R&D effort to offer broader and more customized product lines.

Conclusion on the Strategic Challenges of the 1980s

The need for a change of the strategy concept into its fourth school of thought is described by three major trends influencing the socioeconomic environment in the 1980s and 1990s. These three trends, based on for example Drucker (1990), Lambright and Rahm (1992), and many others are summarized in Table 1-1.

It can be argued that these trends are not new; for example, the life-cycle argument actually seems inconsistent since consumer electronics products are compared with farming equipment. However, as soon as managers accept the challenges outlined and begin to act on them, a climate in which the challenges will be created sooner or later is generated instantly.

EMERGENCE OF THE SCHOOL OF COMPLEX STRATEGIC MANAGEMENT

This section describes the fourth school of strategic management, with emphasis on the evolution from the third to the fourth school.

The evolution from the first three schools to the fourth is illustrated beautifully by Michael E. Porter and H. Igor Ansoff. While Porter in his 1980 book did not include dimensions in strategic management other than portfolio management and marketing, this changed in 1985, where the impact of technology on competition was analyzed and described. In a 1987 article, a warning emerged against naive acceptance of strategic portfolio prescriptions and his own appraisal of competitive forces (Porter,

TABLE 1-1. Strategic Challenges Underlying the Fourth School of Strategy

Technological Trend

Manufacturing technologies for achieving lower through-put times, higher productivity, better quality, and flexibility
Closely related to the emergence of new information technology, which has greatly enhanced the possibilities for communication
New and improved products, which yield competitive advantage for high-technology firms and alters entire industries
New technologies replacing mature ones

Greening trend

Need to reduce use of resources (e.g., energy)
Need to reduce waste and pollution

Internationalization

Need to cope with international competition to a much higher extent than before

1991). Other comments on strategic portfolio management include the following. "Perhaps the most difficult task for managers is to balance the needs of existing . . . [product] . . . lines. This problem requires a portfolio strategic management much more complex than the popular four-box Boston Consulting Group matrix found in most strategic management texts" (Quinn, 1992, p. 81). Another comment comes from Kantrow, who emphasized that the BCG matrix misses many other important factors in a business that should go into a company's strategic management. "It is of great importance to identify and assess the nature of the relationship between a company's distinctive technological competence, its organizational structure, and its overall strategic orientation" (Kantrow, 1983, p. 12). However, Porter has left it to others to expand the contents of the strategic management concept to include, for example, technology.

H. Igor Ansoff represents a somewhat different case. His 1965 book can be viewed as a rigorous perception of strategic management (1965). But in 1976, Ansoff co-authored *From Strategic Planning to Strategic Management* (Ansoff & Hayes, 1976), where the strategic management concept was thoroughly investigated and revised. He continued this work during the 1980s emphasizing issues such as strategic issue management, so-called "weak signals," and many other aspects of strategic management (Ansoff & McDonnell, 1990). He has also stressed the importance of technology and organizational capabilities in strategic management and has thus been an inspiration for a number of authors contributing to the fourth school of strategic management.

What has happened from school 3 to school 4? This question does not have one definite answer; however, as described in the introduction, the way of thinking behind the theoretical contributions has changed. Most notably, the assumptions behind the strategic management task have changed from a relatively simple/stable concept to a complex unstable one, with the company as a collection of resources, rather than a portfolio of product/market combinations. This has, in turn, led to a rather diverse amount of contributions spanning from mission management and behavioral strategic planning processes, as advocated by Campbell and Yeung (1990), to resource/capability-based strategies, as advocated by Hamel and Prahalad (1994). In between these two fields is located technology-based strategic management, which attempts to integrate the other two approaches.

The diversity of the contributions seems to indicate that the school of complex strategic management has not yet reached a state of maturity, which makes it difficult to characterize precisely. Nonetheless, this school is the topic of discussion in the remainder of this chapter.

THE DEVELOPMENT OF STRATEGIC MANAGEMENT OVER TIME

Summary: Four Schools about Strategic Management

Strategy theory can be divided into four different schools of thought, all of which have different assumptions regarding the content and process of strategic management (Table 1-2).

Conclusions

The Structure of the Strategy Concept
The four schools of thought about strategic management are interrelated, as they all offer solutions to problems imposed on corporations by the socioeconomic environment. As such, all of the schools have been developed to cope with one of the four situations in the environment, which in turn have been typical in certain periods of history. This does not imply that, for example, long-range planning is outdated today.

TABLE 1-2.   Summary of the Four Schools of Strategic Management

	School 1: Long-Range Planning	School 2: Strategic Planning	School 3: Product Market Focused Strategic Management	School 4: Complex Strategic Management
Situation	Stable, simple, and expanding	Changing but predictable	Changing, and discontinuous	Changing, discontinuous, unpredictable with new dimensions
Scope	Providing economic resources in orderly fashion	Directing resources into the most promising areas	Balancing cash flow to yield competitive advantage	Managing and integrating problems in areas of economic, technology, environment, etc.
Issues	Financial planning and profit maximization	Satisfy consumer demands to yield profits	Achieve competitive advantage to yield profits	Deal with all the dimensions of the environment to survive
Elements	Budgets and programs in one overall plan	Corporate economic strategic management— choice of products and markets	Corporate, business, and functional strategic plans	Many different strategies along with the ones from school 3

First, there may be markets or market segments that resemble the situation corresponding to that of long-range planning. Second, the methods and concepts of this area have evolved over time and have thus become part of the subsequent schools of thought about strategic management.

This way of thinking about strategic management is illustrated in the framework of the development of the strategic management concept over time (Figure 1-4).

This framework represents a pragmatic approach to strategy: that is, the "great divide" between the complex school and the other schools is deemphasized. Instead, it is speculated whether the evolution of the strategy concept has taken place as a process of gradual improvement. This implies that the process is to continue in the future, that is, that the latest developments in theory are not *the* truth either, which seems to suit my ideal of science quite well. It should not be overlooked, however, that the strategy concept has become much more complex in its most recent developments.

Complexity of the Strategic Management Concept

From our earlier discussion, it is evident that the strategic management concept has become more complex over time. This can be

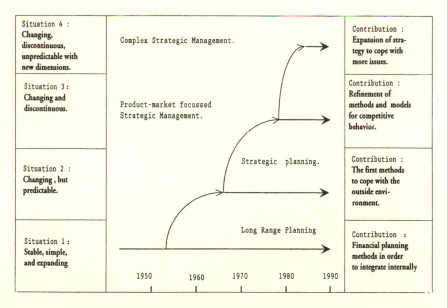

Figure 1-4. Conceptual framework for the evolution of the strategic management concept.

illustrated by both the many different views of the contents of strategic management inherent in the four schools and the many different ways the term *strategic management* is used in textbooks.

In my view, complexity, in terms of the assumed uncertainty of the strategy task as well as the assumed manageability of the strategy process, has increased over three dimensions: scope, issues, and elements.

The *scope* of strategic work has evolved from having only little interest in the outside environment—focus on internal integration—to having very high interest in the external positioning in the environment, but only little interest in internal integration. According to many authors, these developments were the result of the socioeconomic environment losing its stability, simplicity, and growth. Lately, however, both external positioning and internal integration are in focus in school 4, as illustrated by activity area strategies such as manufacturing strategy as well as interfunctional (integrating) strategies such as quality strategy, CIM strategy, and technology strategy. Furthermore, strategies for learning and sustaining core competencies have been advocated in the literature.

Until the emergence of school 4, economic issues were at the center of strategic work; in school 3, these issues were supplemented with competitive analysis and product-market analysis. Within the fourth school in the socioeconomic environment, new issues have been added. Some of the most notable ones are technology, sociopolitical factors (e.g., the "greening" of consumer demands), and internationalization.

Viewing the developments along the other two dimensions, it is hardly surprising that the *elements* in strategic work also have increased in number. In school 1, financial planning was the sole element of strategic management. This evolved in schools 2 and 3 into a more marketing-oriented planning, but still centered on profit and finance. In school 4, both technology and administrative/human resources planning have emerged as parts of strategic management.

2

The Alphabet Soup of Strategic Management

Competencies and competence-based strategy are issues that managers must devote time to as part of their strategic management. However, methods and theories that can be applied in strategic management change at an almost constant rate. Every day seems to bring new management fads conveniently abbreviated to three letters—hence the odd title of this chapter. But are these "new" management fads really something new, or are they merely reflections of each other?

MANAGEMENT FADS

In the introduction it is argued that competence-based strategy should be part of the strategic management of all firms. Nonetheless many theoretical areas that evolve affect the way we perceive and understand competencies and competence-based strategy. Business process reengineering, benchmarking, total quality management, lean production, and vision management are just a few examples of areas that help to evolve competence-based strategy.

At the same time it is clear that new theoretical areas keep emerging. Some prefer to call many of the new areas management fads. E. Shapiro (1966) has written an excellent book on that subject and argues that most of the "new" areas are in fact not new at all. Still, there are areas of a more stable nature with more than 20 years of evolution behind them. Those areas can hardly be labeled "fads," but they still shape our perception of competence-based strategy and need to be considered in a discussion of the alphabet soup that surrounds competence-based strategy.

Some think that the evolution of new and mature areas happen in a pendulum movement. Over the last 10 to 15 years, I have observed how management research attention has gone from being almost exclusively focused on human resources, corporate culture, and other very soft issues to being concerned with IT systems, Enterprise Resource Planning (ERP) systems, advanced manufacturing technologies, and so on. Others argue that the use of research methods—that also to a great extent determines the kind of issues that can be looked at in research—undergoes similar pendulum movements (Spender, 1996). Whether or not the motion is, in fact, in the form of a helix—indicating that we get wiser along the way—remains to be investigated.

Figure 2-1 illustrates some theoretical areas of obvious relevance for competence-based strategy in a system of coordinates that shows time on the Y-axis and whether the areas are mainly focused on technology (hard aspects of management) or human research (soft aspects of management) on the X-axis. I have chosen areas that are directed toward the

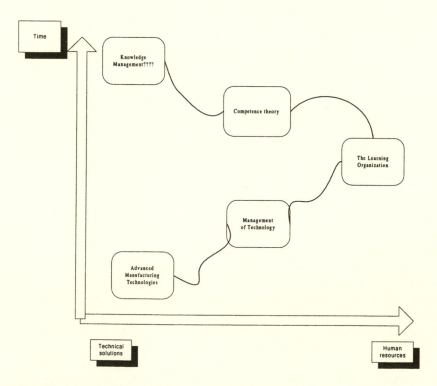

Figure 2-1. Pendulum movement of theoretical areas.

internal activities of the firms in much the same way as competence-based strategy is. I return to this point at the end of the chapter.

In the early 1980s, a large amount of research and managerial attention was directed toward the promise of advanced manufacturing technologies such as robots, automated guided vehicles, and other gadgets that could create the unmanned factory. Computer integrated manufacturing (CIM) was the overarching concept at the time (Drejer, 1996b). However, after these wonderful technologies were actually implemented, few results were realized (Voss, 1988), and attention shifted to a more balanced approach to developing the internal activities of the firm. In fact, several researchers called for a balanced, or integrated, approach to technologic innovation and organizational development (Bessant, 1988; Voss, 1988; Steele, 1989). All of this took place within the theoretical area of management of technology (MoT), which was fashionable in the late 1980s and early 1990s. About 1990 the notion of the learning organization (LO) came into fashion and attention shifted to soft aspects of management (Senge, 1990a), just as ten years earlier, when we talked about motivation, human resources, mission of the firm, and corporate culture. Now, ten years later, the name of the game was learning and organizational learning. Especially MoT and LO keep evolving, even if they are not as much in fashion as they used to be. These are areas that have a degree of staying power and can survive until they will again become fashionable for everyone—remember that the idea of organizational learning is at least 50 years old.

Attention has now been directed at knowledge management (KM) for a couple of years, and this area has directed its attention toward the more technological aspects of management. Information technology in the form of very operational solutions such as ERP systems, Lotus Notes, and many others have become part of the managerial agenda in the past few years. As Figure 2-1 illustrates, I interpret this as a return to the hard, technological world of the early 1980s, albeit that the specific solutions preferred are different from those of 10 to 15 years ago. Of course this begs the question of what will happen next. Will attention swing back toward a more balanced approach? Will that favor the area of competence-based strategy in its current incarnation?

This brief discussion involving some of the well-known theoretical areas of the last 10 to 15 years clearly indicates the pendulum motion of new areas that are either in vogue for just a few years or maintain a stable, if not currently in fashion, status. The question is whether the evolution of research areas is real evolution. If different theoretical areas are different mainly by name and not by content, then it seems highly questionable that we get any better at solving management problems over time. It would seem as if we are merely renaming the same old solutions for a new age. In the remaining part of this chapter, I will investigate that question in some detail.

THE NEED FOR A FRAMEWORK FOR ANALYSIS

Having worked with competence-based strategy, MoT as well as organizational learning, I have often wondered which one is the detour? The two or three management areas have had their separate followers and basically not acknowledged the value of the other areas. I would like to find out whether the three areas are merely reflections of each other—same conception with different names—or important supplements to solving the same problems.

Instant Answers to Everything?

For a manager wanting to be updated on the most recent literature on which tools to apply to improve her organization, it is no longer enough to go on an occasional trip and buy the most recent best seller on management. There are now so many relevant and possible management tools that being updated has become a full-time job for the manager, which obviously is not an acceptable situation. For academics and managers alike, the choice of sticking to one such management fad begs serious consideration of what is gained and lost by focusing on, say, competence development. In this chapter, I discuss the considerations related to focusing on competence-based strategy and the future evolution of that area.

Management Fads and Their Inherent Problems

Business process reengineering, benchmarking, total quality management, lean production, vision management, and many others are examples of recent so-called management fads that all promise to lift industrial firms to new heights of profits and competitive advantage. Which one should we choose? The literature on business process reengineering (BPR) does little or nothing to tell us when to apply BPR and when not to apply BPR or what to apply instead of BPR. Therefore, it is virtually impossible to choose among two or more state-of-the-art management fads.

Furthermore, the development of management fads over time offers even more disturbing evidence of what happens in an age of instant answers to everything. Management fads change extremely often and seem to have no other impact on management practice than booming book sales. The example of business process springs to mind. BPR has been even more "hyped" than the new Gorillaz album these days. The original Hammer and Champy "manifesto for business revolution" sold more than 2 million copies worldwide (Hammer & Champy, 1993), and there was at least one international journal established dedicated to BPR. However, in less than two years Hammer and Champy published follow-up articles to the original or rather attempts to explain and detail the concept of BPR (Champy, 1995; Hammer & Stanton, 1995). Today, bookshops are flooded with "BPR workbooks" and their like. At the same time, others have begun to criticize the notion of BPR as something that does not work in practice or, at least, should be used with caution. These are sure signs of the fall of a management fad, and the replacements are all in place. "Total process improvement," "total improvement," and so on are new fads trying to feed off the BPR "hype" while still criticizing BPR. Management fads, it seems, are in a constant flux. As soon as one management fad is firmly established, the next generation is already on the way.

The Need for an Overview

For a manager wanting to do something to become a better manager—or even an academic trying to keep up—the flux of management fads makes it impossible to maintain any kind of overview on which tools to use for which purposes. Eileen Shapiro has dealt with the problems of management fads in her seminal work: *Fad Surfing the Boardroom—Managing in the Age of Instant Answers* (1996). The notion of "fad surfing" is what Shapiro has defined as: ". . . The practice of riding the crest of the latest management panacea and then paddling out again just in time to ride the next one" (p. 217). Her book is about attempting to maintain an overview of the many different management fads.

As already mentioned, some theoretical areas are of a more lasting nature than the most typical management fads. Therefore, I will use the more generic term *theoretical area* to denote both management fads, such as BPR, and more sustainable fields, such as management of technology, in the remains of this chapter. Such an overview is much needed for several reasons:

- It is obvious that all management fads do not have the same area of application (e.g., BPR is about something other than vision management). Therefore, it would be nice to know the area of application for each management fad.
- Any choice of one management fad should be thoroughly justified. Focusing on one management fad is also choosing not to focus on many others and, hence, ignoring important aspects of a firm's management.

- Some theoretical areas have a similar area of application. For instance MoT and competence-based strategy are both directed at the internal activities of the firm, even on a strategic level in both cases. Thus, those two theoretical areas are bound to influence each other's evolution. In this chapter, I focus on those areas that influence and have influenced the evolution of competence-based strategy.

Purpose: Proving an Overview and a Justification

This section provides an overview of relevant management fads and more stable theoretical areas, and their area of application in the management of firms. It also describes the implications of this alphabet soup for the area of competence-based strategy. Since this is a rather long argument, I start by offering an overview over the entire section.

- By taking the perspective of a firm's competitive advantage and management, I will propose a framework for the possible areas of application for different theoretical areas. Furthermore, I will discuss where some of the dominant theoretical areas of the day belong in the framework.
- The framework makes it possible to argue for focusing on competence-based strategy. This is a complementary activity to product-market competition, which has received the bulk of management attention over the years. Focusing too on competence development secures a more intrafirm and long-term perspective on the firm's management.
- Finally, I will discuss whether or not the development of many new theoretical areas is an advantage or a disadvantage for managers (i.e., are we getting any wiser or just plain confused?). The answer is mixed, as we shall see in the final section of this chapter.

PROPOSING A FRAMEWORK FOR ANALYSIS

There might not be any easy way to create an overview of management fads. One way is to take as a starting-point the notion of competitiveness (since any management fad should contribute to enhancing the competitiveness of the firm—and proudly boasts to do so). This makes it possible to look at different types of, or even levels of, competition for the firm. Furthermore, we propose to view different management activities in a firm's management as different purposes on which to pin management fads.

The Foundation for the Framework—Competitiveness

The thinking behind every management fad and more stable theoretical area available is to improve the competitiveness of firms. There is not one management fad that does not claim to enhance competitiveness, often in unspecified ways. It would also be hard to imagine what would happen if a prospective management fad did not—"management crap reengineering is about losing competitiveness by introducing sloppiness and deliberate error to management"? That would be *the Dilbert principle* for you, but it is hard to take it too seriously. Instead, let us turn to what makes a firm competitive.

More than 30 years of discussing competitiveness and strategic management of firms has resulted in some sort of agreement as to what it takes to be competitive, at least on a product-market level. If we start at this level, consider the following statements:

- The firm's products and services must be in alignment with the demands of the customers.
- The firm's internal activities must be fit to produce its products and services.
- Hence, the internal activities must be in alignment with the demands of the customers.
- Furthermore, the firm must be able to compare itself favorably to at least some of its competitors in all three of these respects; that is, the firm must be competitive.

I have chosen to use the term *internal activities* in this chapter. I could just as well have used the term *competencies*, which is the term I use in the rest of the book. However, in this chapter I prefer to use a more generic term because several other theoretical areas would claim that their object, whether technology or business processes, for instance, is a more natural term to use. Hence, I have chosen a neutral term for the purposes of the discussion in this chapter.

The statements on competitiveness, it seems, cover state-of-the-art thinking in most strategy literature. They combine the work on product-market strategy (for example, Porter, 1980, 1985), with the more recent work on core competencies/capabilities/skills/technologies (for example, Hamel & Prahalad, 1994). If we take a more dynamic environment into consideration, a few more things are needed to secure continuing competitiveness than just succeeding here and now. That is, it is not enough to focus on competing on current markets with current products by means of current internal activities. Hamel and Prahalad (1994) argue that bringing an idea to the product-market level takes a large number of years from the very beginning, essentially an elaboration of the argument that work activities should also be considered in strategy, and that competition, thus, transcends product-market competition and includes competition at other levels. These others levels are:

- *Competition for industry foresight and intellectual leadership.* This is competition to gain a deeper understanding than others on the factors (be they technology, demography, lifestyle or others) that could be used to transform current product-market competition by, for instance, creating new opportunities, new products, new ways of viewing customer needs, etc.
- *Competition to foreshorten migration paths.* In between the battle for intellectual leadership and the battle for market share is competition to influence the direction of industry development, that is, a race to accumulate the necessary competencies, to test and prove alternate product and service concepts, to attract coalition partners with critical complementary resources, and many other things.

These two complement competition for market share on current markets with current products and are no less important than the latter. Hamel and Prahalad comment in this manner: ". . . while much attention has been lavished by managers . . . on . . . competition between rival products or services in the market place, this really represent only the last 100 meters of a much longer race" (Hamel & Prahalad, 1994, pp. 46-47). A race longer not only in distance but also in time horizon makes it necessary to focus on all three kinds of competition.

Management Decisions—the Dimensions in a Framework

I now propose a framework for analysis of relevant theoretical areas aimed at improving the management of a firm—a model that provides the purposes on which to hang individual theoretical areas. The model consists of different management decision areas *combined* with different objectives.

Management Decision Areas
Strategy theory has for a long time been preoccupied with different decision areas in a firm's management (Drejer, 1996b, 2001). The most important strategic decision areas are:

- Corporate strategy
- Product-market strategy
- Development of internal activities

Corporate strategy deals with the decisions on the firm as a whole. This is sometimes called "mission of the firm," dealing with issues such as the following: What are the businesses of the firm? What is the purpose of the firm? What are the future objectives of the firm on different aspects? The important thing is that this is dealt with at the firm level.

Another decision area of the firm at product-market level is dealing with individual *strategic business units*. Michael Porter and others have become very prosperous by teaching us the importance of taking a stand on three issues: (1) which products to produce, (2) in which markets to sell these products, and (3) on which competitive advantage to base the successful sale of the products. In short, Porter and others have argued for the inclusion in the strategic management of firms the notion of several strategic methods, that is, the five-forces model for competition, Porter's generic strategies, portfolio management of the firm's products, and so on. Sometimes, it is as if Porter and others have been so forceful that the notion of the customer has been forgotten; but the recent emergence of total quality management and other fads has restored the customer at the cost of some of the models of strategy making. Hence, a fourth issue has risen: what are the customer demands that we attempt to fulfill? In summary, product-market strategy is about answering the four questions in a dynamic perspective taking into account tomorrow's customers, products, and markets.

In general, an internal activity (= competence = capability = technology) may be defined as a combination of human beings who are organized and function in/under a certain culture, using hard technology to do certain tasks to produce the products/services of the firm (Drejer, 1996b). Internal activities may be physical manufacturing, of course, but also all other sorts of nonmanufacturing activities may be of importance for the firm. The fact that tasks are undertaken makes it possible to compare different internal activities, in-house or with competitor's activities. If an internal activity via its output, and hence the way it is undertaken, provides the firm with a competitive advantage vis-à-vis its competitors in an area of competitive importance, then the internal activity is obviously of strategic importance to the firm. This emphasizes the close link between product-market strategy and development of internal activities. The internal activities of the firm do not exist in a vacuum; they too must provide something of value to the customer and do so better than the competitors. Furthermore, development of internal activities is naturally linked to product development (Andreassen, 1999). For instance, the ability to develop new and innovative products may be a core activity for the firm in itself (Drejer, 2001). Another example is *technology commercializing*, that is, the utilization of technologies and/or competencies in new products (Jolly, 1995).

What is development of internal activities and how is this undertaken? Actually, no one has provided any workable definitions to the concept so far other than the obvious: to develop the internal activities of the firm to maintain a close fit between product-market strategy and the internal activities. However, this tells us nothing about *how* to do so, merely the objective of doing so. Given the emphasis on, most notably, core competencies these days, it seems only natural that the academic community and industry are preoccupied with notions such as "knowledge economy" (Stewart, 1997), "balanced scorecard" (Kaplan & Norton, 1996), "management of innovation" (Drucker, 1985), "technology management" (Solberg & Danielsen, 1992), "organizational change" (Moss Kanter, 1992), and "organizational networks" (Savage, 1990). This book is an attempt to remedy that situation within the theoretical area of competence-based strategy, but as it is obvious that many other theoretical areas also try to do the same thing. Therefore, it is of crucial importance to have a feel for all of these areas so that one can get inspiration from several sources rather than inventing the wheel all over again and again within several different areas.

Objectives of a Firm's Management

In the 1980s, much managerial attention in firms was on downsizing and restructuring. This reflects the failure of one-time industry leaders and other firms to keep up with the accelerated pace of industry change. For many decades managers could count on past trends to continue into the future, making careful planning ahead a major task for management. This is, however, no longer the case as the tides of technological, demographic, and regulatory change have created an entirely different competitive situation of the 1990s (D'Aveni, 1994). It is no longer enough to focus management on restructuring, that is, basically on doing the same tasks with fewer resources. According to Hamel and Prahalad, not even the notion of "reengineering" captures what is essential in today's competition (Hamel & Prahalad, 1994). They note: ". . . Recognizing that restructuring is ultimately a dead end, smart companies have moved on to reengineer their processes. . . . Once again, the stopwatches are out: How do we do things faster and with less waste?" (Hamel & Prahalad, 1994, p. 13). To Hamel and Prahalad, the only difference between traditional restructuring is: " . . . Reengineering offers at least the hope, if not always the reality, of getting better as well as getting smaller" (Hamel & Prahalad, 1994, p. 13). Thus, reengineering can be a good thing for firms, but it is not enough. The example of lean production compels us to ask for even more. The *Machine That Changed the World* (Womack et al., 1990) termed "lean manufacturing" as the extraordinarily efficient manufacturing system pioneered by Toyota. Yet reading the book offers the realization that Toyota started developing lean manufacturing more than 40 years ago, and it has taken more than 40 years for U.S. automobile manufacturers to catch up. Why is that? The answer may be that in many firms, reengineering efforts are more about catching up than getting out in front (Hamel & Prahalad, 1994), leaving a third task unattended. It is necessary for a firm to be able to invent new opportunities as a firm, in product-market competition, and at the competence level. This leaves three objectives for management of a firm:

- Restructure and use fewer resources.
- Improve and become better.
- Invent or reinvent.

The Combined Framework

Combining the two dimensions of types or levels of competition with management objectives, the following framework emerges (Figure 2-2).

Each space in the framework marks a purpose that must be fulfilled by management. Many theoretical areas offer ways to fulfill the different purposes and therefore we have a framework for ordering management fads according to a set of purposes in a firm's management.

The proposed framework has one crucial premise that must not be forgotten. The premise is that a firm should take into account the different types of competition and different types of decisions. If a firm does so continuously and does so better than other firms, then the firm will remain competitive over time.

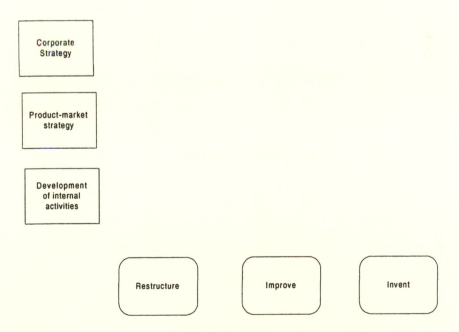

Figure 2-2. A model for categorizing relevant theoretical areas.

PLACING RELEVANT THEORETICAL AREAS IN THE FRAMEWORK

Figure 2-3 places a number of relevant theoretical areas in each of the possible combinations of decision areas and objectives discussed previously. The illustration serves as the starting point for a discussion on where different theoretical areas should be located.

Mission Management and Its Location

The traditional view of the mission of the firm can be expressed by the fundamental question: What is our business and what should it be? (Levit, 1960). In other words was "the mission of the business" traditionally seen as an intellectual discipline that defines the firm's commercial rationale and target market? In this way mission is linked to (product-market) strategy, but at a higher level, as a first step in conducting product-market-focused strategic management.

Another view of mission, however, has also become apparent in the literature. In this view, the mission of the business is the "cultural clue," which enables an organization to function as a collective unity (Campbell & Yeung, 1991a). In this view, the mission consists of strong norms

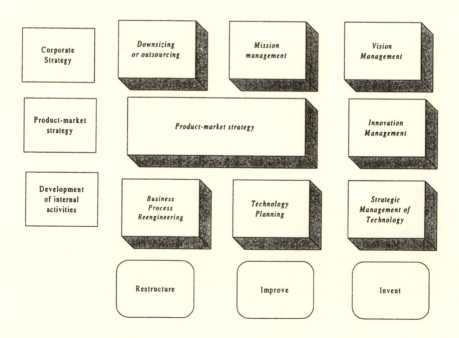

Figure 2-3. The framework for relevant theoretical areas.

and values that influence the way in which people behave, how people work together, and how people pursue the objectives of the organization. Compared with the traditional view, this view sees mission as capturing some of the emotional aspects of the organization, and generating cooperation among people through shared values and standards of behavior.

Much of the recent literature on mission management combines these two different views in a manner expanding both of them to deal with both business logic and emotional aspects of external positioning strategies. A number of authors have contributed to this theoretical area, most notably Andrew Campbell, Fred David and Jack Pearce, and James C. Collins. Unfortunately, these authors do not agree on the contents of important conceptions such as mission, vision, purpose, and values.

Before 1992, the most important contributions was that of Peter Drucker, who in 1973 stated: ". . . mission and philosophy is the key starting point in a business" (Drucker, 1973, p. 47). Drucker's view clearly subscribes to the traditional approach to external positioning, since he mainly considers the customer and the rationale behind the existence of the company. In 1982, Jack Pearce published his article "The Company Mission as a Strategic Tool" in *Sloan Management Review* (Pearce, 1996). This was the first major contribution on the new perception of mission management, even though the contributions within this area clearly draw heavily on a number of earlier contributions from famous authors such as Maslow, Herzberg, Schein, Peters and Watermann, Ouchi, Deal and Kennedy, and others. This is outlined in the book *Mission and Business Philosophy* by Andrew Campbell and Kiran Tawadey (1990), which may be seen as a state-of-the-art contribution on strategic mission management by the Ashridge Center.

As already mentioned in Chapter 1, mission management focused on values and norms as a valuable supplement to the more "hard" aspects of management and analysis. Returning to Figure 2-3, mission management seems to deal with corporate strategy (Campbell & Yeung, 1991a). To be even more specific, I believe that part of this work—that one mission of the firm—covers one part of the three objectives (improve), whereas another part—visions for the future (Collins & Lazier, 1993)—covers another part of the objectives (invent). It seems, though, that the third objective (remove) is hardly covered by any part of the mission management movement.

Perhaps another management fad of relatively recent glory may help us. There has been much talk about "corporate down-sizing," "right-sizing," and so on (Shapiro, 1996; Hamel & Prahalad, 1994), and I propose to locate that management fad in the upper-left corner of Figure 2-3.

Product-Market Strategy

Since we have already discussed product-market strategy in great detail, I will not describe that area any further here, but merely conclude that as we move toward the middle part of Figure 2-3, we also move toward competition on product-market level. The successful work on product-market strategy (or business strategy) that peaked in the 1980s (Porter, 1980, 1985) covers at least the two objectives of removing and improving. However, it should be noted that, for example, the Boston matrix does by no means tell the spectator which new products to introduce at which markets or, for that matter, how to go about doing so (Drejer, 1996b). Perhaps the tools of product-market strategy can point toward the need for inventing new product-market combinations, but the *how* and *what* of that is never really covered by the tools.

Management of Technology

Part of MoT, however, may be appropriate for covering the what and how of selecting new products for new markets (Drejer, 2001). Innovation management or simply the management fad of product development is a discipline that probably covers the objective of inventing new product-market combinations, especially as more recent work on both fads emphasize strongly the link to marketing and the customer (Hein & Andreasen, 1985; Andreassen, 1999).

Over the last few years, a perception of MoT as a part of strategic management has become evident in the literature (Drejer, 1997). This seems to be the culmination of a historical development. A review of the MoT literature reveals that many authors do not share a common understanding of the subject or the nature of technology and management of technology. Thus, the literature on MoT is rich both in different perceptions of MoT and in work within each of these perceptions. Each of the many contributions to the MoT field has something to offer. An overview of the different perceptions of MoT and their implications is, therefore, much needed.

Some authors state that the field of MoT has existed since the early 1980s in its present form (Ulhøi & Madsen, 1993), but that the field can be traced back to the early 1970s under labels such as R&D management, innovation management, engineering management, industrial engineering, and operations management. The argument that MoT now embraces all of these different fields is that MoT is an umbrella concept that has the purpose of creating competitive advantage for firms by means of the internal activities in the firm. This has also been (part of) the purpose of operations management, but to me the strength of having MoT as the umbrella concept is that it allows for many different approaches to creating competitive advantage. This is in line with my rather pragmatic view that in practice many different approaches are needed to secure and create competitive advantage.

In 1987, the U.S. National Research Council (NRC) published *Management of Technology: The Hidden Advantage*, a research project aimed at discussing some current tendencies within international competition. NRC defines MoT as

> . . . Management of technology links engineering, science, and management disciplines to plan, develop, and implement technological capabilities to shape and accomplish the strategic and operational objectives of an organisation. . . . Key elements of MoT in industrial practice are (1) the identification and evaluation of technological options; (2) management of R&D itself, including determining project feasibility; (3) integration of technology into the company's overall operations; (4) implementation of new technologies in a product and/or process; and (5) obsolescence and replacement. (National Research Council, 1987, p. 15)

This is one of a number of explicit definitions of MoT. Another definition within the same tradition is:

> . . . [MoT should] explicitly incorporate mechanisms to deal with management's understanding of new and emerging technologies, organisational and workforce issues, and factors external to the firm. . . . [MoT should be] "integrated" because it . . . [should] . . . combine the management of organisational issues related to technological innovation and implementation with the technical issues. (Monger, 1988, p. 39)

These definitions seem to consider technology one of the important resources of a corporation. G. H. Gaynor states:

> . . . MoT at the academic level implies: developing an understanding as to how all of the technologies of a business can be integrated, directed towards some specific objectives, and optimised with all the other business resources . . . as an example, marketing, financial, and human resource management must be included. (Gaynor, 1991, p. 21)

However, other definitions concentrate on the invention and innovation of technology.

> . . . Management of technology is the timely creation and improvement of the products and productive capability of the corporation. The problem of managing technology . . . divides into two parts: encouraging invention and managing successful innovation. (Betz, 1987, pp. 6-7)

... There is a growing realisation that the adoption of new technology is a highly complex process. Success is dependent not only on the management of change in the technology itself but also upon the changes within the business that are necessary to exploit the potential of the technology. It is these technology-induced organisational changes which management often has great difficulty in coming to terms with. Frequently it involves the culture of the business, its strategies, the organisational structure, managerial attitudes, and personal policies. (Twiss & Goodridge, 1989, pp. xv)

In a third category are authors who see technology as a strategic factor and, therefore, MoT as an explicit part of strategic management.

The integration of business and technology is critical to success in today's environment of stiff competition, changing social values, and fast development of new technologies. Success in integrating these functions will depend on a corporation's ability to:

- Create a mutual understanding between business and technology, recognising each other's needs and constraints.
- Recognise the limitations of strategic business planning process.
- Incorporate technology as a part of corporate strategic planning process.
- Recognise that the effective utilization of human resources may be the only strategic advantage of a business or corporation. (Bhalla, 1987, p. 85)

... management of technology is actually the practice of integrating technology strategy with business strategy in the company. This integration requires the deliberate co-ordination of the research, production, and service functions with the marketing, finance, and human resources functions of the firm. (Badawy, 1991, quoted in Gaynor, 1991, p. xi)

Few people have provided an overall view of the management of technology as a discipline. Among those who have are Paul Adler (1989), and John P. Ulhøi (Ulhøi & Madsen, 1992). My own work and reviews of the literature (Drejer, 1996b, 1997) support the conclusion that there are several different perceptions of what MoT is in the current research community. For the purposes of this chapter it is particularly relevant that MoT can be divided into four schools of thought (Drejer, 1996a):

- R&D management
- Innovation management
- Technology planning
- Strategic MoT

The schools have been evolving since the early 1970s. Table 2-1 summarizes this historical account of the MoT discipline.

Without going into too much detail with each of the four schools of thought within MoT, it seems to be natural to locate the school of innovation management in the middle-right part of Figure 2-3, thereby covering the invention-purpose at the product-market level. More recent development in the field of innovation management suggests that this corresponds to a traditional perception of innovation management (Drejer, 2001), and that this perception is currently being supplemented with the idea that innovation should also take place at the internal level—competencies—of the firm.

Furthermore, MoT has traditionally focused on the internal level of the firm. I would choose to locate the area of technology planning in the improve-internal activities square, whereas the more advanced area of strategic MoT could be located in the invent-internal activities square. This may be a stretch, as there is a degree of overlap between the two areas; however, it seems clear that they do not fill the restructure-internal activities square.

Business Process Reengineering

BPR is one of the latest stars to appear on the management scene, launched by Michael Hammer in 1990 and later quickly adopted by consultants all over the world. The aim of BPR is radical improvements, where 10% is seen as a little improvement in performance. In fact,

TABLE 2-1. Summary of the Four Schools of Management of Technology

	School 1 R&D Management	School 2: Innovation Management	School 3 : Technology Planning	School 4: Strategic MoT
Perceived environment	Stable, simple and expanding	Changing, but predictable	Changing and discontinuous	Changing, discontinuous, unpredictable with new dimensions
Scope	Manage R&D resources	Manage innovation in the entire company	Manage technology across the company	Manage and integrate technology with other aspects
Issues	People, ideas, funds, culture	Conception, invention and exploitation of technology	Analyze and plan the complex process of technological development	Deal with all the dimensions of technological evolution
Tools for making decisions	Technology forecasting, budgeting	Delphi-forecasting, technology forecasting, project management of the innovation process	Scenario forecasting, technology analysis and planning	Strategic MoT, O-T approach to MoT, and integrated MoT

Hammer and Champy advise us to choose ordinary quality control techniques, if we "merely" desire 10% better performance. In other words: "... at the hearth of business reengineering lies the notion of discontinuous thinking—identifying and abandoning the outdated rules and fundamental assumptions that underlie current business operations" (Hammer & Champy, 1993, p. 3). In his 1993 book (with Champy), Hammer defines BPR as: "... the fundamental rethinking and radical redesign of business processes to acheive dramatic improvements in critical contemporary measures of performance, such as cost, quality, service, and speed" (Hammer & Champy, 1993, p. 32). Other pioneers of BPR include Davenport and Short (1990) and Harrington (1991).

In the area of BPR, organizations are perceived as a set of so-called business processes, that is, a set of logically connected tasks performed to achieve a specific business outcome (Hviid & Sant, 1994). A process consists of the logical organization of people, procedures, materials, equipment, and so forth into work activities designed to produce a specified end result. What is new is that business processes, according to, for example Hviid and Sant (1994), is the way customers view the firm as cross-functional processes aimed at providing value to the customer. By focusing on business processes, the customer and her needs return to the focus of strategy. Figure 2-4 illustrates some of the business processes within a firm. Business processes can be characterized by quantitative measures such as cycle time, quality in output, total costs per activity area, and capacity and resources (Hammer & Champy, 1993), which makes it possible to reengineer business processes.

According to Rigby (1993), there are always four characteristics of business process reengineering:

- A fundamental rethinking of the way work gets done, process redesign, leading to improvements in productivity and cycle times.
- A structural reorganization typically breaking functional hierarchies into cross-functional teams.
- A new information and measurement system using more advanced technology to drive improved data collection and improved decision making.
- A new cultural value system typically placing higher emphasis on the customers.

What I find the most important about BPR, however, is the view of processes that cross functional boundaries in a traditional, hierarchical organization. This view of the actual activities of organizations makes it possible to focus on the customer as the end-user of processes. This

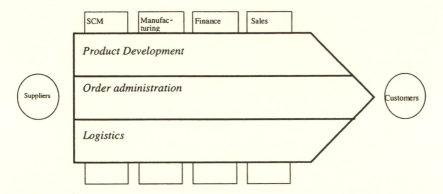

Figure 2-4. Examples of business processes across the functional organization.

is in line with the thinking behind competence-based strategy and certainly has been a great influence on the area of competence-based strategy as we know it today.

In light of the description of BPR, I find it natural that BPR should be located in the internal activities part of Figure 2-3. Whether or not it occupies the invent-internal activities square, the improve-internal activities square, or restructure-internal activities square depends on perspective. No doubt, the theoretical idea of BPR has a natural place in the invent-internal activities because of its emphasis on innovation; however, the actual practice of BPR in firms (Champy, 1995; Hammer & Stanton, 1995) seems to support that BPR should be located in either restructure or improve internal activities.

CONCLUSIONS

Competence-Based Strategy and the Other Areas

As has already been shown, competence-based strategy is far from the only theoretical area that claims to deal with the development of internal activities of firms, not even on the strategic level. In this section, we have discussed MoT and BPR in great detail, and later I will return to organizational learning as another relevant area in this respect. I believe that competence-based strategy should occupy the entire lower row of the framework for analysis of theoretical areas. This implies that competence-based strategy is concerned with the restructuring (destruction perhaps), improvement, and invention (innovation) of the competencies of the firm. What can we learn from those other areas that occupy the same space in the model?

I think we can learn something from every theoretical area that is concerned with the same area of application as competence-based strategy. BPR has taught us to consider processes that work across the functional boundaries of our hierarchical organizations and interact directly with the customers of the firm. Undoubtedly, that is an important lesson when we start looking for what core competencies are; that is, we should not just look for competencies inside departments but also across departments. As for MoT, this area has many things to offer. First, several definitions of technology traditionally emphasize the interplay between hard technology and human resources. This is of major importance when we talk about competencies as well. Second, the area of MoT is based on a firm grasp of the dynamics of technologies and derived need for developing and destroying technologies over time. As we shall see, this is also an important lesson for competence-based strategy, and several models for analysis and planning of technology development can be used as inspiration for the area of competence-based strategy. Third, organizational learning is an area that I will return to later, when we discuss competence development. The case for that is simply that it must be the human element that improves its knowledge over time, rather than, for instance, the technological element of competencies. Organizational learning as a theoretical area has been concerned with this issue for more than 50 years, so why not seek inspiration there?

The overall message of this discussion is that we must avoid reinventing everything from scratch just because we work in a rather new theoretical area. There are so many theoretical areas and fields in management today that there is bound to be overlap in interests, area of application, research traditions, and so on.

The Evolution of Competence-Based Strategy

Competence-based strategy does not exist in a vacuum. In Figure 2-5, I have attempted to illustrate the context in which the theoretical area of competence-based strategy is located.

The area of competence-based strategy is based on a certain rationale, much of which I believe is captured by the ideas of competitiveness that have been formulated in strategic management. It is particularly important to note the idea that competitiveness needs to be sustainable over time; this leads to the conclusion that competencies cannot be assumed to be stable, eternal entities but that they need to change over time. In turn that leads to the important conclusion that competence-based strategy should be concerned with improvement, invention, and destruction (restructuring) of competencies. This signals a different rationale than that for BPR, at least in my interpretation, where BPR is more concerned with restructuring than

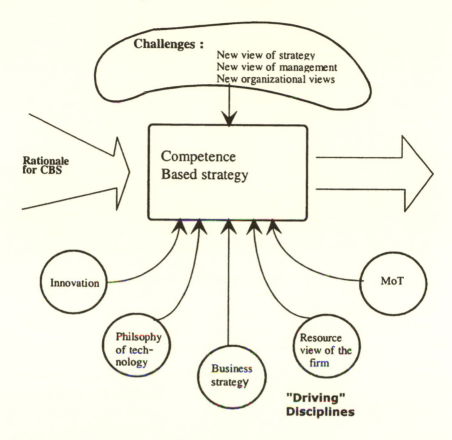

Figure 2-5. Context of competence-based strategy.

invention. There are several other important points about the rationale of competence-based strategy, but for now the emphasis on competitiveness is the most important one.

Furthermore, competence-based strategy is driven by the strong influence of the area of strategic management in general. In particular, this chapter has emphasized how the concept of strategic management has changed over time. The emphasis on the internal activities—whether capabilities, technology or resources—that started in the 1980s certainly has been one of the major drivers of the entire area of competence-based strategy. That continues to have a strong impact on the area and will do so in the future as well. Another important development in strategic management and management in general is that of the role of management itself. In the introduction I emphasized the emergence of new kinds of employees as one key to the change in attitude and ideas about managers and management. The new economy and its emphasis on innovation—and hence nonhierarchical organizations—probably also adds to this trend. Perhaps it is just that pendulum motion that now swings toward the softer aspects of management and human resources again. In any case the emphasis on human resources, organizational learning, and knowledge of the 1990s is also a major driver of the area of competence-based strategy.

The final point is that a number of other theoretical areas also shape and drive competence-based strategy. As already mentioned, areas such as BPR, MoT, and organizational learning seem to be of particular importance. There is, however, another set of theoretical areas that I have not yet mentioned. These are the ancestors of competence-based strategy. Even though, for instance, Hamel and Prahalad (1994) do not acknowledge that there was something before "core competence" as a concept, a historical analysis reveals that there have been several attempts to formulate a theoretical area based on the same background and rationale as competence-based strategy. The two major attempts are the resource-based view of the firm and critical capabilities. In the next chapter, I will look at what competence-based strategy of today can learn from the work of those areas. The two areas are not just those that have a certain overlap with competence-based strategy, such as BPR, but areas that almost totally have the same purpose, same basic concepts (albeit with different names), and the same rationale. Therefore, there must be much to learn from those two areas, which is the purpose of the next chapter.

3

What Shaped Competence-Based Strategy?

The ultimate purpose of strategic management is to secure competitive advantage of the organization in question. Therefore it seems natural to take a look at both the concept of competitive advantage and the idea of sustainable competitive advantage. Recent development in the thinking related to those concepts has been part of what shaped competence-based strategy as we know it today. Thus, the discussion of competitive advantage acts as a prelude to a discussion of the theoretical areas that shaped competence-based strategy.

WHAT IS COMPETITIVE ADVANTAGE?

The development over time of the concept of *(sustainable) competitive advantage* is one of the main reasons why the concept of strategic management has evolved into its recent state. In this section I make three attempts to define competitiveness before discussing sustainable competitive advantage.

Value to the Customer

According to Michael Porter, competitiveness is what the customer is willing to pay for. Thus, a first attempt to define competitiveness could be to look at value to the customer derived from the products and services of the firm. Some would say that this is fairly easy to answer as a firm offers (physical) product to its customers. But is it really so simple? James Brian Quinn, in his 1992 book, makes a great effort to convince us that it is not. For instance, he cites Ted Levitt's famous paraphrase, ". . . millions of quarter-inch drill bits are sold not because people want quarter-inch drill bits but because they want quarter-inch holes. People don't buy products, they buy the expectation of future benefits . . ." (Levitt, 1969, quoted in Quinn, 1992, p. 175). Consequently, a firm may offer a given (physical) product, but the customer, who defines the competitiveness of the company by his actions, may perceive the value of the product very differently from the company.

This has been common knowledge in marketing theory for some time. For instance, Phillip Koetler, in his 1999 marketing book, defines a product as: ". . . anything than can be offered to a market for attention, acquisition, use, or consumption that might satisfy a want or need . . ." (Kotler, 1999, p. 429). Furthermore, Kotler elaborates on this definition by proposing that the offering a company must be thought about on five different product-levels (Figure 3-1).

- *The basic need* is the need that is fulfilled by the offering.
- *The generic product* defines the basic, physical elements of the product.
- *The expected product* is what the customer expects from the offering.
- *The expanded product* is the elements that extend the expected product.
- *The potential product* contains what may be included in the offering in the future.

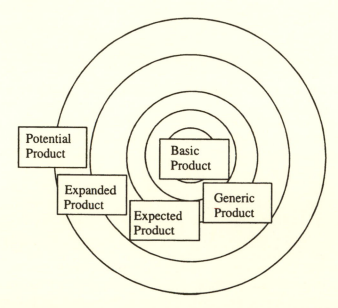

Figure 3-1:   Kotler's five product-levels. (Adapted from Kotler, 1999)

To me, a division of a product/offering into levels is not necessarily an adequate way of describing products and the value derived from products because customers rarely make such distinctions between the different parts of the product/offering. For instance, a customer who buys a holiday will not distinguish between the generic product (flight travel and hotel room) and the expanded product (easy access to a beach, nightclubs or museums) when she decides how satisfied she is with the product. It is possible that each of the elements may be weighted differently, but they will be part of one judgment and one decision-making process.

However, Kotler has one very important message for those who believe that what the company offers to its customers is an easy matter to characterize—the customer's perception of the product is enormously complex and perhaps no all-encompassing definition can be offered. However, we can say that customer's perception of a product depends on a number of factors, as the following equation attempts to illustrate.

$$\text{Product} = \text{the physical product} + \text{marketing} + \text{service} + \text{delivery} + \text{image} + ...$$

Each of these factors can provide value to the customer. Consequently, the competitiveness of what a company offers to its customers depends on how the customer judges each of the many factors constituting the offering and how well she thinks these factors contribute to the fulfillment of her needs and wishes.

Naturally, evaluating competitiveness of a product offering is a very complex process that cannot be reduced to purely economic considerations. We may well define the costs of the physical product and compare this to the actual cost obtained in the marketplace—but is this market price really what the customer is willing to pay, and what about the more intangible elements of the offering? James Brian Quinn refers to these as "services," somewhat a broadening of the traditional concept of services, but still, how can we measure the effects of a good marketing campaign? Or the value of the company image? Clearly, evaluating the competitiveness of an offering is a complex process indeed.

All of this point towards the idea that a firm can achieve competitive advantage based on several kinds of positional advantage. There are three main forms:

- *Positional advantage from an attractive industry structure.* In some cases all firms in an industry benefit from that industry's structure. For example, there are industries with very few firms (that typically are more profitable than industries with many firms). Airbus and Boeing, as the only manufacturers of large, commercial aircraft in the world, are examples of this kind of advantage.

- *Positional advantage from heterogeneity within the industry.* Often positions within an industry create advantages for the firms occupying them. For instance, a firm with a dominant position in an otherwise fragmented industry is usually more profitable than the other firms. An example could be the advantages that large fast-food chains have enjoyed over small, independent fast-food outlets. The smaller firms have higher costs and less brand equity than their dominant rivals that leverage economies of scale in operations and branding to sustain their position.
- *Positional advantage from a network of relations.* A firm may derive positional advantage from its relationship with buyers, suppliers, or competitors. For example, most car manufacturers have been able to define and manage their supply chains from (almost) raw material to end-user in an advantageous and efficient manner.

In the real world, of course, it may not be trivial to assign specific instances of positional advantage to one of the three generic forms of positional advantage. The following list of examples provides a broader perspective on positional advantage:

- *Brand name.* A firm with widely recognized and appreciated brand has positional advantage over other firms in the industry whose brands are weaker. A strong brand lets the firm command premium shelf space, wider customer attention, and higher prices.
- *Customer relationships.* A firm with an established reputation for "fair trading" and consistent high quality has a positional advantage over firms whose customers think that the firm is being opportunistic.
- *Government support and protection.* Firms may derive positional advantage from government intervention in many ways from direct economic support to indirect support by means of legislation, taxation, and so on.
- *Distribution channels.* A firm may derive status as the dominant firm within its industry via its distribution channels and thereby access to customers.
- *Installed base and de facto standards.* In markets where product compatibility is important, firms with a large installed base have a positional advantage. Those firms can even use this base to create de facto standards for products, thereby forcing other firms to apply those standards, often at a high cost.

Based on these examples, I believe that we can say something more general about positional advantage. First, many instances of positional advantages stem from the ability and will to move first, as do many failures in generating a positional advantage. Thus, the ability and willingness to spot opportunities and move in first are connected to the whole notion of positional advantage. Second, positional advantage is defined only relative to actual and potential competitors—it is not something absolute.

Assets and Resources Needed to Produce the Offering

Too often scholars of strategic management believe that competitive advantage can be gained merely by analyzing value creation and advise firms to maximize the value created for the customers. The preceding discussions deal with the issue of external productivity, that is, the value delivered to the customer in terms of satisfaction of needs and wishes. Of course, the customer is the ultimate judge of just how much value a given offering delivers to him. However, if there is such a thing as external productivity, then there must be such a thing as internal productivity, and perhaps this concept may help us to evaluate what creates competitive advantage beyond positional advantage.

Internal productivity may be stated as:

$$\text{Internal Productivity} = \text{Output/Cost of Resources used.}$$

Our man with the shovel digs with a certain (given) value of m^3 per hour, for instance. Knowing this, one might calculate how much two men will dig in five hours, and so on. However, here we find the first obstacle: the soil may be hard and rocky at times and soft at others. Consequently, a measure of internal productivity must also include a specification of the task to which work is related, as well as the methods used for the task. This makes it, for one thing, difficult to compare internal productivity for different tasks and, thus, difficult to calculate one company measure of internal productivity. For instance, the number of working hours per cost is not a sensible measure to apply to the departments of a company in order to decide who is behind in productivity.

There is another, and much greater, difficulty when the use of so-called capital resources or assets has to be taken into account. Consider, for instance, the situation where the digging is done with a tractor. Then one will have to take into account the cost of the tractor when determining internal productivity:

$$\text{Internal Productivity} = \text{Output/(Cost of Resources used}$$
$$\text{+ Cost of Assets used).}$$

In traditional management accounting costs of assets used are labeled "overhead," and a peculiar situation arises when overhead can no longer be ignored. For instance, consider a multiproduct factory with a substantial amount of total costs as overhead. Then one has to add overhead to a given product to determine internal productivity. But overhead costs are of an elusive nature that may not be directly connected to each product. For instance: what about R&D costs? Should R&D costs be split equally among all products or merely on "new" products? Not even the cost of "hard assets" like a milling machine that is only used for one product can easily be split this way. If the number of products manufactured decreases, the prices on the remaining products will have to increase to cover the overhead costs of the milling machine. There are numerous problems like these in management accounting today, where more than 95% of internal costs may be outside of the physical transformation of materials and other resources, that is, outside manufacturing (Quinn, 1992). Quinn calls all nonmanufacturing resources "services" and claims that these constitute the major part of the U.S. and European economy (Quinn, 1992). Of course, this has not been unnoticed in academic circles and a lot of attempts to deal with overhead costs have been thought out, for instance activity-based costing. See Johnson and Kaplan (1987) for an excellent review of much of this debate or Kaplan (1990) for a proposal for new measures and methods for improvement of management accounting.

Despite measurement problems and their varying solutions it can be concluded that internal productivity leads us to look at core competencies as a source of competitive advantage. Consider the example of a firm that derives competitive advantage from manufacturing products at low cost. This we can objectively see (in stores or in the marketplace), but we cannot see how firms achieve low cost. It may be because of positional advantage. For instance, the firm may have access to cheap labor or resources or may be government subsidized. But again this may not be the case. The history of strategic management is full of cases in which it has been impossible to explain the apparent competitive advantage of firms by means of positional advantage; some firms simply perform better than other firms with similar positional advantages. In fact, I would call it the great failure of the school of product-market strategy that it has failed to explain such cases.

The latest school of thought about strategic management has provided an explanation. No matter the name given to the concepts at work, it is possible to explain why some firms have competitive advantage over others with similar positional characteristics and advantages, because the former firms have learned to combine their resources and assets more efficiently than the latter firms. Our low-cost manufacturer may be extremely good at planning production, have a superior quality program, be able to integrate product development and manufacturing in superior ways compared with other firms in the industry. The more competitive firm has one or more core competencies that it can use to create value for its customers and/or achieve lower internal costs, thereby creating overall competitive advantage relative to its competitors.

As we shall see later, there are many different kinds of competencies and, hence, many different ways that these competencies can help create competitive advantage (see Chapter 4). Competencies are an important supplement to positional advantages when it comes to explaining competitive advantage.

An Overall View of Competitive Advantage

Competitiveness is derived from external factors—or positional advantage—*and* internal factors—or resources and assets used. The latter is the effect of the competencies of the firm. Thus, a definition of competitiveness might be: competitiveness is a measure of the ability of the company to deliver value to the customer divided with the resources used relative to the competitors of that particular company. This measure may be illustrated by Figure 3-2.

This measure of competitiveness is not an operational measure and should not be taken as such. However, it does focus attention on two different issues that must be seen in connection in strategic management: the position enjoyed by the firm and the internal competencies of the firm, which together form the basis for judging the competitive advantage of the firm. Evidently, both measures must be taken relative to the competitors of the company.

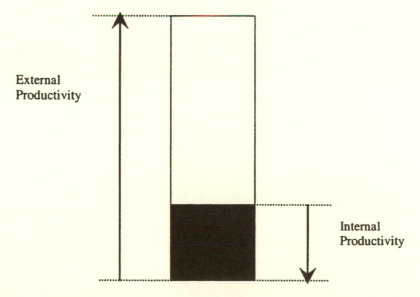

Figure 3-2. An illustration of total competitiveness.

Finally, to add even more to the complexity of this issue a note on competitors is called for. Regarding product offerings it may be relatively easy to deduce who the competitors are even though the multi-element conception of products may render this quite difficult. For instance, substituting products may be in vast numbers and kinds. Furthermore, regarding internal measures, Quinn advises us to consider each competence area as an area where the company must excel in competition with all the companies that offer this competence as a product offering (Quinn, 1992). For instance, one may consider outsourcing all sorts of competence areas (e.g., R&D, finance, inventory control) if one's internal productivity is too low compared with others (see, for example, Venkatesan, 1992).

WHAT, THEN, IS SUSTAINABLE COMPETITIVE ADVANTAGE?

At this point in the discussion of competitive advantage, two important issues are of interest. First, the conception of competitiveness as dictated by the customers alone may be questioned from a number of sides, perhaps most notably from the environment side, for example do customers know, or even care, what is good for the environment? Second, what creates sustainable competitive advantage? This may be either products or underlying competencies. Even though a much more adequate discussion follows later, I argue that sustainable competitive advantage is created in the interplay between so-called product-market and competence considerations.

Is the Customer the Ultimate Judge of Quality?

According to the preceding discussion and most theory on strategic management, the customer is the ultimate judge of competitiveness; that is, by buying the products of a firm, the customer indirectly decides which firms will continue to exist and which firms will go bankrupt. This corresponds to the famous slogan by Alfred Sloan of General Motors: *doing better by doing good*; that is, if a firm makes money then that is good for society (Mintzberg & Quinn, 1990). However, quite a few scholars have questioned this, for instance, the entire line of research in vision management (Andersen, 1995; Campbell & Yeung, 1990, to name a few of the seminal references), which claims that a corporation has more than just economic responsibilities. In fact, Andersen claims that taking no responsibility for larger societal issues equals lack of responsibility (Andersen, 1995), a rather serious claim toward managers of today. And, in fact, there are some serious questions to be asked regarding the entire set of stakeholders in a firm and their claims. For instance, one very hot topic of today is that of sustainable environmental development, which in many cases will not correspond to sustainable economic development—environmental protection costs money.

This discussion is divided into two parts: first, the shareholders, who may or may not share interests with customers, and, second, all other stakeholders, who may or may not have noneconomic stakes in the firm.

Although both competitiveness and shareholder value are typically measured in economic terms, there has been considerable argument regarding whether either should be the key to managing a firm. Typically, management is said to have to do with the fact that shareholders focus on short-term profits, while competitive advantage—and strategic management—should focus on long-term profitability of the firm. Thus, this discussion has to do with strategy (mostly of U.S. corporations) being focused on short-term issues instead of long-term issues (as, it is said, Japanese firms) (Abegglen & Stalk, 1985). This focus has been blamed to be, at least partly, the cause of the decline of U.S. competitiveness (Kantrow, 1983).

The problems of shareholder value versus sustainable competitive advantage are related to the problems discussed previously regarding accounting methods (Johnson & Kaplan, 1987), which seem to show an imprecise picture of the economic state of a corporation. Furthermore, Rappaport devotes an entire *Harvard Business Review* article to the demonstration of the fact that: ". . . establishing competitive advantage and creating shareholder value . . . stem from a common economic framework . . ." (Rappaport, 1992, p. 84). Rappaport's basic argument is that shareholders evaluate the prospects of long-term profitability of a firm when they decide to buy or sell stocks, and that it is only unexpected short-term results, such as a bad quarterly report, that make them change their minds. Consequently, the stories of shareholder panic caused by a bad quarterly report, which in part has caused some to claim that shareholder value and competitive advantage are different, are simply misinterpretation of shareholders. In Rappaport's words: ". . . long-term productivity lies at the root of both sustainable competitive advantage and consistent results for the shareholder . . ." (Rappaport, 1992, p. 84). Consequently, if top managers maximize, or at least do better than competitors, the shareholders will be pleased as well:

$$\text{Total productivity} = \text{Value to the customer} / \text{Resources and assets used.}$$

It has now been established that shareholder value and customer value are two sides of the same coin. This may also be the case for other stakeholders of a corporation, for instance, suppliers, who have a natural interest in the long-term competitiveness of their customers. However, there may be other interests besides economic results. An excellent example is that of sustainable environmental protection that may cost more money than it saves, which works against the maximization of the above equation. A number of other examples like this one may be cited: employee well-being, philanthropy, and so on; and the question is what can be done to incorporate such issues in the equation of, and thinking behind, total productivity? This interesting question may not have a simple answer.

In a "mathematical" way of thinking, the concept of constraints can be of great assistance. If issues such as environmental protection are formulated as constraints to the original equation of total productivity, such issues can be taken into consideration without fundamentally changing the thinking behind competitive advantage. Total productivity is still supposed to be maximized, but now with regard to some constraints; that is, solving the equation yields a local, not global, optimum point.

Of course, this is a simplistic way of looking at such difficult problems as environmental protection, mainly because the equations of this section are not solvable, "hard" equations, but rather conceptual ones. However, it is of crucial importance that a link is established between competitive advantage and societal responsibilities, a link that can be established by using (conceptual) constraints to the economic equation of total productivity.

What Creates Sustainable Competitive Advantage?

At this point in the discussion, an interesting question is, what is competitive advantage? And how is it created? Any firm is interested in competitive advantage; actually it may be said to be the very purpose of strategic management, especially if the advantage proves to be sustainable. Hall defines this: ". . . companies have sustainable competitive advantage when they consistently produce product/delivery systems with attributes which correspond to the key buying criteria for the majority of customers in their targeted market . . ." (Hall, 1992a, p. 135). Thus, if a company has sustainable competitive advantage, customers will prefer its product offerings to those of the competition; that is, external and internal productivity will be greater than that of other firms in the targeted market.

Of course, this is a simple view of competitive advantage. For instance, what about substituting products, that is, other offerings that may be preferred to the offering of the corporation? This and many other examples must remind one that competition and strategy never deal with simple issues. However, for the sake of illustrating that competitiveness is decided by the customers—and the customers alone—the preceding discussion functions perfectly and leads to another question: What creates sustainable competitive advantage? There are different views regarding the source of competitive advantage.

For the purposes here, I have chosen to focus on two views: the product-market view and the competence view. The dominant line of research is that of product-market focused strategic management, most prominently represented by Michael Porter, who focuses on maintaining market positions within a given industry. According to Porter, competition within an industry can be described by five forces—the famous five forces model—and the individual firm is seen essentially as a black box. Consequently, competitive advantage stems from building entry barriers to the firm's market segment, and sustainability is secured by managing a balanced portfolio of product/market segments. This view is the *product-market view* of strategy.

Over the years it has become evident that the competitive power of the products in the marketplace is not synonymous with sustainable competitive advantage. Michael Porter (1991) has been one of those to admit this. Furthermore, in practice it may be hard to "translate" the selection of a selected product-market strategy into organizational action. This has led a number of recent authors to propose another view of the firm: the competence view (Prahalad & Hamel, 1990; Prahalad, 1993; Eriksen, 1993a; Grant, 1991). Within this view the level of analysis is taken to be the company, and differences in competitive power are explained in terms of company-specific core competencies. Aaker summarizes the arguments of this line quite nicely: ". . . competing the right way in the right arena can be extremely profitable, but only for a limited time. The . . . [core competencies] . . . of the corporation, which are the basis of competition, provide the foundation of a sustainable competitive advantage . . . and long term performance. Unless there is an advantage over competitors that is not easily duplicated or countered, long term performance is likely to be elusive . . ." (Aaker, 1989, p. 91). Strategy theory based on core competencies—or technology, since these two words are not clearly defined as mutually exclusive conceptions— has become an alternative approach to strategy making. For obvious reasons this approach has been labeled the competence view of strategy theory.

The two alternative approaches to strategic management cannot deal with the entire task of strategy alone. Aaker's argument regarding the profitability of competing the right way in the right arena can be turned upside down. You may have world-class competencies in many areas, but if this does not correspond to what the customers want or if it is offered to the wrong customers, long-term performance is likely to be elusive. For instance, what competencies contribute to a given product line? What are the demands for competence development resulting from expanding this product line? On the other hand, what possibilities result from the development of a new core competence, for example, high-speed manufacturing? The questions illustrate that while product-market strategy cannot explain sustainable competitive advantage, competence development does not automatically lead to the creation of business. There is, therefore, a need for an integration of the two approaches to strategic management in order to secure sustainable competitive advantage.

Summary and Conclusion on Sustainable Competitive Advantage

To summarize this section on sustainable competitive advantage, it can be concluded:

- To evaluate competitiveness, both external and internal productivity should be considered relative to customer demands and competitors.
- However, evaluating the value of these is very difficult owing to the fact that there are many complex issues to consider when making an evaluation.
- The discussion of competitiveness leaves one with basically three options: (1) provide more value to the customer, (2) lower internal costs, and (3) do both to improve competitiveness.
- While value to the customer has no limits, one can only lower internal costs to a certain extent. This is particularly true if one focuses on manufacturing costs that have been the subject of "optimization" for many decades.

These conclusions lead us to considering alternatives to the traditional approach to describing competitive advantage, that is, away from Porter's microeconomic universe and thus toward newer approaches to strategic management that have shaped competence-based strategy.

THEORETICAL AREAS THAT HAVE SHAPED COMPETENCE-BASED STRATEGY

What are core competencies? By what characteristics can we describe them?

Different Names for Different Conceptions

If one takes competence-based strategy as a part of strategy theory that has the basic premise that strategy must be directed inside the corporation toward resources, capabilities, and/or competencies, a scan of the literature will reveal that different authors have different names for the issues to be dealt with in strategic management. A more precise literature analysis and synthesis will follow, but in this section my intent is to illustrate the diversity and complexity of the literature.

Some authors refer to the new view of the corporation as the *resource-based view* of the firm, even though most recent publishers generally attribute: "... the intellectual roots of the resource-based view of the firm ... to Penrose (1959) ..." (Eriksen, 1993, p. 3). Conner has summarized the main idea of the resource-based view of the firm as: "... a resource-based approach to strategic management focuses on costly-to-copy attributes of the firm as sources of economic rents and, therefore, as the fundamental drivers of performance and competitive advantage. ... According to this perspective, a firm's ability to attain and keep profitable markets segments depends on its ability to gain and defend advantageous positions in underlying resources important to production and distribution ..." (Conner, 1991, pp. 121-122). This corresponds to Penrose's theory of the firm as a collection of productive resources, which is decided upon by administrative decisions (Penrose, 1959). These resources range from the physical resources of the corporation, financial resources, human resources, reputation, technological resources and intellectual probate, and organizational resources (Grant, 1991; Eriksen, 1993). A number of authors subscribe to the resource-based view of the firm and attempt to define strategic management in terms of resources.

However, others seem to have evolved from the resource-based view of the firm into something slightly different. For instance, Aaker defines that sustainable competitive advantage must be derived from: " ... assets or skills possessed by the business. An asset is something your firm possesses such as a brand name or a retail location that is superior to the competition. A skill is something that your firm does better than competitors such as advertising or efficient manufacturing ..." (Aaker, 1989, p. 91). From this quotation it is easy to see that a distinction has been made between "hard" and "soft" resources. This is taken one step further by, for instance, Amit and Schoemaker (1993) who make a distinction between resources and capabilities. To these authors, resources are transferable, while capabilities are firm specific. Consequently, sustainable competitive advantage is more likely to be derived from capabilities than from resources; this is also clear from Barney

(1991) and others. In my view, the main difference between Penrose's resource-based view of the firm and the contributions treated here is the question of the conditions under which a resource or capability can constitute the basis of competitive advantage. Penrose and others following her make no distinction between the different kinds of resources, whereas Aaker et al. and others clearly subscribe to the view that truly sustainable competitive advantage flows from firm-specific, difficult-to-imitate, resources.

Finally, there is a third trend within this area of research—the contributions on core competencies. Their origin, or at least the origin of the term *core competence*, can be traced to 1990. Most of the contributions on core competencies either acknowledge the work of Penrose as an inspiration or account for why it is not taken into account. If the latter, the concept of core competencies is presented as the invention of different authors; generally, the concept is attributed to Prahalad and Hamel (1990, 1993). In 1990, they defined core competencies as: ". . . the collective learning in the organisation, especially how to co-ordinate diverse production skills and integrate multiple streams of technologies . . ." (p. 82). It should be noted, though, that in his 1992 book James Brian Quinn attempts to attribute the invention of core competencies to himself. His explanation is that *Harvard Business Review* delayed publication of his articles introducing core competencies until Prahalad and Hamel's work was published first (Quinn, 1992). Still, in his 1992 book it is difficult to find any concrete definition of core competencies. Apart from the sad, but still rather amusing, story of authors' "copyright" to new fads, what can be concluded from this third approach to resource/capability/competence strategy is that it has contributed to lack of clarity. For instance, the notion of core competencies has quite a lot in common with more recent definitions of technology, to such a large extent that later I will argue that core competencies and strategic management of technology deal with basically the same issues, and consequently must be one and same. However, it is time for a more concrete and in-depth analysis of the literature.

Literature Analysis

Literature can tell us quite a lot. Here, I have decided to focus on five pieces of information that seem interesting based on the discussion so far:

1. Most authors seem to propose competence development as a supplement to business strategy. However, which authors seem to think that strategy can exist without business strategy?
2. Do authors recognize the earlier work by Penrose?

3. Which authors prefer "soft," intangible, costly-to-copy, resources/capabilities as the basis for competitive advantage?
4. What is their name for the basis of competition?
5. Do they include case examples for detailed information?

In Table 3-1, I have attempted to display information resulting from the literature analysis on these questions. The literature analysis provides answers to the five questions. In the next section, I will attempt to provide a deeper meaning to the analysis.

Literature Synthesis

Three issues stand out as crucially important at this stage:

- What is the relationship between product-market strategy and competence-based strategy?
- What is the meaning of the many different terms for resources/capabilities/competencies?
- What about technology and the theory area of management of technology?

In the literature, two approaches to strategy theory seem to collide: the product-market focused and the competence-based approach. What is the background of the apparent conflict between the two approaches? The product-market strategy approach is the well-known and very dominant strategy theory put forth by Michael Porter and others (see for instance Porter, 1980, 1985). This approach has celebrated a number of triumphs, for instance the advantages of a, more or less, unified concept of strategy spread to a vast amount of corporations worldwide. However, product-market strategy has been criticized heavily both for being theoretical unsound and for being insufficient. As for theoretically unsoundness, this goes for the process of conceiving, planning, and implementing strategic decisions in a rational manner—something Henry Mintzberg has been the most notable advocator of (Mintzberg, 1994). I focus here on the criticism that claims that product-market strategy is insufficient. Grant is a often cited as an example of this sort of criticism: "... during the 1980s, the principal developments in strategy analysis focused upon the link between strategy and the external environment ... by contrast, the link between strategy and the firm's resources and skills have suffered comparative neglect ..." (Grant, 1991, p. 114). In other words, there is a need to consider the competencies of the firm as well as its product/market applications.

Of course, product-market strategy has a view of the firm, but to quote Eriksen: "... the firm in the neo-classical theory of the firm ...

TABLE 3-1. Literature Analysis on Competence-Based Strategy

Reference	Competence and business strategy?	Recognizes Penrose and earlier work?	Intangibles is the basis of competitive advantage?	Name for resources/ capabilities/ competencies?	Examples include?
Aaker, 1989.	Yes	No	Not alone	Skills (intangible) and assets (tangible)	Yes
Amit & Schoemaker, 1993.	Yes	Yes	Yes	Resources and capabilities (the capacity to deploy resources)	No
Barney, 1986	Yes	No	Yes	Unique skills	No
Barney, 1991	Yes	Yes	Yes	Firm resources (rare, inimitable)	No
Bowonder & Miyake, 1994	Yes	No	Yes	Innovations (product, process, and applications)	Yes
Burgelman & Rosenbloom, 1989	Yes	No	Yes	Capabilities creates technologies	No
Chester, 1994	Yes	No	Yes	Technology	Survey analysis
Clark, 1989	Yes	No	Yes	Technologies and technical competence	Yes
Cleveland et al., 1989	Yes	No	Not alone	Production competence, consists of nine areas of which some are tangible and others are not	No
Corbet et al., 1993	Yes	No	No	Manufacturing competence in time, quality and cost	No
Delapierre, 1988	Yes	No	Yes	Technology bunching	Yes
Eriksen, 1993a & 1993b	Yes	Yes	No	Resources and capabilities	No
Eriksen & Mikkelsen, 1993	Yes	Yes	Not alone	Resources, social capital and organizational capital	No
Ford, 1988	Yes	No	Yes	Technology strategy = knowledge and abilities	No
Foss, 1993	Yes	Yes	Yes	Resources and capabilities	No
Frohman, 1985	Yes	No	Yes	Distinctive technological competencies	No
Grant, 1991	Yes	Yes	Yes	Resources (inputs) and capabilities (the capacity of a team of resources to perform an activity	No
Hamel & Prahalad, 1993	Yes	No	Yes	Resources = core competencies	No

TABLE 3-1. continued

Reference	Competence and business strategy?	Recognizes Penrose and earlier work?	Intangibles is the basis of competitive advantage?	Name for resources/ capabilities/ competencies?	Examples include?
Hall, 1992	Yes	No	Yes	Intangible resources of whichs some are skilles and others assets	No
Hayes & Pisano, 1994	Yes	No	Yes	Critical capabilities = core competencies	No
Hitt & Ireland, 1985	Yes	No	Yes	Distinctive competence	Survey analysis
Irwin & Michals III, 1989	Yes	No references	Yes	Critical capabilities and skills (difficult to replicate)	Yes
Madsen, 1994	Yes	Yes	Yes	Same as Grant, 91	No
Miyazaki, 1994	Yes	No	Yes	Generic technologies = core competencies	No
Morone, 1989	Yes	No	Yes	Technology	No
Normann & Ramirez, 1993	Yes	No	Yes	Competencies	Yes
Prahalad & Hamel, 1990	Yes	No	Yes	Core competencies	Yes
Prahalad, 1993	Yes	No	Yes	Core competencies	Yes
Sterne, 1992	Yes	No references	Yes	Unique core competencies	Yes
Schoemaker, 1992	Yes	Yes	Yes	Core capabilities some of which are skills and others assets	Yes
Teece et al., 1990	Yes	Yes	Yes	Resources and firm capabilities	No
Wernerfelt, 1984	Yes	Yes	No	Resources (tangible and intangible assets)	No
Wernerfelt, 1989	Yes	Yes	Yes	Critical resources (unique)	Yes

[Porter and others within the school of product-market strategy] . . . does not resemble the real-world firm in many ways. The real-world firm is often operating in many product-markets, and the firm changes over time, e.g. through internal growth or mergers. Thus the real-world firm seldom experiences the restrictive and static conditions of the neo-classical theory of the firm . . ." (Eriksen, 1993b, p. 3). Instead, there is clearly a need to consider the dynamic competencies and processes of the real-world firm when conducting strategic management. In the words of Teece, Pisano and Schuen: ". . . we suggest that building into strategy analysis a dynamic view of the business enterprise. . . . enhances the probability of building an acceptable descriptive theory of strategy, as well as a normative theory that has some promise of yielding long-run advantage to its practitioners" (Teece et al., 1990, pp. 12-13).

It is evident that product-market strategy and competence-based strategy cannot exist without contributions from each other. In other words, product markets and competencies are two sides of the same coin and, furthermore, the work on competencies is a necessary and valuable supplement to business strategy theory. Foss (1993) discusses this in much greater detail and concludes that: ". . . the two approaches do actually supplement each other in may ways, for instance when it comes to time horizon and type of strategy. . ." (p. 16). Foss seems to claim that the inward view of competence development is a necessary supplement to the outward view of business strategy. This also seems to be the view of Teece, Pisano and Schuen, who write: ". . . competitive success can flow from both classes of strategy . . ." (Teece et al., 1990, p. 31). This assumption is shared by virtually all the writers reviewed here. However, many of them seem to refer to different concepts when they discuss how this is to be done, for example, what is a critical capability as compared to a core competence? Furthermore, few authors offer any kind of case examples regarding how to do this, which leads readers to reflect on whether they have a concrete idea of how to achieve integration of business strategy and core competencies. Figure 3-3 summarizes the meaning of different concepts within this area of theory.

First of all, strategy is about *where you compete*, that is, the issues of choosing proper market segments and dealing with competitors. Furthermore, strategy deals with *the way you compete*, that is, essentially a selection of one of Porter's three generic strategies. These two issues are the traditional contents of business strategy. Finally, there is core competencies, which are the basis of competition. The latter is the subject of the next section.

The Meaning of Different Concepts

As Table 3-1 shows us, there seems to be a lot of confusion about the terms used among the authors within this area. However, it is possible to create meaning from the many different labels used.

First, the authors who subscribe to the work of Penrose (and, of course, Penrose herself) recognize the resource-based view of the firm as a way to view the firm (Eriksen, 1993a, 1993b; Eriksen & Mikkelsen, 1993; Foss, 1993). In my view, however, this is merely a statement of the necessity to take an inward view of the firm when making strategic decisions. In the work of the previously mentioned authors, little is said about *how* competitive advantage is to be derived from the company viewed as a bundle of resources. An example of this approach may be taken to be that of Amit and Schoemaker: ". . . the challenge is to

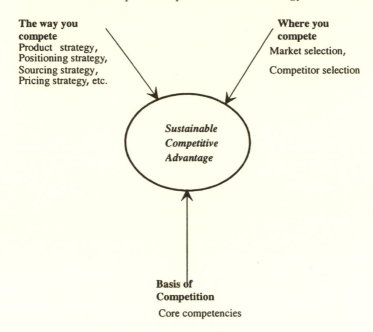

The way you compete
Product strategy,
Positioning strategy,
Sourcing strategy,
Pricing strategy, etc.

Where you compete
Market selection,

Competitor selection

Sustainable Competitive Advantage

Basis of Competition
Core competencies

Figure 3-3. Core competencies and competition.

identify, develop, protect, and deploy resources and capabilities in a way that provides the firm with a sustainable competitive advantage . . ." (1993, p. 33).

However, others have taken these considerations on the resource-based view a step further. For instance, Teece et al. (1990) claim that their work builds on the resource-based view of the firm, but is distinct from it. In my view, these authors and a few others (Grant, 1991; Barney, 1991) conclude that to create sustainable competitive advantage, resources must be firm specific, difficult to imitate, and/or intangible. For instance, Hall notes: ". . . sustainable competitive advantage results from the possession of relevant capacity differentials. The feed stock of these capability differentials is intangible resources . . ." (1992, p. 135). In other words, within this approach there is an important distinction between resources that are easily copied, for example, robot technologies, and resources that are hard to copy, for example, a brand name, reputation, etc., where the latter is most capable of creating sustainable competitive advantage. Barney notes that: ". . . whether or not a competitive advantage is sustained depends upon the possibility of competitive duplication . . ." (1991, p. 32).

Even though some of the authors have taken it a step further, the authors cited here all build on the resource-based view of the firm.

There is a final group of authors who do not recognize the resource-based view of the firm. This group is centered around Prahalad and Hamel, Quinn, and others. To authors in this group, sustainable competitive advantage must be derived from so-called core competencies, which Prahalad, in his 1993 publication (p. 45) described as:

(technology • governance process • collective learning)

Regarding a core competence, it must be subject to three tests:

- Is it a significant source of competitive advantage?
- Does it transcend a single business?
- Is it hard for competitors to imitate?

Consequently, I find it difficult to distinguish between a core competence and, for instance, a critical skill or a unique capability. Thus, in the definition and understanding of core competencies/capabilities and their effect on competitiveness, there seems to be little difference between core competencies and capabilities. Consequently, the main difference between the work on core competencies and the work of capabilities/intangible resources seems to be in the recognition of Penrose or any other prior work.

To summarize the conclusions of this section, it appears that resources are a better way to identify the corporation that is better suited for strategic management than is the traditional black-box view within business strategy. However, sustainable competitive advantage is created by: "... blending the different types of resources in ways that multiply the value of each ..." (Hamel & Prahalad, 1994, p. 81). This implies that resources must be combined, or integrated, to provide competitive advantage, or in Grant's words: "... a capability is the capacity for a team of resources to perform some task or activity. While resources are the source of a firm's capabilities, capabilities are the main source of its competitive advantage ..." (Grant, 1991, p. 119). Furthermore, capabilities and core competencies seem to be one and the same concept and will be treated as such in this thesis. I have chosen to use the term *core competence*, mainly because it secures complete separation from the terms *resources, critical resources*, and so on. Finally, to create sustainable competitive advantage, core competencies must be intangible. This, among other things, is indicated by the keywords of the definition of core competencies: *collective learning, coordinate*, and *integrate*.

Especially interesting is that competencies by nature seem to be the result of a creative blending of "hard" technologies, that is, tangible resources such as equipment and skills/knowledge under the influence of the culture of the corporation.

Technology and Competencies

Now that we have discussed the meaning of core competencies, it may be an appropriate time to reflect on the concept of technology in relation to core competencies. The reader must forgive me for bringing this up—I have worked within the field of MoT for quite a few years.

One of the problems with more recent definitions of technology within the MoT area is that technology seems to contain "everything," that is, physical tools, procedures for use, and knowledge (Gaynor, 1991; Dussage et al., 1992; Bhalla, 1987). In this manner it becomes very difficult to distinguish between what technology is and what is not technology and/or core competencies. However, having defined core competence as above, it is possible to view technology solely as: tools and support for people used in an organized/systematic manner in order to create competence. Thus, core competence becomes a motherhood concept for technology.

COMPETENCIES—THE OBJECT OF COMPETENCE-BASED STRATEGY

Since it seems as if several theoretical areas are concerned with the same concept—let us call it competence hence forward—I would like to end this chapter by synthesizing the theoretical contributions on competencies. I will do so by defining the characteristics of competencies. First, three important distinctions are introduced between different types of competencies. This makes it possible to propose a competence grid. This, in turn, leads to a number of examples of competencies based on the competence grid. Finally, I discuss development patterns for different types of competencies: core and support competencies.

Distinctions in a Discussion of Core Competence

When discussion is on competencies, it is important to note that different authors may talk about different issues when they argue. Thus, it may be a good idea to attempt to "map" the different possible meanings of the *core competence*. To do so, I propose that three distinctions may be of use.

Firm Specific versus Public Domain

A fairly easily comprehensible distinction is between core competencies that are firm specific and core competencies that are public domain. A number of authors in the literature analysis make this distinction. Aaker (1989) distinguishes between intangible skills and tangible assets; Wernerfelt (1984), one of the very first authors of the resource-based view of the firm, distinguishes between tangible resources and intangible assets. Quite a few other authors make this distinction. Some of them put forward the proposition that firm-specific competencies build more sustainable competitive advantage. Others note that working with intangible competencies may be more difficult than working with tangible assets. As we shall see later, there may be different development patterns over time of firm specific-competencies and public-domain competencies.

Human versus Technological

Another distinction is between core competencies as primarily based on human skills or on technological hardware. Again, we may look in the literature to find the reason for this. Some authors distinguish between assets and skills (Hall, 1995; Aaker, 1989), where the former is technological (hardware) and the latter human (software). One reason for this difference may be the starting-point of the different authors. Some authors (Burgelman & Rosenbloom, 1989) originate within the MoT area and they may, perhaps, make the classic mistake of defining technology as consisting of both human and technical hardware but fail to incorporate the human dimension in their normative models. Others (Irwin & Michaels, 1989) have a background in consulting where it may be more tempting to focus on human resource issues. At any rate, it is important to know whether an author thinks of core competencies as "distinctive technological competencies" (Frohman, 1985) or as "unique skills" (Barney, 1986).

Product, Process, and Administrative Competencies

Finally, there is the classical distinction between product technology and process technology, (Hayes & Wheelwright, 1979), which within this context is between product-based competencies and process-based competencies. This is seen from a MoT viewpoint, where it often is sensible to distinguish between the actual product and the technology with which the product was produced: process technology (Bhalla, 1987; Dussage et al., 1991). However, the literature on core competencies point to a third category which is often missing in much of the literature. For instance Eriksen and Mikkelsen (1993) talk of organizational and social capital, while Cleveland et al. (1989) define "production competence" as divided into nine areas of which some are clearly organizational. Consequently, I propose a third category within this context: administrative competencies. Inspired by Miles and Snow (1978), I see administrative competencies as "everything" apart from product and process. This may be organizational structure, management systems, human procedures, and so on.

The Core Competence Grid

Applying the distinctions discussion yields the so-called core competence grid, which consists of all the different possible meanings of core competencies that authors may or may not imply when they talk of core competencies (Figure 3-4).

It may be rather important to know where one is located in the grid to comprehend the full meaning of what an author writes about core competencies. The core competence grid in Figure 3-4 is designed to capture all the possible meanings of the term *core competencies* as it has been used in the literature. In the next section a number of examples will be presented for node instances of core competencies, that is, types of competencies that fit just one box in the grid. This is followed by a discussion of development patterns over time for firm-specific and public-domain competencies. I argue that core competencies should be kept firm specific to create sustainable competitive advantage.

Different Types of Competencies

In accordance with the core competence grid, we will discuss product, process, and administrative competencies separately.

Product-Based Competencies

If one investigates product-based core competencies alone, the following set of examples of product-based competencies may be de-

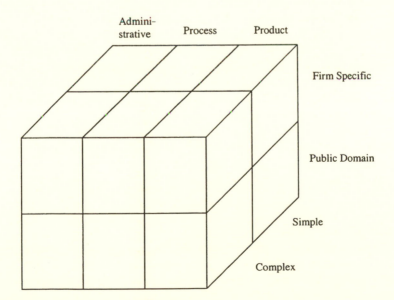

Figure 3-4. The core competence grid.

duced. First, it should be noted that discussing product-based core competencies is entirely different from discussing product-market strategy, mainly because product-market strategy is concerned with the product-market portfolio and adequate generation of cash to sustain business. In contrast, product-based core competencies is about competencies in making and/or marketing the products.

An example of a firm-specific product competency that may be the most difficult to imagine may be that of a patented product technology. For instance, many firms have patented technologies. Such technology, which usually spans a number of different product applications, may be labeled company specific because competitors are not allowed to copy it. If we move on to firm-specific human-based core competencies, an example is the great knowledge and experience that the Danish firm Bang & Olufsen has about their customers. In Bang & Olufsen, there is a clear vision of who the customers are and what preferences they have. This vision is used for product development and marketing. This competence is firm specific because Bang & Olufsen is a niche producer of very special products, whereas the knowledge of their customers may be of very little use to competitors.

If we move to the public domain kind of core competencies, an example of a technological competence would be that of superior products in terms of customer satisfaction. For instance, Bang & Olufsen, within their market niche, offers products that are clearly superior to the competition. As proof is the fact that Bang & Olufsen's customers return, that is, have great loyalty toward Bang & Olufsen. Of course, this may be different from market to market, but almost certainly Bang & Olufsen's products are perceived as superior in their home market of Denmark. Regarding core competencies, which are human-based, an example may be a reputation or a brand name. For instance, another prominent Danish firm, Grundfos, has the reputation of making the best waterpumps in the world, while Coca-Cola has named an entire industry. Such a competence may be of enormous advantage when marketing one's products, but it is difficult to develop competence in such an area. Another example is advertising where, for instance, the owner or CEO of the firm takes an active part. Richard Branson of Virgin Records, with his virtually death-defying balloon stunts, is an example of this kind of competence.

Process-Based Competencies

On the technological side, firm-specific process core competencies may be patented process technology. The Danish medical firm Coloplast provides an excellent example, as the company has a specialized department for developing its own process technologies, which, in turn, are patented. Consequently, the technology may be viewed as firm specific. Regarding human-based competencies, evidently the knowledge of members of Coloplast's technology department regarding their self-designed process technologies is an example of such competencies. This also applies to the blue-collar workers of Coloplast, as they learn to operate the highly specialized equipment with great expertise—an expertise and knowledge that may be of little value outside Coloplast.

Regarding public domain processes, AMT technologies such as robots is an example of technological competencies. If a company has implemented the very latest technology, this may offer great competitive advantage for the company compared with other companies—at least until they purchase the equipment. As for human-based process technologies in the public domain, an example would be well-defined procedures for operating AMT technologies. For instance, Japanese car manufacturers have never been hesitant to invite Western competitors to observe their procedures for Kanban control, quality control, use of robots, and so on. Such more-or-less well-defined procedures for production were thereby free on the public "market" for anyone wishing to copy them. The ultimate example of this trend may be the 1990 book *The Machine That Changed the World* by Womack, Jones and Ross in which "all" of the Japanese procedures are revealed. Of course, as history has shown, "copying" or "implementing" the so-called lean production is not as easy as many imagined. For instance, Jones and Ross (1994) claim that the apparent lack of success of lean production is due to the fact that the entire value-chain or industry of a firm has to be "lean" to secure success. Obviously procedures and practices of one country may be very difficult to implement successfully in another culture and country, in accordance with ideas put forward by Schein (1986) and Hofstede (1981). However, simple procedures and elements of what one company does may very well be implemented in another culture, as the many attempts to implement just-in-time production control in Danish companies as well as other European firms bear witness (Johansen & Mitsens, 1987).

Administration-Based Competencies

Technological, firm-specific core competencies might include an internally designed management information system (MIS) (using the latest information technology), which may be difficult to transfer to another firm. Such an MIS may involve company-specific productivity measures, communication links, customized user interface, and so on, which would be useless in another company. The opposite example, technological competence in the public domain, could simply be the latest information technology, the latest production planning tool, and so on. Such technologies may be advantageous for the company, even though the competitors could easily buy them and, thus, catch up with the company using the latest technology.

If one moves to the human category of administrative competencies, public domain competencies may be well-defined procedures for administrative activities, for instance organizational structure. Organizational structure is almost always identifiable in the public domain, at least to some extent, which makes it public domain. Of course, the formal structure of an organization is just one aspect of organizational practices. Furthermore, contingency factors for organizations may vary greatly from industry to industry; however, there may be administrative competencies that are transferable and formalized. The final category, firm-specific administrative competencies, consists of organizational culture and values. These are, in almost all cases, intangible and difficult to describe and, thus, firm specific. Still, organization culture can be a powerful source of competitive advantage, for instance, if it is used actively in a change process. Bang and Olufsen is a clear example of this, as they have used the company culture to make a major turnaround of the corporation, including technology and organizational structure, since 1990.

Development Patterns of Competencies

Here I would like to discuss the distinction between firm-specific and public domain core competencies in greater detail. These two categories will evolve differently over time. No matter whether competencies are related to product, process, or administrative, development patterns put different emphasis on core competencies of the two categories of firm-specific and public domain competencies.

Firm-specific Core Competencies

Firm-specific core competencies is, according to many authors, the major source of competitive advantage (Table 3-1). The reason for this is that firm-specific competencies cannot be imitated and, thus, they are likely to last longer, see for instance Amit and Schoemaker (1993), Prahalad and Hamel (1990), and Ford (1988). According to this view, firm-specific core competencies evolve only when the company and/or the customers desire it. Coloplast's patented competencies provide an example of such a development. As described previously, the competence is patented in many different ways ensuring that competitors cannot copy it. This does not mean that the competence is not developed further or that competitors do not try to copy the technology. In this case, Coloplast has done a good deal of research and developed the core competencies into new product applications and new levels of performance.

Public Domain Core Competencies

Public domain core competencies have a less encouraging development pattern. An example of this may be ISO 9000 quality management systems. Only 10 years ago, having an ISO 9000 certificate was a major source of competitive advantage, and quality was virtually an industry in itself. Five years later, however, at least in some industries, ISO 9000 was reduced to a qualifying factor for taking part in competition and today no one seems to care whether firms have a ISO 9000 quality system, although customers may care if a firm does not have such a system. In other words, there seems to be a "slide" from a competitive factor toward a qualifying factor as time progresses and more and more competitors transfer the public domain competence to their activities. This is probably why many authors within this field insist that sustainable competitive advantage is best achieved by building firm-specific core competencies. This does not mean, however, that it is any easier to build public domain competencies. Consequently, the builder of core competencies, which are public, should be even more discouraged.

Introducing Core and Support Competencies

In light of the preceding discussion, this is the time to introduce another distinction: the distinction between core competencies and support competencies. Of course, it should be evident that not all competencies are core competencies. In fact, Prahalad (1993) argues that a company may be able to deal with and develop only five to six core competencies at any one time because of the enormous resources and commitment required for working with core competencies. Resources may include financial, research, management, technology, and so on.

Consequently, there must be a concept of noncore competencies, that is, competencies that are not core competencies, but act as support for them. I propose to label such noncore competencies as support competencies. Support competencies may include all the categories of core competencies already described, which implies that they have the same characteristics as core competencies. The question of which competencies to select as core or support competencies is, thus, a matter of which competencies give the largest contribution to the competitiveness of the corporation. For instance, Bang & Olufsen have determined that the competencies that have a high impact on both internal and external productivity are to be treated as core competencies. Other competencies have a high impact on external productivity but low impact on internal productivity, that is, the customers think they are important, but Bang & Olufsen are not performing them at world-class level. This kind of competencies are supposed to be elevated to core competence status. However, Bang & Olufsen has not defined any place in its procedures for support competencies, even though they clearly state that the company cannot deal with all the competencies it possess and has to out-source some competencies.

This illustrates one of the basic points of support competencies. A firm cannot concentrate its scarce resources on everything, that is, too many core competencies. Consequently, some competencies should be defined as support competencies and/or be out-sourced. Recalling the discussion on public domain competencies, the conclusion that public domain competencies should be defined as support competencies and, if possible, be out-sourced is not far off. I would prefer not to use such a strong formulation because there may be good reasons for out-sourcing a core competence. For instance, Bang & Olufsen has out-sourced some competencies of which several probably would be considered core competencies. To secure these competencies, the company has built strong strategic alliances with the suppliers of the competencies and involves the suppliers actively in strategic competence development and so on.

CONCLUSIONS ON WHAT SHAPED COMPETENCE-BASED STRATEGY

This chapter has discussed what has shaped competence-based strategy. These general conclusions can be made:

- Core competencies should provide sustainable competitive advantage within the areas of products, processes, and administrative execution of tasks.
- Core competencies have both a human and a technological element. Even though I have emphasized the interplay between these elements, it may be of use to distinguish between mainly technological and mainly human competencies.
- To provide truly sustainable competitive advantage, core competencies should be kept firm-specific. This implies that they are rare, intangible, costly to copy, inimitable, and so on. Alternatively, core competencies may be public domain. However, public domain competencies have shown a historical tendency to "slide" from being highly differentiating to becoming qualifying factors in competition.
- Firms may concentrate their scarce resources on only a few— perhaps five to six—core competencies. Thus, unless there are special circumstances, it would be natural to focus on firm-specific core competencies and define other competencies as support competencies.

Finally, it can be concluded that the core competence grid proposed earlier may not have much relevance as an operational tool, but not as a way of capturing the many different perceptions of core competencies in the literature. However, as a tool for describing the characteristics of core competencies, two of the distinctions seem to lack relevance. First, the distinction between firm-specific and public domain competencies is not relevant, since I have argued that core competencies should be of the former category. Second, the distinction between human and technological competencies may be of little practical relevance. In practice, a competence will almost always be composed of both. Of course, a special case is purely technological solutions to a problem (e.g. a welding robot), but despite serious attempts, no one has yet made a robot function effectively without the involvement of some sort of human expertise and knowledge.

To summarize the discussion of core competencies and their characteristics a number of characteristics are described in Table 3-2. The characteristics are:

- *Degree of specificity:* How difficult is the competence to describe and analyze? For instance, reputation is difficult to analyze and describe, whereas product technology is easier to analyze and describe according to well-known models and tools.
- *The complexity of a core competence:* How difficult is it to manage? For instance, company reputation is highly complex and difficult to manage, whereas process technologies are manageable to a much larger extent. Please note that process technologies such as welding robots are very advanced and, thus, complex to manage, even though they are "hard." Over time it will become easier to manage such competencies as knowledge of them increases and models and tools are developed.
- *Effect on external productivity:* How does possession of a core competence within a given category affect the value provided to the customer? For instance, reputation for quality products may have an unlimited effect on value to the customer while the mastery of CNC machinery only has a low impact on external productivity.
- *Effect on internal productivity:* How does possession of a core competence affect internal productivity? For instance, reputation will have a low impact on internal productivity, whereas product technology may have a high impact on both external and internal productivity. The latter is due to the well-known fact that a large amount of total life cycle costs are decided in product development, that is, by the choice of product technologies.
- *Mode of access:* How does one access a competence within a given area? Reputation must be accumulated; it is difficult to buy. On the

other hand, process technologies such as welding robots may be acquired.

I have attempted to characterize the different categories of core competencies according to this set of categories. The results are shown in Table 3-2, which illustrates six basic categories of core competencies and their characteristics. Of course, the conclusions may, at best, be taken as simplistic. First, every example of a true core competence will be firm-specific and will, thus, have its own set of characteristics. Second, there is no guarantee that every core competence fits the six categories in the table. Some competencies may be a mixture, whereas others may simply belong to other categories.

TABLE 3-2. Characteristics of Core Competencies

Category	Example	Degree of specificity	Complexity	Effect on external productivity	Effect on internal productivity	Mode of access.
Soft product competence	Reputation	Low	High	Unlimited/high	Low	
Hard product competence	Plaster for ostomy products	High	Advanced	High	High	Acquire or accumulate
Soft process competence	Knowledge of robots	Low	High	Low	High	
Hard process competence	Welding robots	High	Advanced	Low	High	Acquire or accumulate
Soft adm. competence	Knowledge of management	Low	High	Unlimited/high	High	
Hard adm. competence	Management information systems	High	Advanced	Low	High	Acquire or accumulate

4

Competence-Based Strategy So Far

In the last chapter I arrived at the notion that competencies and competence-based strategy are essential for strategic management. Of course, I did not invent that notion, and in this chapter I will discuss the seminal contributions to the field of competence-based strategy and attempt to outline where work is still needed.

FUNCTIONAL DEFINITIONS OF COMPETENCIES

Generally, the concept of core competencies is attributed to Prahalad and Hamel (1990) and Prahalad (1993), so why not start there. In 1990, Hamel and Prahalad defined core competencies as: ". . . the collective learning in the organization, especially how to co-ordinate diverse production skills and integrate multiple streams of technologies . . ." (p. 82). Furthermore, Prahalad elaborated on this in his 1993 publication as (p. 45):

$$\text{Competence} = (\text{technology} \bullet \text{governance process} \bullet \text{collective learning})$$

Regarding a core competence, Hamel and Prahalad say it must be subject to three tests:

- Is it a significant source of competitive advantage?
- Does it transcend a single business?
- Is it hard for competitors to imitate?

This points toward the main contribution from Hamel and Prahalad and their followers—the definition of competencies as a part of strategic management. From a strategic viewpoint, *core* competencies are those that provide the firm with a competitive advantage via the execution of the competence, for instance the way in which Nike manages its world-wide net of subsuppliers. Core competencies have been built up over time and are not easily imitated. For instance, it will be difficult to get access to the knowledge of Nike managers on subsuppliers, not to mention imitate Nike's credibility with the suppliers. Core competencies are distinct from competencies that are not "core." Such other competencies may be either enabling or supplemental competencies.

Supplemental competencies are those that add value to the core competencies but that could be imitated, for example, the distribution channels of Nike or its strong but not unique packaging design skills. *Enabling* competencies are necessary but not sufficient in themselves to competitively distinguish a firm. For instance, quality management skills and systems are increasingly the price for entering the competitive game rather than the road to superiority. Evidently, some core competencies will over time slip and become enabling competencies if nothing is done to preserve the core competence and make it impossible to imitate, for instance, if the core competence contains proprietary knowledge (unavailable from public sources) or is developed constantly beyond the competitor's competencies.

There has been much debate over whether core competencies should be defined at the corporate level only or whether a core competence can be located at a division or function of the firm. For instance, is Toyota's production systems (one of) its core competence; or does this competence, in fact, consist of several core competencies residing in, for instance, quality management, production planning, inventory control, and many other places? Given the idea of different levels of competition discussed in the introduction to this book, it seems only natural that a core competence may reside at any level and that it is a matter of convenience that defines the level of the competence. Returning to the Toyota example, it would probably make life somewhat easier for the firm's management if competencies were not defined as the entire production system but at a lower level. On the other hand, defining the competence at too low a level destroys overview. Prahalad and Hamel have noted that a firm probably has only six to ten core competencies, since this number makes it possible to focus on the competencies while still maintaining the necessary operational focus.

Still, something is missing here. The work of Hamel and Prahalad fails to explain how core competencies are linked to other aspects internally within the firm. For instance, what about knowledge and knowledge workers? Or what about technology? Furthermore, Hamel and Prahalad's definition of competencies is clearly a functional definition. By this I mean a definition that is concerned with what the competence does—is it important to our customers?—rather than why this is done. The latter would be a structural definition, and in the next section, I will argue that such a definition is much needed.

ALTERNATIVE DEFINITIONS OF COMPETENCIES

Leonard-Barton's Definition

Dorothy Leonard-Barton (1995) has written an excellent book on core competencies, knowledge, and innovation. Part of her starting point is that competencies should not be defined as static entities, since: "... organizations, like the people who populate them, have invested in knowledge building over the years and have developed particular skills, they still must continue to build and change those skills in response to changing environments ..." (p. 17). In other words, competencies need to be changed all the time. In order to do that, however, managers need at least two abilities: "... they must 1) know how to manage the activities that create knowledge and 2) posses an understanding of exactly what constitutes a core capability ... [competence] ... " (p. 4). Therefore, Leonard-Barton's book is centered around two main contributions: a definition of the dimensions or elements of competencies and a thorough discussion of the processes that can lead to development of competencies.

One reason for the emphasis of developing competencies all the time ties in with the second part of Leonard-Barton's starting-point—innovation. She quotes Gary Hamel, who believes that competence provides a gateway to new opportunities that the organization must exploit in order to survive (Leonard-Barton, 1995). However, in doing so, the knowledge and competencies that the firm is based on must also change as: "... even seemingly minor innovations that alter the architecture of a product can undermine the usefulness of deeply embedded knowledge ..." (Leonard-Barton, 1995, p. 17). Thus, innovation, even in the form of not creative destructive, is a key factor in rendering current core competencies obsolete. This phenomenon is called *core rigidities* by Leonard-Barton.

Based on these considerations, Leonard-Barton defines what she labels a core technical capability (noting that core competence and core technical capability are interchangeable) by means of four elements, or dimensions as she calls them:

- Employee knowledge and skill. This is the most obvious dimension according to Leonard-Barton. This is because Leonard-Barton perceives organizations as knowledge. She writes that firms are knowledge as well as financial institutions and that they are repositories as well as wellsprings of knowledge. Expertise collects in employees' heads and is embodied in technology, and this knowledge is the starting point of core competencies.

- Physical technical systems. Technological competence accumulates not only in the heads of people, but also in the technical/physical systems that people build over time: databases, machinery, software, and so on.
- Managerial systems. The accumulation of employee knowledge is guided and monitored by the company's system of education, rewards, and incentives. These systems are often called management systems, and they create the channels by which knowledge is accessed and flows—and barriers to the same.
- Values and norms determine the kind of knowledge that is sought and nurtured, what kinds of knowledge activities are tolerated and encouraged, and so on. In organizations, there are informal systems of caste and status, rituals of behavior, and passionate beliefs associated with various kinds of knowledge. Often the systems in organizations are no less rigid and complex than systems of religion in society as a whole. Thus, values and norms serve as knowledge screening and control mechanisms.

These four elements are a first step toward a structural definition of competence. The four elements can be identified and manipulated by certain processes, thereby enabling us to go one step further than Hamel and Prahalad allow us. The processes by which the four elements are to be changed are, to Leonard-Barton, processes related to organizational learning. Leonard-Barton focuses on four such processes: problem solving, implementing and integrating knowledge, experimenting, and importing knowledge. I discuss organizational learning as a means for developing competencies at a later stage, so we will skip that discussion for now.

Competencies as Systems of Knowledge

Based on much of Leonard-Barton's thinking, a lot of promising work has gone into perceiving competencies as different forms of knowledge or systems of knowledge, thereby linking core competence development to the vast learning literature. For instance, Drejer and Henriksen propose that development of (human) knowledge is the all-important element to be developed in a competence and that this must be done differently than developing the technological element of a competence (Drejer et al., 1998). Here Drejer and Henriksen clearly view technology in its constrained sense to mean (only) hardware and tools. However, Anders Nielsen (1998) and a number of other authors take a slightly different approach by proposing that competence in itself is a manifestation of different kinds of knowledge: specific knowledge, integrative knowledge, and deployment knowledge. Based on this perception, the step toward arguing that organizational learning is the key to developing the core competencies of the firm is straightforward and has been made by several authors (Nielsen, 1998; Spender, 1996; Kogut & Zander, 1996).

Nielsen's starting point is that: "...It has been chosen to use knowledge as the central building-block as knowledge is conceived to be independent of the medium carrying the knowledge. As such knowledge might reside in and be reproduced in organizational processes or forms of collaboration, in hardware, e.g., equipment as well as in software, procedures and organizational routines and heuristics. Technology can also be seen as having a very close connection to knowledge..." (Nielsen, 1998, p. 161). Specifically, Nielsen proposes to view a competence as consistent of three different kinds of knowledge, specific knowledge, integrative knowledge and deployment knowledge.

Nielsen views a competence in terms of specific knowledge, for example, stand-alone technologies (seen as structured and highly formalized knowledge) or knowledge about specific areas such as FEM analysis or composite materials. Normally, there will be several areas of specific knowledge in a single competence. Specific knowledge can best be described as "deep," as it consists of deep understanding of scientific areas or technologies. This kind of knowledge can usually be codified and articulated quite easily, for example, in the form of drawings, and can thus be exchanged between firms easily. Therefore, specific knowledge can rarely lead to sustainable competitive advantage (Barney, 1991; Clark, 1989). The second kind of knowledge is integrative knowledge and is concerned with how the different areas of specific knowledge can best be integrated and coordinated to function together as a whole, for example, as a functional planning system. Furthermore, it is integrative knowledge that makes a firm capable of internalizing external knowledge and/or technology (Cohen & Levinthal, 1990). Integrative knowledge is knowledge about how the "deep" areas of knowledge interact and work together and can be best coordinated. Integrative knowledge will be difficult to transfer between firms and will, therefore, contribute significantly to the creation of competitive advantage. The third and final kind of knowledge is deployment knowledge, which is concerned with how specific knowledge and integrative knowledge can be used to create commercial value for the company and its customers. This kind of knowledge is, hence, concerned with the link from competencies to market/customers. Deployment knowledge is about customers, customer demands, and how specific/integrative knowledge can be used to fulfill the demands (Nevis et al., 1995). Such knowledge will often be company-specific and tacit.

Even though the operational definitions offered here have not divided knowledge about a competence into knowledge about each of its elements—technology, people, organization, and culture—there is some resemblance between Nielsen's views and the obvious move from the competence definition of Leonard-Barton. For instance, specific knowledge is knowledge about technology, as well as something else. Furthermore, knowledge about people, organization and culture will be included in integrative knowledge. Thus, Nielsen's view is different from the previous view, where a core competence is seen as a system of technology, knowledge, management systems and values; but the two views do not exclude each other. By viewing a competence as a system of three different kinds of knowledge, it is made clear that to develop a competence, learning must be the prime tool.

Technological Definitions

In Chapter 3, I described how the area of Management of Technology (MoT) to a large extent is concerned with many of the same issues as competence-based strategy. In that light, I would like to describe how some definitions of technology dating before 1990 have close to the same content as competencies. Consider, for instance, the seminal definition of technology by Milan Zeleny (1989), where he defines technology as:

$$\text{Technology} = \text{hardware} + \text{software} + \text{heartware} + \text{technology supportnet}$$

To make matters even more interesting, what does Zeleny mean by the term *technology supportnet*? Technology supportnet are the parts of organizational structure, culture, employees, and so on that are related to the technology in question.

It is safe to assume that technology in this definition (and many others as there is quite a tradition for that) is perceived in broad terms. It reminds us of how competencies have been defined from Prahalad/Hamel to Leonard-Barton. Consider Leonard-Barton's definition of a competence. Is it different from Zeleny's? This tells us that a lot can be gained from including models and theories from the area of MoT into the considerations of this book and, for now, that it is interesting to take a further look at how technology has been defined over time.

Even the most superficial review of the literature on MoT reveals that there are many different perceptions of how technology should be defined, hidden in and behind research on MoT (Drejer, 1997; Dussage et al., 1991).

The starting point for a discussion of management of technology could be the concept of technology itself. In 1974, Maack (1974) described three definitions of technology, to which I feel that there has to be added one. As a result, four definitions of technology are presented:

- Technology as a tool
- Technology as a value
- Technology as a system
- Technology as a meta-tool

Technology may be viewed as physical tools such as machines and robots. This perception underlines the systematic and rational aspects of technology. However, it is not possible to ignore the fact that technology will affect the user, the tasks it is used to solve, and other factors; that is, technology is more than a hammer, a tool. This recognition has probably been one of the reasons why another perception—technology as a system—is also visible in the literature. Dussage and others refer to the systems view as "allusive," since technology is treated as a system without giving too much consideration to its subsystems and specific contents. The third perception is viewing technology as a value. Here the focal point is to assess technology in relation to something, usually without offering detailed definitions of technology. By such assessment, it will become evident whether technology is "good" or "bad" seen in relation to something. This perception gave rise to the technology assessment movement in the late 1970s and early 1980s, where technology was to be assessed on a societal level. This is only of marginal interest within this context, since the author is dealing with managing technology at the corporate level.

Maack wrote his book in 1974 and although it is full of insight, I wish to add another perception of technology to the list—the perception of technology as a meta-tool. What is meant by this view is that by studying literature from 1974 onward, it has become evident that many authors have attempted to combine the tool view and the systems view with the value view (Bhalla, 1987; Dussage et al., 1991). Please note that these perceptions are not incompatible. As for the tool view and the systems view, these may be viewed as a total and detail view of technology. With a systems view, it is possible to see technology in relation to, for example, culture, society, humans, and so on, as Leavitt does with his famous model (1965). With a tool view it is possible to describe and study different specific technologies, such as so-called advanced manufacturing technologies (Sun, 1994). Furthermore, it is possible to combine the view of technologies as hard or soft, that is, also methods and heuristics, with a view of specific categories, for example, product, manufacturing, and management technologies. This can be combined with assessment of technology on a corporate or lower level; the increased use of Leavitt's model for such purposes is an example of this trend. I have chosen the term *meta-tool* to illustrate that technology is seen as a tool, but also more than a tool.

It can be noted that the definition of technology in the broad sense seems to correspond to the preceding definition of core competence; however, in the hard, constrained sense of technology as tools, technology may be perceived as only part of a core competence. It is necessary therefore to specify whether technology is viewed in the broad sense, when discussing competence-based strategy and/or management of technology.

Recently, Dussage et al. have attempted to summarize the different perceptions of technology found in the literature. They propose that definitions fall into three categories (Dussage et al., 1991):

- *Allusive* definitions, where technology is viewed as a key factor of success, but where no specific definition of technology is made.
- *Extensive* definitions, where technology is defined but extended to all areas of expertise existing in a corporation, thus making it difficult to differentiate between what is technology and what is not.
- *Specific* definitions, where technology is placed somewhere between science on one hand and the commercial products or processes derived from the application of scientific knowledge on the other. All processes and products are thus related to the various technologies they integrate, which in turn are linked to science. One might add that most definitions in the references fall into the category of specific definitions.

Technology has now been discussed in some detail. I usually prefer to define technology in the most constrained sense. The reason for this is quite simple and can be explained using Zeleny's technology definition discussed previously. If technology is defined to be as broadly perceived as Zeleny does, then it seems hard to comprehend and explain what is *not* technology. An all-encompassing concept seems of as little value as no concept at all. Therefore, I prefer to define technology as the tools of human beings. In the case of the industrial enterprise, examples of technology include traditional machinery, computer numerical control (CNC) machines, computer-aided design (CAD) stations and software, and so on. This definition, however, does not imply that technology can be regarded in isolation. On the contrary, technology is in a systemic relationship with the formal organization, the organizational culture, the people, and so on of the individual enterprise. By defining technology as tools, however, I am able to regard the elements of the system and their relationships with other elements as distinguishable entities, rather than merely as a whole.

If one wants to look at systems of technology, organization, and people, I prefer to use the term *competence*. This enables a distinction between technology (tools) and the systems in which technology are a part, and still enables the important discussion of how technologies being used can contribute to the creation of competitive advantage for the firm.

There is just one hitch in this perception of technology. It is not shared with all authors contributing to the area of MoT. This means that in some cases, I can take models and theories from MoT and use them directly for inspiration in this book. In some cases, the terms technology and competence can be used interchangeably. However, this is not always the case, so other models and theories from MoT must be approached with great caution before being applied to competence-based strategy. This means that whenever I use theories from MoT in this book, I will carefully point out the relationship between definitions of technology and competence in each case.

From Products to Competencies—Hierarchical Definitions

Prahalad and Hamel (1990) provided one of the first attempts in analyzing the diversified corporation in a competence context, by comparing a diversified corporation with a tree: "... the trunk and major limbs are core products, the smaller branches are business units, the leaves, flowers and fruit are end-products. The root system that provides nourishment, sustenance and stability is the core competence ..." (p. 24). This hierarchical approach has similarities to other contributions to the field of MoT. For instance, Giget uses a tree structure to visualize the integration of technical capabilities into products: "... with the roots representing technologies, the trunk the firm's technological and industrial potential, the branches representing sectors and sub-sectors of valorisation, and the fruit representing products ..." (Giget, 1988, p. 35). Giget's way of thinking, in turn, is inspired by the way Japanese corporations used to illustrate how their products/markets were created by internal capabilities, the so-called bonsai tree view of the firms (Dussage et al., 1991).

Based on this way of thinking about competencies and their relationship to end-products, it should come as no surprise that competencies in general should provide potential access to a variety of markets and enable the firm to compete in diversified businesses; however, this is not a characteristic that will separate noncore competencies from core competencies.

Hierarchical approaches have been empirically tested (Knott et al., 1996; Lewis and Gregory, 1996), and a number of difficulties have been found. For instance, difficulties arose because of the blurring between skills and competencies; it was frequently difficult to find a distinction as to what are competencies and what were skills. Furthermore, the core product and competence concepts are also difficult to separate, especially in smaller firms. Finally, it is difficult to use the hierarchical model on smaller units (small and medium-sized enterprises [SMEs] or a business unit).

Despite the difficulties associated with a hierarchical approach, it still constitutes the foundation for much of the present-day competence thinking. The approach creates a critical link to the products of the firm and, thereby, enables the identification process to discuss competencies in light of the customers. This becomes critical when one wants to identify core competencies. Furthermore, a strong link to the customers is also a means for avoiding validity problems in the identification and analysis process. On the difficulty side, it is obvious that many of the identified problems of hierarchical models deal with what these models do not take into account—what is inside identified competencies.

FRAMEWORKS FOR COMPETENCE-BASED STRATEGY

Just as there have been definitions of concepts related to competence-based strategy before, there have been proposals of frameworks for competence-based strategy. Again a look at the relevant literature (a broad look) will reveal that many more people than Hamel and Prahalad have proposed relevant frameworks.

In this section, I discuss a few relevant frameworks. To compare them to the work of Hamel and Prahalad, I will describe each framework along the following dimensions:

- The starting point of the framework; that is, what is the basic idea of the work?
- What is their key concept and how is that related to competence?
- What is the task of the framework?
- What is the managerial process of the framework?

Miles and Snow's Model

Starting Point

Miles and Snow's model is an example of a framework taken from the area of strategy theory that has as its starting point that integration of business strategy and competence development has to do with another concept related to integration, namely that of balancing the many different disciplines relevant to strategic management. Miles and Snow emphasize balancing choice of product-market domain, production and distribution technologies, and administrative structure and processes (Miles and Snow, 1978), whereas others, for instance Sun, emphasize balancing of strategy (product/market strategy), organization, and technology (Sun, 1994).

Relation to the Definition of Core Competencies

This leads to considering the next dimension—the way in which technology and/or competence is defined. A relatively vertically broad definition of technology is encountered as Miles and Snow define technology as: "... the combination of skills, equipment, and relevant technical knowledge needed to bring about desired transformations in materials, information, or people..." (Davis, 1971, quoted in Miles & Snow, 1978, p. 256). This encompasses the people of the organization and, therefore, structure (or organization) may be perceived as the characteristics of organizational subunits and the relationships between them.

The Task of Miles and Snow's Model

Raymond E. Miles and Charles C. Snow's model of what they refer to as "organizational adaptation" is a widely quoted conceptual model regarding integration mainly between technology and organization (Figure 4-1). The model is usually also referred to as a model for "strategic adaptation" by others (e.g., Stacy, 1993). The model is based mainly on conceptual thinking, but also on a number of case studies. The purpose of the model is to describe and diagnose existing organizational behaviors and to prescribe alternative directions for change when necessary. The model is based on the following three basic ideas (Miles & Snow, 1978):

- Organizations can act to create (or choose) their environment.
- Management's strategic choices shape the organization's structure and processes.
- On the other hand, once chosen, structure and process constrain strategy.

These basic ideas follow the work of authors such as Thompson (1967), Lawrence and Lorsh (1967), Galbraith (1973, 1979), and Mintzberg (1983) and should not be too hard to comprehend. Furthermore, the ideas also describe the change in attitude toward strategy in the school of product-market strategy as opposed to the school of strategic planning, where the environment was assumed to be given.

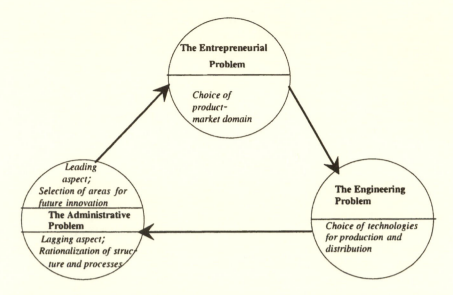

Figure 4-1. Miles and Snow's framework for organizational adaptation. (Adapted from Miles and Snow, 1978)

The Process of Applying Miles and Snow's Model

Miles and Snow describe strategy as the idea of strategic choice, that is, that organizational structure is only partially preordained by the environmental conditions, which implies that top management has an important role to play as the primary link between the firms and their environment. Thus, the effectiveness of organizational adaptation hinges on top managers' perceptions of the environmental conditions and the decisions they make concerning how the organization should cope with these conditions. The complex and dynamic process of strategic adaptation is broken down into three major problems, which management must continually solve: entrepreneurial, engineering, and administrative. According to Miles and Snow (1978), these problems typically occur simultaneously. However, they are discussed sequentially here.

The entrepreneurial problem involves defining the organization's domain, often in terms of a specific product or service and a target market or market segment. In mature and ongoing organizations, attempts to modify the products or markets may be constrained by the organization's existing manufacturing and management technologies/competencies.

The engineering problem involves the creation of a system that puts into actual operation management's solution to the entrepreneurial problem. The creation of such a system requires management to select appropriate technologies for manufacturing and distribution of the products or services and to form new information, communication, and control linkages to ensure proper operation of this technology.

The administrative problem is primarily that of reducing uncertainty within the organization, that is, rationalizing and stabilizing those activities that successfully solved problems faced by the organization during the entrepreneurial and engineering phases. Furthermore, solving the administrative problem also involves formulating and implementing those processes that will enable the organization to continue to evolve (innovation).

Apart from describing the adaptive cycle, Miles and Snow also divide successful organizations into three types according to their adaptive behavior, with one additional unsuccessful type (Table 4-1).

As illustrated in Table 4-1, there is also an unsuccessful organization—the reactor. This type of organization is not able to respond effectively to environmental changes and must, ultimately, change or give up.Within this context it might be important to note that the solutions to the three problems, apart from being part of organizational adaptation, can be viewed as a choice of the three categories of competence, that is, product, process, and administrative competencies, respectively. In other words, by choosing different solutions to the entrepreneurial problem, different business strategies are selected.

Bhalla's Framework for Integrated Strategic Management

An example of another approach often proposed in the literature is that of Bhalla's framework for integration of technology and business. This approach originates within the area of management of technology and discusses, thus, technology rather than competencies. Bhallas framework is a typical example of a number of other publications, most notably those of Steele (1989), Twiss and Goodridge (1989), Dussage et al. (1991), and Gaynor (1991). Along with a number of more recent articles, these contributions form the basis of this discussion.

The Starting Point of Bhalla's Framework

The starting point for technology-based strategy is the recognition that product-market applications, that is, "businesses," are related to a set of core technologies that provide the foundation for the production capabilities of the corporation. This starting point is equivalent to the technology bonsai-tree view advocated by Japanese corporations—a way of perceiving a corporation that has been adopted by a number of Western firms during the 1980s (Dussage et al., 1991). This

TABLE 4-1.   Types of Organizational Adaptation

Kind of organization	Kind of adaptional behavior
Defenders	Organizations with narrow product-market domains. As a result of this narrow focus, defenders seldom need to make major adjustments in their technology, structure, or methods of integration. Instead they devote primary attention to improving the efficiency of their existing operations.
Prospectors	Organizations that almost continually search for market opportunities and regularly experiment with potential responses to emerging environmental trends. Thus, these organizations are often the creators of changes and uncertainty to which their competitors must respond. However, they are usually not completely efficient.
Analyzers	Organizations that operate in two types of domains: one relatively stable and one changing. In the stable area, analyzers operate routinely and efficiently through the use of formalized structures and procedures. In the more turbulent area, top managers watch competitors closely for new ideas, and then rapidly adopt those that appear to be the most promising.
Reactors	Unsuccessful organizations in which top managers frequently perceive change and uncertainty occurring in their organizational environment, but are unable to respond effectively. Because this type of organization lacks a consistent strategy-structure relationship, it seldom makes adjustment of any sort until forced to do so by environmental pressures.

Inspired by Miles and Snow, 1978

has led to an illustration of firms as a tree, where the top of the tree is the firm's product-market applications and the roots are the firm's core competencies.

Relationship with the Concept of Core Competencies

It is evident that competitive advantage is assumed to exceed that of product-market strategy. However, there is no clear distinction between competencies and technology in the publications mentioned. This is due to the relatively broad definitions of technology offered by the contributions. Typically, technology is defined as a combination of tools and knowledge, that is, as both human and technical hardware.

The Task of Bhalla's Framework

The starting point for this kind of approach is most clearly illustrated by Bhalla's 1987 book. Bhalla devotes three chapters to an analysis of methods for product-market strategy and one chapter to describing the increased strategic importance of technology in the industrial competitive environment of the 1980s, before moving on to propose a parallel stream model for integration of business strategy and competence development (Bhalla, 1987). Thus, parallel stream models acknowledge the importance of both technology and business issues of strategy. Another characteristic is that the models are analytical and planning-oriented; that is, integration of business strategy and competence development is the result of parallel stream planning processes. Bhalla claims that: ". . . the integration of business and technology is critical to success in today's environment of stiff competition, changing social values, and fast development of new technologies . . ." (Bhalla, 1987, p. 85). Typically, it is noted that success in this integration requires:

- Creation of mutual understanding between business and technology, recognizing each other's needs and constraints.
- Recognition of the limitation of the (traditional) strategic business planning approach.
- Incorporation of technology as a part of the corporate strategic planning process.

Within the publications mentioned, traditional strategic management is seen as product-market focused strategy, hence the first three chapters of Bhalla's book. As for technology and/or competencies, technology seems to be confined to the product and process domains of the corporation in question. Vertically, technology is seen broadly as the link between science and end-products.

The Process of Bhalla's Framework

Bhalla's integrated framework for corporate strategic planning might be one of the first suggested frameworks for integrating technology into strategic management. The framework is built on the assumption that technology planning must be undertaken simultaneously with product-market strategy. Bhalla notes: ". . . it is almost impossible to prepare a business/technology plan unless the whole organization participates . . ." (1987, p. 83). Thus, the framework is designed to bring technology and business together at the same level with equal emphasis and start thinking about technology as an integral part of business planning. It is implied in the model that Bhalla sees product-market strategy as only a part of strategy and that methods within that area used alone will result in the firm not being able to use its resources to the fullest, in turn resulting in loss of competitive advantage. Bhalla therefore moves to suggest a simplified framework that consists of a parallel stream of product-market planning and technology planning. I will not bother to illustrate the framework for integrated strategic management (Bhalla, 1987), as the general idea probably is clear by now.

The process of the framework is divided into a number of phases. The *fundamental organization purpose* reflects the type of business in which top management would like to be. This is based on their evaluation of strengths and weaknesses of the firm and the strategic fit of various businesses. The formulation and reexamination of the fundamental organization purpose leads to outlining the *overall organization objectives* for both financial and nonfinancial issues.

Together these two issues function as input to the strategic planning process, which in Bhalla's framework addresses both business and technological issues as equally important in the evaluation of product lines, new products, and acquisitions. An important part of such a consideration is to assure the exploitation of synergistic effects of different technologies and to place an emphasis on effective utilization of technology, while taking into account skills, talents, and communications (organization). These are key factors to be considered as the planning process moves to functional and organizational levels, and in turn generates short- and long-term program and budgets. The planning process also addresses implementation and evaluation, which is fed back to the original plan and reiterated until most of the organization is in concert with the plans.

Mr. Bhalla notes: ". . . it is not wise to quick fix strategies for integrating business and technology since this will dilute the thinking process essential to the whole idea of the planning exercise . . ." (1987, p. 80).

Eriksen's Framework for Resource-Based Strategy

Several people have contributed to the area of competence-based strategy via the idea of the resource-based view of the firm. One example of that is Eriksen, who has been one of the few to propose an operational framework.

Starting Point of Eriksen's Framework

In his work, Eriksen places emphasis on investments in human and organizational resources as sources of competitive advantage (Eriksen, 1993). This is seen as in contrast to product-market strategy. To Eriksen, organizational and human resources may be an important source of sustainable competitive advantage compared with some of the firm's more tangible resources. Furthermore, human and organizational resources play an important role for the efficiency of the firm. This is obviously the case for human resources (e.g., better skilled workers are a potential sources of advantage). In general, Eriksen claims that: "... firm-specific skills are those that endow the firm with the largest sustainable competitive advantage ..." (1993a, p. 8). Regarding organizational resources, the case may not be as obvious. However, organizational resources may be viewed as a form of social capital, which functions as a resource that enables the organization to do something it would not be capable of doing otherwise (i.e., corporate culture).

Relationship to Competence

Even though Eriksen refers to the basis of competition as "resources," he seems to agree that such resources should be costly to copy. Furthermore, Eriksen emphasizes human and organizational resources in favor of physical resources for the same reason. Consequently, Eriksen's perception of resources is similar to the definition of core competencies offered by Leonard-Barton.

The Task of Eriksen's Framework

Eriksen's 1993 contribution on what he refers to as "resource-based strategy" is furthermore founded on a set of three propositions regarding the sources of competitive advantage: behavior of strategic decision makers, resources, and analytical focus of strategy.

What is the behavior of strategic decision makers?

Eriksen's proposition regarding the behavior of strategic decision makers can be summarized to the concept of *bounded rationality*. According to Eriksen, this is an important concept in understanding some of the limitations of strategy and why, for instance, firms are path-dependent in their development. In the traditional accounts of strategic management, managers typically know all possible actions and the corresponding outcomes and, being rational, they always choose the dominant strategy. Past commitments count only as factors in the analysis, but do not affect the process of decision making. However, Eriksen claims that this is not the case and that managers do not have either full information or the ability to choose the best possible strategy.

What is the nature of resources?

Resources are heterogeneous and immobile. First, it should be noted that some of the firm's human resources are of general nature, for example, accountants and bookkeepers. Such skills are unlikely to offer the corporation any sustained competitive advantage, as they are not particularly scarce. On the other hand, skilled workers and managers who have accumulated many firm-specific skills and knowledge are likely to be more scarce and heterogeneous, and thus endow the firm with sustainable competitive advantage. As for immobility, human resources may be transferred to other firms. Indeed, this takes place every day. However, the more firm-specific the skills, the lower the employee's value to outsiders is likely to be. There is a need to avoid transfer of firm-specific skills, as a valuable asset will be lost to both the corporation and to the employee. Thus, it appears natural to conclude that firm-specific skills are generally less mobile.

What is the analytical focus of strategic management?

The analytical focus of Eriksen's approach is much more closely tied to managerial control variables than competitive forces and entry barriers. According to the traditional approaches to strategic management, the accumulation process itself is not central to the development of sustainable competitive advantage, as resources are viewed as essentially homogeneous and mobile. Thus, the focus of traditional approaches is directed outside the corporation. However, Eriksen's approach has its focus on what is inside the firm, namely resources and skills, whereas traditional accounts do not focus on understanding essential differences among firms.

The Process of Eriksen's Framework

Eriksen reaches the conclusion that a resource-based strategy must be characterized by the following points (Eriksen, 1993a):

- Cognitive limitations
- Building a resource portfolio
- Building human and organizational resources
- Connection to organization design
- Connection to the environment.

This allows Eriksen to propose the following framework for resource-based strategy (Figure 4-2).

Cognitive limitations

Managers are boundedly rational, although not intentionally so, and strategic decision making may be seen as a way of dealing with cognitive and informational limitations in a systematic way. A realistic framework for strategic management should be directed at understanding these cognitive limitations, such as decision-making heuristics and different types of biases. Furthermore, if normative use is intended, such a framework should also be concerned about how the cognitive limitations can be dealt with.

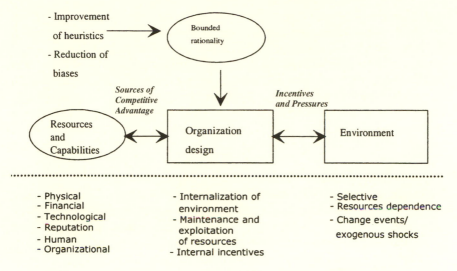

Figure 4-2. Eriksen's framework for resource-based strategy. (Adapted from Eriksen, 1993)

Building a resource portfolio

Managers should focus more on building and leveraging the corporation's portfolio of resources. Given the assumptions on path dependence and administrative heritage, incremental development is assumed to be most efficient (Eriksen, 1993a). However, few resources are free from imitation or substitution, and without further development the firm's resources will become obsolete in the long run. Thus, development and experimenting activities are important for the continued well-being of the firm. This may include both product or process innovation, as well as diversification.

Building human and organizational resources

In Eriksen's approach, strategic management concerns both the economic and organizational issues of management, and a central link is how the firm can create valuable human and organizational resources, as such resources may offer the corporation sustainable competitive advantage. Human and organizational resources have a number of advantages; they seem to be better protected from their inherent heterogeneous characteristics than do, for example, physical resources; they are more causally ambiguous than other types of resources; and they are usually firmly embedded in a unique social structure.

Connection to organization design

The process of creating, exploiting, and maintaining the corporation's resources is intimately related to the organization design process. A central issue here is to maintain the proper incentives for managers and employees. Therefore, Eriksen sees the corporation as not only a collection of resources, but also a collection of intraorganizational incentives. These incentives range from explicit contracts to job enrichment, empowerment, and other attempts to motivate people in the organization. Eriksen notes: ". . . assuming some degree of moral hazard, then proper incentives are necessary in order to increase the firm's efficiency, and prevent dysfunctional behaviour . . ." (1993, p. 22).

Connection to the environment

Finally, a framework for strategy should focus on the role of the environment. However, unlike the structure-conduct-performance assumptions of schools 1 to 3 on strategic management, Eriksen views industry structure as not determining the firm's strategies, even though industry structure may have a selective effect on firms (Eriksen, 1993). Thus, change events or exogenous shocks may have a major influence on firms; for example, major technological breakthroughs may destroy some industries while creating new ones.

Prahalad and Hamel's Framework

Finally, there is the framework that Prahalad and Hamel have proposed. I hope that it is clear to the reader by now that this is far from the only, or even an authorative, framework. Nonetheless, it is certainly worth mentioning, as it is an interesting piece of work.

Starting Point of Prahalad and Hamel's Framework
According to Prahalad and Hamel (1993), the view of competition as market power no longer suffices in the long run. This is due to the fact the survivors of decades of fierce global competition all seem to be converging on similar and formidable standards for product cost, quality, and timeliness; see for example, the contributions on world-class manufacturing (Roth et al., 1992) and others. Therefore, managers need to look at the internal competencies of their corporations to secure long-term survival.

The Task of Prahalad and Hamel's Model
It is evident that the competitive advantages of tomorrow must be derived from elsewhere. Prahalad and Hamel note: ". . . the critical task for management . . . [in the 1990s] . . . is to create an organization capable of infusing products with irresistible functionality or, better yet, creating products that customers need but have yet not imagined . . ." (Prahalad and Hamel, 1990, p. 278).

Competition has more than one side to it. Apart from competition on end-products, firms can compete on core products and core competencies. Prahalad and Hamel advocate an expanded view of a firm where the business strategist sees the firm as a portfolio of product-market combinations; there is additionally a need to view the firm as a collection of core competencies and core products (Prahalad, 1993; Prahalad & Hamel, 1990).

Relationship to the Definition of Core Competencies

According to Prahalad and Hamel, a core competence can be identified by applying three simple tests: 1) Is it a significant source of competitive differentiation? 2) Does it transcend a single business? 3) Is it hard for competitors to imitate?

The difference between, for instance, technology and competence is that technology can stand alone, while competence is more or less tacit knowledge in human minds. Thus, core competence may be perceived as: ". . . communication, involvement, and a deep commitment to working across organizational boundaries . . ." (Prahalad & Hamel, 1990, p. 283). The key to understanding the competence concept is that it involves more than just technology. In a 1993 publication, Prahalad conceptualizes competence as:

$$\text{Competence} = (\text{Technology} \bullet \text{Governance Process} \bullet \text{Collective Learning})$$

It is evident from this equation that all three components are equally important, underlining the importance of organization. Furthermore, the concept of learning becomes important as seen from the definition of competence. Core products are defined as: ". . . the physical embodiments of one or more core competencies . . ." (Prahalad & Hamel, 1990, p. 288). In this way, core products act as linchpins between competencies and end-products, that is, what the customer receives and pays for. Another definition of core products is that they are the components or subassemblies that actually contribute to the value of the products. An example, taken from Prahalad and Hamel (1990), is that core competencies can be know-how in miniaturization, material science, and so on for Sony. Regarding core products, an example would be Honda's engines (Prahalad & Hamel, 1990).

The Process of Prahalad and Hamel's Framework

In the view of Prahalad (1993), competence-based strategy should be characterized by the following points:

• It should challenge existing price-performance assumptions.

- It should be customer-led.
- It should not be based solely on the current business strategy; that is, it should be possible to invent something that the customers have not yet imagined they needed.

In their views, Prahalad and Hamel clearly subscribe to the critique of the traditional approach to strategic management as being too bureaucratic. Firms should compete on all three levels of competition: the level of existing businesses, the level of core products, and the level of core competencies. These considerations led Prahalad and Hamel to propose a framework for integration of business strategy and competence development (Figure 4-3).

The framework has four related parts:

- Strategic intent
- Strategic architecture
- Creation of new competitive space
- Energization of the entire organization

Strategic intent is equal to the aspiration level for the organization. All the employees of the firm can identify with and feel committed to the strategic intent of the firm. Aspirations must represent a stretch and by definition exceed the current resources of the company. By design,

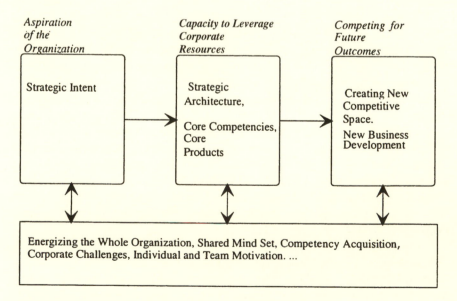

Figure 4-3. Prahalad and Hamel's framework for competence-based strategy. (Adapted from Prahalad, 1993)

strategic intent must cause a "misfit" between aspirations and current resources and current approaches to using resources. Thus, the strategic intent must focus the energies of the organization toward innovation, for example, changing the rules of the game, in the way the corporation competes.

A high aspiration level (compared with available resources) leads to the need for resource leverage. The issue for managers is how to create the capacity in a large organization to leverage corporate resources. The process of corporate leverage is accomplished through the development of a strategic architecture, that is, a way to capture the pattern of likely industry evolution, and by identifying core competencies and core products of the corporation. Reusability of invisible assets, as well as core products, in new and imaginative configurations to create new market opportunities is at the heart of the process of leverage.

An internal capacity to leverage resources is a prerequisite for inventing new businesses and creating new competitive space. This is competing for the future and requires a framework for identifying new opportunities, focusing on functionalities rather than on current products and services, and dramatically altering the price-performance relationships of the industry.

This approach is not just a technical task or a senior management task; it is a task for the entire organization. The role of top management, thus, is essentially one of energizing the whole organization—all people, at all levels, in all functions, and in all parts of the world. This process involves developing a shared mindset and shared goals and developing strategies for acquiring competency. Top managers must focus on stretching the imagination of the employees, challenging the organization, and motivating individuals and teams.

NOW WHAT?

I have now defined, described, and discussed the theoretical basis for competence-based strategy. Now we are ready to understand how to apply the theory.

The next chapter is the bridge between the theoretical and the practical. That chapter describes my definition of competencies—a definition that combines a functional and structural approach. The definition is illustrated with a number of examples from the real world.

I have divided the application of competence-based strategy into three parts. First, I define what I mean by competence-based strategy from a managerial and strategic perspective and propose a framework for a managerial activity. Second, I discuss the identification and analysis of the competencies of the firm. Third, I discuss the development of existing and new competencies of the firm.

5

Toward a New Perception of Competencies

In view of the dynamics of both market and technology development, the notion of competencies may play an important role as a bridge between market and technology. However, a more differentiated view is needed. Based on a definition of competencies as a system of human beings, technology, organization, and culture, I will propose three kinds of competencies and illustrate these by means of case examples. This will form the basis for discussing issues related to competence-based strategy and the important drivers of competence-based strategy The chapter concludes with a model for competence-based strategy in the context of the firm and its environment.

WHY WE NEED A STRUCTURAL DEFINITION OF COMPETENCE

Core competencies, critical capabilities, and/or key technologies have all become household names within the management scene over the past decade or even more. However, so far very little has emerged to reveal for managers and researchers how they function or how competencies should be developed over time. Therefore, it is question-able whether competence is an operational concept for managers to use in their *ex ante* strategic management of firms or whether competence in fact is a nice idea that can only be used *ex post* to explain the differences in firm performance in an industry?

So far, as I have argued in this book, very little research has emerged that goes beyond the latter use of the competence concept. Certainly, the success of several firms has been explained in terms of the core competencies of those firms in many competence publications (Hamel & Prahalad, 1994). However, this is always a historical account, and, more important, the descriptions of core competencies of those firms rarely go beyond the abstract level. We are never told precisely what technologies were applied, how employees were recruited or dispensed with, how the organization was changed, and so on.

Take for instance the definition of competence offered by Hamel & Prahalad: ". . . the collective learning in the organisation, especially how to coordinate diverse production skills and integrate multiple streams of technologies . . ." (Prahalad & Hamel, 1990, p. 82). Aaker submits that sustainable competitive advantage must be derived from: ". . . assets or skills possessed by the business. An asset is something your firm possesses such as a brand name or a retail location that is superior to the competition. A skill is something that your firm does better than competitors such as advertising or efficient manufacturing . . ." (1989, p. 91). From these and many other definitions, it is hard to define in precise terms what a firm's competencies actually are—and are not—as well as difficult to plan for the development of those competencies. We need much more detailed definitions of competencies, something that a few, for example Leonard-Barton (1995), have started to offer (see Chapter 4).

What is especially worrying is the more or less implicit claim that core competencies need not be developed over time. This claim comes from the assumption that core competencies should be impossible to imitate for competitors (i.e., unique). Consider, for instance, the three tests that a competence should pass to be considered a core competence (Prahalad & Hamel, 1990):

- Is the competence a significant source of competitive advantage?
- Does the competence transcend a single business?
- Is the competence hard for competitors to imitate?

Also Barney notes that core competencies should provide the firm with a sustainable competitive advantages and writes that: ". . . whether or not a competitive advantage is sustained depends upon the possibility of competitive duplication . . ." (Barney, 1991, p. 102). From such ideas comes a focus on identifying and exploiting the core competencies of the firm—and not at all on developing and changing the core competencies of the firm. I do not agree. For several reasons I find it necessary to discuss competence development as part of competence theory as well as competence identification and exploitation.

For now, I offer two reasons why competencies cannot be impossible to imitate. First, technology is usually a part of the competencies of the firm. This applies not only to manufacturing competencies; for instance, information technology penetrates most of the organization in any modern firm. As it is well known in the technology management literature, technology has a tendency to evolve over time according to an S-shaped life cycle. Thus, part of the foundation for a firm's competencies certainly changes over time and is even replaced occasionally as a technology change happens.

A second important part of competencies will almost certainly be the employees of the firm. It is employees that apply technology, communicate with others, and make most of the decisions related to the functioning of a core competence. And employees change as well. Employees follow a life cycle, as well as technologies, even though key employees have been known to have car accidents, retire, or in other ways change. Today employees change jobs more often. Therefore, key employees will certainly leave the firm and take their knowledge with them. This opens the opportunity for other firms to get access to key knowledge about the competencies of the firm and imitate them. Furthermore, the world has never been more open with respect to knowledge than it is now. From wandering employees to Internet communication, possible explanations abound. Thus, it will usually be possible for competitors to get access to critical knowledge about the competencies of a firm. Therefore, competence development is a crucial activity in the strategic management of firms today.

In this chapter, I focus on competence development as a bridge between market requirement and opportunities, on the one hand, and technological developments on the other. However, the definitions of competencies offered in the literature focus on either the output of competencies (e.g., that they create value for the customer) or the attributes of competencies (e.g., that they are difficult to imitate). This makes it difficult for managers to include competence-based thinking in their managerial activities. First, I define competencies by means of their elements and introduce three different kinds of competencies.

UNDERSTANDING COMPETENCE

Since the first ideas of viewing strategic management in terms of "resources" (Wernerfelt, 1984), "critical capabilities" (Grant, 1991), and "competencies" (Prahalad & Hamel, 1990), few substantial contributions have addressed the operational aspects. Therefore, it is difficult for managers to actually apply competence-based thinking in their management efforts. I shall make use of one of the few operational definitions of core competencies to argue that competencies can be developed by using operational "handles."

In the literature, competencies, capabilities, and technologies all refer to the same thing (Leonard-Barton, 1995; Drejer, 1996a). *Core* competencies are usually defined as those competencies that provide the firm with a competitive advantage via the execution of the competence, for instance the way in which Nike manages its worldwide net of suppliers. Core competencies have been built over time and are not easily imitated. For instance, it will be difficult to get access to Nike's knowledge of suppliers, not to mention to imitate Nike's credibility with the suppliers. The traditional definition of a competence looks at either the output of the competence (value, competitive advantage) or its attributes (difficult to imitate). Little is said about how the output is created or how the attributes are achieved.

In my previous work, I have defined competencies as a system of human beings, using (hard) technology in an organized way and under the influence of a culture to create an output that yields a competitive advantage for the firm (Drejer, 1996b; Drejer & Riis, 2000). This definition focuses on the *elements* of a competence and can provide a comprehensive basis for discussing competence development. This definition emphasizes the internal characteristics of competencies and should be seen as a supplement to the more traditional output-oriented definitions, rather than as a replacement.

A competence consists of the following four generic elements:

- *Technology* is often the most visible part of a competence, because it represents the tools that human beings use to do activities. I prefer to view technology as physical systems or tools—restricting the softer perspectives on technology to be skills and knowledge of human beings. "Hard" technology, then, becomes machinery, tools, equipment, software programs, databases, and so on.
- *Human beings* are the most obvious part of competence; if no humans use the technologies, then nothing will happen. Therefore, human beings are the focal point of competence development.
- *Organization* refers to the formal organizational structure and management systems under which human beings function. For instance, planning and control systems, reward and pay systems, communication channels, hierarchy of responsibilities and tasks, and other formal organizational manifestations will greatly influence the human beings and their actions.
- *Culture* refers to the informal organization of the organizational unit considered. The corporate culture influences the human beings via shared values and norms guiding activities.

These elements interact in a systemic relationship (i.e., competencies are constituted by systems of the four elements). This implies that there is actually a fifth element of some importance—the relations between the four generic elements.

As Leonard-Barton notes, a competence may be viewed as a system (i.e., it is difficult to focus solely on individual elements as they are related to each other) (Leonard-Barton, 1995). This points to the need to focus on not only the individual elements, but in particular on their mutual interplay. The definition proposed here provides a context in which specific technologies may be seen and discussed, for instance, in terms of their strategic importance to the firm. Also, the definition emphasizes the formal and informal way in which human beings interact as an essential constituent of a competence, thus pointing to the area of organizational learning as a relevant part of competence development. In this way, the definition of competence makes it possible to relate technological development and organizational learning to the development of competencies.

A TYPOLOGY FOR DIFFERENT TYPES OF COMPETENCIES

One can think of a variety of different competencies in firms associated with different organizational units, such as:

- A production plant consisting of everything from management to shop floor and consisting of many different work cells and sections.
- A production group or workshop inside the plant.
- A product development section (e.g., specializing in the engineering design of mechanical parts).
- A quality assurance department (e.g., working with total quality control or preventive maintenance).
- The whole firm with all of its departments and production plants.
- A logistic supply chain consisting of several firms that work together in a complex network of relations.

The spectrum of different competencies may be expressed by the nature and role of the elements of a competency. I have identified three distinctly different types of competencies representing three points on a continuous scale.

A Single Technology and a Few People

This may be a workshop operating a few machining tools within a special type of production processes. Or it may be a production group capable of processing a certain group of parts. The competence is rather easy to identify, and especially for the process-oriented workshop the technology part is rather well defined.

Interwoven Technologies in a Larger Organizational Unit

This may be the production engineering capability to design a new tool for plastic molding machines. This may include different capabilities (or competencies), such as the application of simulation software for the extruding process, a CAD system with the specification of the product parts, a CAM system for preparing instructions for the machining of the tool, and know-how to make use of the previously mentioned capabilities in an appropriate and integrative way. The technologies are interwoven because alone their utility may be limited, but combined a significant synergy is obtained. Organizational structure and formal processes are necessary for the coordinated use and interplay of the various technologies.

Complex Systems Connecting Many Persons in Different Departments and Organizational Units

This may be the capability of an industrial enterprise to deliver customer orders at the promised day and with the specified quality and customization. Obviously, this competence is at the heart of the competitive strength of the firm; however, it is difficult to identify. Some examples are:

- A quality management system with procedures and rules but also the norms and values related to quality. Such a system will often work across departments and functions.
- A production management system including order handling, planning, purchasing, and inventory control. Again such a system has many manifestations in different departments.

Such complex competencies may include a number of complementary competencies, for example, the tacit knowledge of individual employees interacting collectively. The resulting competence will be greater than the sum of the individual competencies.

Ordinarily, technology is the major part of the first type of competence. However, in the other two types of competencies, technology interacts with other elements, and the role of a specific technology is difficult to assess explicitly.

CASE EXAMPLES ILLUSTRATING THE DIFFERENT TYPES OF COMPETENCIES

To illustrate the nature of competence development for each of the three types of competence, a number of illustrative case examples are presented and discussed in this section.

A Single Technology and a Few People

Case Albatros

A company, which I will call Albatros, produces paper tissue for diapers and other personal hygienic products. Through an international merger with an American firm a few years ago, Albatros has become one of the major manufacturers of this type of material. It employs a well-proven manufacturing technology that has been improved over the years. Together with the people and other organizational elements this forms a simple competence for the firm. However, recently the only major competitor has invested in a new technology with a better performance than the traditional technology. Furthermore, it eliminates a process at the proceeding companies that produce the diapers; however, the traditional technology is capable of providing features that may not be achieved by the new technology.

The new technology requires a rather large investment. So Albatros is considering what to do. The manufacturers of the traditional technology have been able to increase the speed of the process without loss of quality, and it may be expected that continued effort will lead to even better performance.

In many respects, Albatros has been involved in a fierce race between two different technologies of major strategic importance. Consequently, Albatros has increased its effort in technological forecasting. In view of the difficulties of predicting what will happen in the future, the focus has been to understand the underlying technological and scientific developments behind each of the two technologies. This approach has also provided useful insight into the operation of the current technology.

In addition, the product development department has directed its attention to Albatros' customers to prevent drastic moves and to forecast what functional properties they would prefer in the coming years. This effort is focusing on the opposite end than that of traditional technological forecasting. I call this form of forecasting functional forecasting.

In this case it is easy to identify the strategic role of production technology as a significant part of the competencies of the firm. Furthermore, the key competence of the company is dominated by this production technology. The human and organizational elements of the competence play a supporting role, and the nature of organizational learning is primarily skill development.

Case Bounty

This industrial company develops and manufactures pumps of different types. Traditionally, Bounty has for many years practiced the policy of using primarily stainless steel for its rotors. However, competitors have started to introduce plastics for the lower end of the pump program (small, low performance, low price, and high volume). For some years Bounty has been engaged in developing rotors of plastic, which has included experimenting with different kinds of plastics with respect to functionality and producibility. The problem of long-term durability has imposed difficulties and uncertainties.

The effort had two directions. First, technology forecasting was intensified with respect to new sorts of plastics that also included composite plastics. Vendors were involved as well as international R&D centers. The second direction of effort was the customer side. A QFD (quality function deployment) study was made to map the shift of material and technology for the rotor onto customers' expectations, of both plumbers and end-users. One aspect of functional forecasting in this case example was concerned with the reaction of customers to the introduction of plastic parts instead of stainless steel, which was so closely related to the image of Bounty.

Thus, the nature of competence development in this case was primarily a technological forecasting issue combined with a projection onto customer expectations and with functional forecasting on specific issues. The major uncertainties were associated with the long-term properties of the selected types of plastics.

Case Care

This company manufactures components for hydraulic systems for mobile equipment, such as engines and pumps, proportional valves, and control units. Whereas engines, pumps, and proportional valves are standard products marketed to the entire market, control units are products designed specifically for engineering heavy machinery and in alliance with partners within that industry.

The actuator plays an important role in a hydraulic system. For a number of years, magnetic valves have been the only technology available for actuation of hydraulic products. As time has passed, however, a number of new technologies have begun to emerge as possible alternatives (e.g., ultrasound engines as used in camera zooms). Thus, at some point the management of Care decided to conduct an evaluation of alternatives to magnet-valves as actuator units. The key question in this case example is, therefore, not how to develop a competence/technology further, but whether to replace a competence with another competence.

First, the system in which an actuator is to function was investigated. Criteria of robustness, that is, immunity to disturbance from oil, dirt, and high/low temperatures, were seen as the most important criteria, along with ability to manufacture and economy. The next step was to evaluate a number of alternatives, according to the formulated criteria. However, before undertaking this step, the issue of maturity and time horizons became important.

Typically, a technology is developed through a number of stages from basic research to applied technology, that is, the S-curve phenomenon; and in this case, it was evident from the start that the alternative technologies were located rather early in their life cycle. Thus, an important question for Care was whether it should commit itself to the development of alternative technologies into a core product.

It was decided to see if other industries would be in the same situation in terms of being challenged to seek alternative technologies. It was discovered that magnet-valves for fuel injection of car engines have great resemblance to those of Care. The requirements to magnet-valves were also similar, for example, in terms of working environment.

Since the automotive industry operates with a much higher volume than Care, it was argued that Care should follow the development in this industry and be prepared to quickly adopt a new technology when the automotive industry first has decided which technology to adopt. In this way, Care would not invest in technology development in the early and risky stages. It was argued that Care would not lose market share in its business area if it shifted to the new technology one or two years after the automotive industry.

In this case it was possible to position a technology in relation to the development of another industry. The analysis also implied the need to develop competence in adopting a new technology with speed and precision. Thus, both hard and soft elements of competencies were involved.

Interwoven Technologies in a Larger Organizational Unit

Case Dorton

This industrial enterprise produces farming equipment. Several years ago it introduced robots to assist in welding some of the more complex parts. A system of four pallets was installed in front of the robot to allow for mounting pieces on fixtures for the subsequent parts to be welded. Programming was carried out by the operator by moving the robot along the desired trajectory. The robot functioned well, but was considered a stand-alone piece of equipment, initiated and run by the production engineering section. After two years of successful operation it was realized that the greatest benefit of the robot was the possibility of cutting the batch size to just one, which simplified production planning and control significantly while at the same time improving customer service.

The technological development soon brought into focus off-line programming that would significantly increase the up-time of the robot. However, it presupposed the existence of precise drawings and software for programming the robot on the basis of CAD drawings. If at the same time vision control could be introduced, the robot would be able to allow for minor deviations between the drawing and the actual physical form.

Thus, what started as a single piece of technology evolved into a set of interwoven technologies. A given competence, for example, to weld complex parts with high quality and with a batch size of one, depends on the development of several technologies. As a consequence, it is difficult to justify investment in a specific technology because it was used as an integral part in several competencies. Furthermore, more cross-functional cooperation was needed to fully utilize the potentials of technology.

The case example points to the benefit of considering a competence as a unit of planning, because of the possibility of connecting the capability to customers' expectations. This cannot be done directly for individual technologies. Hence, the notion of competence clearly demonstrates its usefulness as an intermediate unit between technologies and the customers.

Several organizational issues are associated with this type of competence, for example, the need to be able to use different technologies. We find that an effort spent for functional forecasting may help formulate motivating goals for competence development and stimulate a more holistic thinking in the unit. Organizational learning should be directed toward the combined operation of using several technologies.

Complex Systems Connecting Many Persons in Different Departments and Units

Case Everton

This industrial enterprise produces equipment for food processing. In recent years customers had requested shorter delivery times and a higher degree of customization at the same time. Management had identified this shift and noticed the widespread dissatisfaction with the current production planning and control system. Assisted by external consultants, the information technology department preparepared a proposal for a new computer-based production planning and control system. After some discussion it was decided to acquire the new system with the hope that it would remedy the identified deficiencies.

With the joint effort of several employees, the new system was installed and instructions were offered on how to operate the new system;

however, the overall performance did not increase as expected. Management called on other external consultants, who concluded that the new system basically was geared to a batch, forecast type of production and not the customer ordered, project oriented mode of production that was characteristic of the way the organization was carrying out its processes, for example, handling customer orders, in the same way as it had always done.

Management started to realize that the production planning and control system was, in fact, only supporting the organization's behavior, and, as a consequence, the main effort should be directed toward training the many persons involved in new ways of doing things. Handling customer orders required a complex interaction of persons from different sections and disciplines. Hence, focus should be placed on developing and implementing cross-functional working modes.

Management would readily admit that the capability to deliver customer orders on time and in a customized version was one of the key competencies of the company. At the same time, management realized that this competence was difficult to identify. First, it involved many persons, and second, it was primarily informal (tacit) and difficult to capture and measure. Next, a production planning and control system was to be considered as an important means for guiding the daily operation and business processes associated with the handling of customer orders, purchasing, and capacity planning. The system also should be seen as a means for capturing cross-functional experiences.

As the case example illustrates, organizational learning is a key element in the development of competence of this type. This is not to say that technological forecasting should be neglected. To the contrary, new technologies will play an important role for competence development, not only as an significant enabler but also as a potential driver of organizational development. However, technologies should be considered as a part of the overall competence with organizational learning across functions and disciplines as another major part.

WHAT IS THE CONTEXT OF COMPETENCIES?

Based on the three different kinds of competencies and examples of each, I would like to discuss some issues related to the context of competencies in a firm. As noted in the introduction, firms are confronted with several external forces from the environment and have to deal with these forces. Two forces are particularly important in relation to competencies—market and technological development, respectively.

Each may represent a threat to the firm but may also constitute an opportunity. One the one hand, it is important to understand these external developments and perhaps be able to anticipate future developments. On the other hand, it is not sufficient to study market development or technology development alone; it is the combination of the two developments that is important.

In light of these external dynamic forces, I see competence-based strategy as a link between market and technology development. As pointed out earlier, a competence rests on technologies brought to use by means of organizational learning. At the same time, a competence should be used to increase the firm's competitive strength. I believe that it is possible to develop a model that relates technology and market development with organizational learning and competence development. This will place each of the concepts in a meaningful context and allow for a constructive discussion of the direction and importance of each of the concepts and provide a foundation for the application part of this book.

The Role of Technology and Forecasting

If we start by looking at technological dynamics, the case examples earlier underlined the importance of technology for certain types of competencies. Thus, changes in technology in the environment can be potentially important to the competencies of the firm. Luckily, there is a lot of relevant literature regarding anticipating technological changes.

Technology Forecasting

In the literature, technology forecasting (TF) is seen as a means for predicting the development of technologies. According to Jantsch ". . . Technology forecasting is the probalistic assessment on a relatively high confidence level of future technology transfer . . ." (Jantsch, 1967, p. 1). Empirical observations of performance changes over time of technologies in the chemical business led to the proposal of the S-curve phenomenon (Bhalla, 1987). Accepting that a technology typically will evolve along an S-curve makes it possible to predict the future development of a given technology.

Ordinarily, a distinction is made between two basically different kinds of forecasting: explorative and normative forecasting. Jantsch writes about the two: ". . . Exploratory technological forecasting starts from today's assured basis of knowledge and is oriented towards the future, while normative technological forecasting first assesses future goals, needs, desires, mission, etc., and works backwards to the present . . ." (Jantsch, 1967, p. 4). Examples of explorative TF techniques are extrapolation, morphology, Delphi methods, and scenario forecasting. Examples of normative TF techniques are network analysis, relevance tree, and decision matrices. Whereas explorative forecasting deals only with prediction of how technologies may evolve along the predetermined S-curve, normative forecasting attempts to be more proactive. It is not assumed that technological evolution is predetermined. Instead, it can be created and it is important to discuss how. The focus of normative forecasting, however, is still technology and technological possibilities alone.

Despite the extensive literature on TF, few firms make systematic use of TF techniques and methods. One reason may be ascribed to the passive nature of the concept. Technological forecasting has been considered as a rather technical activity mainly concerned with measuring development of given technologies and offering a prediction about the future. As some of the case examples show, it is often difficult to make a prediction of the development of a specific technology, for example, in the shape of an S-curve. On the other hand, it is important to understand the underlying technological and scientific determinants. This calls for a continuous monitoring of the driving forces behind the specific technology.

Another reason for the limited application of TF is the little attention given to the way in which technologies may be tied to corporate strategy and market opportunities. As we shall discuss later, TF should be related to these elements through a constructive dialogue.

Functional Forecasting

Just as it is important to focus on the development of existing and emerging technology pertinent to the firm, it is also useful for the firm to make a forecast of functionalities that may be needed or wanted in society. As mentioned previously, the case company Albatros engaged in an effort to identify future desired functional properties. It was seen as complementary to technological forecasting and can be called functional forecasting.

The first activity of functional forecasting would be to predict the future preferences of current customers. For example, what may customers like to see in future products? Could new customers be attracted with the same functionalities of the products or with completely new functional properties? In the case of Bounty, it was important to estimate the reaction of customers to a shift from stainless steel rotors to rotors of plastic.

Functional forecasting should also go beyond the present customers to a more open discussion of identifying new ways of assisting customers in their activities, shifts of values in general, emergence of a new type of customer, new needs, etc. These questions are central to the marketing function, but should be included into a broader dialogue in which the technical functions also play an active role.

Forecasting versus Visioneering

I have introduced the notion of functional forecasting as an activity opposed to technological forecasting. However, forecasting—whether technology or functional forecasting—is usually considered a passive activity. There is a need for a more active and innovative way of discussing future technologies and/or product functionalities. Thus I introduce the notion of "visioneering" as a complementary activity to forecasting. Visioneering has been proposed earlier in the TF literature, often using the term *backcasting* for the activity of starting with some future desirable solution and deriving the necessary developments leading to a future solution. Visioneering should also apply to the output side of the firm—to customer demands and expectations. Some firms already attempt to create a market need rather than wait for a need to appear. This may be used actively by management and enable the firm to build its future core competencies and products.

I view visioneering as an idea that supplements the Hamel and Prahalad concept of long-term competition for the future of the firm's industry (Hamel & Prahalad, 1994) and not a seminal idea in its own right. However, the relevance of visioneering is supported by the existing work on competence-based strategy, and I mention it here to make the point that forecasting alone will not make the firm proactive.

When Technological Changes Enforce a Shift of Paradigm

Sometimes technologies do not only evolve slightly, they change completely. This situation will enforce a shift of paradigm with respect to the competencies that are based on the technology in question.

On the basis of empirical studies, Boston Consulting Group found that technologies seemed to have a life cycle similar to the well-known product life cycle with an S-shaped curve for performance measured as a function of either time or resources used for developing the technology (Bhalla, 1987; Drejer, 1996a). In recent years, it has even been argued that technologies change faster and faster (Drejer, 1996a), and since entire industries sometimes are based on one or a few key competencies, the effects of technological changes have become stronger. How is technological dynamics related to knowledge and learning? To address this question, we need to go beyond the empirical pattern of technological diffusion and see how the S-curve comes about. As summarized by Kate Blackmon: ". . . technological change is used to describe changes in knowledge that increase the volume of output or allow a qualitatively superior output from a given amount of resources. . . . It is one of the key forces shaping organizational environments and thus in driving organizational evolution . . ." (Blackmon, 1996, p. 6). Based on case studies, Tushman and Anderson proposed that technological change: ". . . constitutes an evolutionary system punctuated by discontinuous change . . ." (Tushman & Anderson, 1990, p. 440). A more recent refinement aimed at explaining technological change has been made by the same two authors in the form of the technology cycle model (Anderson & Tushman, 1990). In this model, it is proposed that technological change is characterized by sociocultural evolutionary processes of variation, selection and retention (Campbell, 1969). The model explains the S-curve phenomena by dividing the life cycle into four elements: technological discontinuity, era of ferment, dominant design, and era of incremental improvement (Rosenkopf & Tushman, 1994).

A technological discontinuity, for example, a major product or process breakthrough, provides a source of variation either by substituting an old technology or rendering possible a new one. This initiates an era of ferment in which different variations compete. Furthermore, there will be technological rivalry between an old and a new technology, as seen in the case of Albatros. At some point, a dominant design emerges as one variation "wins" the selection process. This initiates the era of discontinuous improvement of the dominant design that eventually leads to a new technological discontinuity. A technological discontinuity is fundamentally different from other types of environmental change (Freeman, 1981), as a discontinuity represents a dramatic break with existing practice, and hence knowledge, in an industry. Thus, technological changes are clearly important for the competencies of firms.

Technological dynamics is clearly important for all three types of competencies. It poses several questions to organizational learning. For example, with which speed should employees associated with a specific competence be capable of changing their qualifications in the face of rapid changes of the technologies used? Will new qualifications be required, or may existing qualifications be used in a new way? Will a shift to a complete new technology also imply adoption of a new paradigm of operation?

Some of the questions address general managerial questions: When should continuous improvement of current operation be stimulated? When should the company prepare for a shift of paradigm that implies abandonment of present skills and working modes?

Linking Competencies and Product-Market Strategy

If we take a look at the "other side" of the firm, there are the market and customers. As defined in the introduction, the strategic way to reach customers in the marketplace is by means of the firm's product-market strategy. But the product-market strategy should not exist in isolation from the competencies of the firm, so the question here is how can firms integrate or link product-market strategy and competence-based strategy?

Based on my previous work (Drejer, 1996a&b), I have found that there are several different models and theories that directly or indirectly attempt to deal with this question. I have divided those into three different perspectives on linking competencies and product-market strategy, focusing on the integration of activities, aspects, and time horizons, respectively.

Integration of aspects implies establishing coherence among a number of different viewpoints regarding strategic management of the firm, that is, linking customer demands, products, manufacturing processes, quality, productivity, and delivery. It often involves seeking a balance between conflicting criteria and disciplines.

As one of their many contributions to the area of core competencies, Prahalad and Hamel have proposed a model for linking products with core competencies. Prahalad and Hamel note: "... the critical task for management ... [in the 1990s] ... is to create an organization capable of infusing products with irresistible functionality or, better yet, creating products that customers need, but have yet not imagined ..." (Prahalad & Hamel, 1990, p. 278). Thus, competition has more than one side. Apart from competition on end-products, corporations can compete on core products and core competencies. Prahalad and Hamel's way of linking products and core competencies provides a strong conceptual illustration. However, the model is very focused on products, that is, end-products and manufacturing processes, and it gives us very little idea of other kinds of core competencies. This need is fulfilled by Miles and Snow's *adaptive circle* (1978), where strategic management is seen as a matter of balancing (integrating) solutions of the entrepreneurial problem (products), engineering problem (manufacturing processes), and the administrative problem (administrative and control competencies). This provides an intuitive understanding of what products are to be linked with. Still, Miles and Snow's model is conceptual and not operational.

A discussion of integration of aspects may help identify core competencies of a firm and how they are linked to product functionalities.

Integration of activities attempts to view competencies along a chain of activities in the firm. An activity chain is a continuous chain of activities associated with essential tasks of a firm (Frick & Riis, 1990), most notably product development, handling of customer orders, and materials flow.

By means of *activity chains,* it becomes possible to discuss and integrate the set of activities that contribute to the fulfillment of customer demands and, furthermore, to link underlying competencies to those activities. In a firm, top managers had discussed how to ensure that new competencies were developed in time so as not to delay fulfillment of customer orders. By analyzing the relevant activity chains, it was possible to discuss whether or not competence development would delay present orders and to decide when to apply new competencies.

The activity chain perspective may also be used to discuss which competence on an activity chain to outsource and which to insource.

The contributions of *business process reengineering* and *time-based management* have much in common with the notion of activity chain view. The strength of taking such a view is twofold: first, competencies are linked to activities producing the firm's products and services. It is possible to evaluate the strategic necessity of competencies, and to discuss the time involved in a chain of activities. Second, it becomes possible to map and discuss cross-functional competencies cutting across organizational boundaries and thereby to capture a number of competencies that would probably not have been identified.

It can easily take 5 to 10 years to change the organization and culture of a firm. To realize this, activities with different time horizons need to be initiated. An important challenge for company development is to *integrate decisions related to different time horizons.*

The literature on strategy is scarce with respect to the issue of where to *commit* the firm to certain actions and where to establish *readiness* for action in light of the uncertainties of the firm's environment. Most of the literature assumes that there is some fixed, hierarchical division between decisions of strategic, tactical, and operational importance. We believe, however, that it is vital to discuss the degrees of freedom and time horizons associated with customer needs, the products of the firm, and the competencies of the firm. As illustrated in the case stories earlier in this chapter, different sorts of portfolios for competencies may be used to deal with the issue of achieving *coherence between readiness for action and commitment of the firm.* By means of such portfolios, of which Bhalla (1987) has proposed a few, it is possible to discuss the diffusion of competencies, the performance of the firm as it is compared to that of competitors, and the need for further development of competencies.

The dimension of integration suggests that competencies must be placed into their proper context of time and action, that is, the issue of which competencies to develop, desirable levels of performance compared to competitors, when development should be done. Thus, the need for competence development, and perhaps also product development, will arise from the choice of commitment/readiness.

COMPETENCIES IN CONTEXT

Competence-based strategy may be studied in its own right as an important part of corporate strategy. In addition, competence-based strategy should be seen as an intermediate element capable of bridging the gap between technological development and market development. In turn, the study of technological and market development may provide a basis for identifying the direction of competence development.

In the preceding section, several factors affecting competence-based strategy were discussed. These elements may be put together in a model shown in Figure 1 of the introduction. As the model attempts to capture, competence-based strategy is seen as a force field of a number of interrelated drivers, and the notion of organizational learning is a useful concept for capturing the way that firms can work with this force field. This concept is discussed in detail in Chapter 8. For now, accept the claim that learning is the prime means for working dynamically with identification, analysis, and development of competencies.

As illustrated by some of the case examples, technological development often is a strong driving force. The discussion in this chapter, however, suggests that the technology perspective be complemented by a functional forecasting point of view and by an organizational learning perspective. Similarly, when competence development is dominated by informal, collective learning processes, as in the case of complex competencies in Everton, a technology and market perspective may provide useful focus and direction.

The nature of the complex interaction among drivers may vary according to the type of competence in questions. To be provocative, I will claim that competence of the complementary type may only be developed if it is driven by required functionality. In other words, it is the visualization of customers' expectations that drives the organization to cooperate across functions. I have seen many examples where employee loyalty and a clear vision of customers' expectations have created a special enthusiasm, often encountering an informal introduction of innovative working modes. This should be the case not only for traditionally entrepreneurial firms but for in all kinds of firms (Drejer, 2001).

CONCLUSIONS

In this chapter, I have argued that a competence should be defined with respect to its output (its benefit to for instance customers), as well as with respect to its internal elements and characteristics. The former view enables us to define which competencies are core competencies. In this way, competence-based strategy certainly supports strategic management of firms; however, the output-oriented view cannot stand alone. The internally oriented view enables us to differentiate between different types of competencies, to discuss the development of competencies in an equally differentiated manner, and to discuss factors determining competence development.

Toward a More Differentiated View of Competencies

I have argued that it is necessary to look at the inner workings of competencies in order to discuss the development over time of competencies. I have also proposed that the key elements of a competence are:

- One or more technologies
- Actors (employees)
- Formal organization (e.g., organizational structure and management systems)
- Organizational culture and informal aspects of the organization

I then concluded that competencies have different characteristics; for instance, technology plays different parts in different competencies. To be able to discuss this more explicitly, I classified competencies into three different types:

- A single technology and a few people
- Interwoven technologies in a larger organizational unit
- Complex systems connecting many persons in different departments and organizational units

Although the three types are only points on a scale of different competencies, they enable us to distinguish between different competencies and to discuss the development of different types of competencies in more detail than if we should discuss competence development in general.

The Development of Competencies

I have also discussed issues of competence-based strategy based on the three types of competencies. Three factors were identified with a major influence on competence-based strategy:

- Technological dynamics
- Functional requirements
- Organizational learning

The role of these factors for competence-based strategy depends on the type of competence. By means of case examples, I have shown that there are large differences among the three types of competencies. For example, technology is often important for type one competence (a single technology and a few people), whereas organizational learning holds the key to competence development for type three (complex systems connecting many persons in different departments and organizational units). In other words, by means of the proposed classification into three types of competencies, we are able to discuss competence development in a much more differentiated manner.

What about Competence-Based Strategy per se?

Competencies are the key to competitive advantage. This conclusion is based on two lines of argument. First, several authors express growing dissatisfaction with the static equilibrium framework of much of the product-market strategy literature (Wernerfelt, 1984; Barney, 1986). This seems to be a logical stance to take in light of the discussions of the new competitive situation (see introduction). The second line of argument is the increasingly persuasive case examples of successful organizations, such as 3M, Honda, and Canon, that appear to have developed strategy around their existing and future competencies rather than simply market and competitor analysis (Prahalad & Hamel, 1990).

Typically, a core competence is defined in relation to the competitive impact of its output; that is, a core competence provides the firm with (sustainable) competitive advantage via the way it is executed (Prahalad & Hamel, 1990; Grant, 1991), or via its attributes; for example, a core competence is firm-specific and hence difficult to imitate (Barney, 1991; Grant, 1991). However useful these definitions are in terms of competition and strategy; they are not operational (Leonard-Barton, 1995), which creates some serious difficulties in identifying and developing the core competencies of a firm (Drejer & Riis, 2000).

Recent work has moved us toward a more operational perception of core competencies—a supplementary definition of competencies based on their structural characteristics. First, Leonard-Barton defines a core competence as a system with the elements—physical hardware, knowledge, organization and culture (Leonard-Barton, 1995)—and proposes that many of the effects of core competencies are generated via the relations between the elements, hence the systemic nature of competencies. I have used this as a starting point for my discussions on competencies and competence-based strategy in this chapter. For now it is important to know that competitive advantage can be achieved by means of competencies of the firm.

We can also return to the definition of competence-based strategy as offered in the introduction. Competence-based strategy is the subset of strategic management that deals with competition at the competence level and is concerned with identifying, selecting and developing the right competencies to support the current and future product-market strategy of the firm.

Chapter 6 provides a framework for competence-based strategy that I have formulated and worked with over the past four years. Chapter 7 contains a thorough discussion of the identification and selection of important competencies that is the first part of competence-based strategy. Chapter 8 explains how to develop competencies of the firm.

A Framework for Competence-Based Strategy

In this chapter, I propose that competence-based strategy should be applied as a separate decision area in the strategic management of firms. I present a framework for competence-based strategy that will guide the remaining part of the book. First, however, let us discuss the relevance of applying competence-based strategy.

WHY A COMPETENCE-BASED STRATEGY?

The why of competence-based strategy has two starting points. One is that competencies must be seen as the starting point for competitive advantage; the other is the empirical challenges of the postindustrial age that many firms face today.

The Starting Point: Competencies as the Key to Competitive Advantage

I have said that competencies can be perceived as the key to competitive advantage, based on two observations. First, several authors have expressed dissatisfaction with the static equilibrium framework of much of the product-market strategy literature (Wernerfelt, 1984; Barney, 1986). This seems to be a logical stance to take in light of the discussions on the new competitive situation in the introduction to this book. The second inspirational source of work is the increasingly persuasive case examples of successful organizations that appear to have developed strategy around their existing and future competencies rather than simply market and competitor analysis (3M, Honda, and Canon are examples) (Prahalad & Hamel, 1990).

For all practical purposes, *core competencies* seem to be the same concept as *critical capabilities, resources* and the other possible fads that all advocate the building of competitive advantage based on "something" internal to the firm. At least, Dorothy Leonard-Barton claims so (1995), and even quotes Gary Hamel as saying the same thing. Furthermore, the claim of competitive advantage even goes for—at least some of—the perceptions of technology within work on management of technology (Drejer, 1997). For instance, Zeleny's definition of technology as software, hardware, brainware, and technology supportnet (including organizational structure, culture, etc.) (1986) certainly seems to be the same as core competence. Thus, the work discussed in this book stems from several different sources that share the emphasis on some intrafirm element to generate competitive advantage.

Strategic management is concerned with the overall direction of the firm and with those issues that require a substantial portion of the organization's resources to deal with and play themselves out over a long period. Strategic management is also about ensuring the success and survival of the organization by adapting the organization to changes in its environment and making sure that the organization is competitive. Therefore, we can say that strategy is the link between the organization and its environment and that the task of strategic management is to determine how the organization should deploy its resources in the environment and adapt the organization to satisfy the long-term objectives of the firm.

It is important to note that strategic management deals with several time spans. The organization needs to be more than just competitive today. The competition for industry leadership is just as crucial to firms as is the competition for developing the right competencies in the right time. Thus, strategic management is also about integrating time horizons and activities related to all three kinds of competition. This often means finding those issues that should be kept invariant for the time being and adjusting other activities and issues accordingly. For instance, a company could choose to maintain its current customer base and then develop new products and competencies to account for changes in customer demands. Or a company could choose to stick to its current product portfolio and find new markets and customers for that portfolio.

As opposed to strategic management, operational management is about the short-term operation of the activities in the organization within the context of strategic management. In operational management, strategic decisions are executed and short-term results created. But this happens within the confinements of the current strategy of the company. This also implies that strategic management is about innovation for firms. Innovation, in short, breaks with the assumptions of how

things are currently done and, hence, always points toward the reformulation of the strategies of a firm. Therefore, strategic management is
also about innovation.

In summary, the role of strategic management is:

- To guide the organization in the long term.
- To provide context for the operational management and daily
  activities of the firm.
- To balance the three forms of competition by choosing what is to
  be kept invariant.
- To secure innovation in the activities, markets, products, or competencies of the firm.

In general, the new competitive situation has important ramifications
on how firms operate and are managed, as the many *different* fads on
management theory all offered with a rationalization in competition
show (Shapiro, 1996). In the new competitive situation as discussed
previously, there seems to be near universal agreement among theorists
that the focus on product-market competition (as advocated by Michael
Porter and others in the 1980s (1980, 1985) no longer suffices (Barney,
1991; Grant, 1991; Kiernan, 1995). Product-market competition needs to
be supplemented with other forms of competition (Drejer, 1996a) with
different time horizons and characteristics in order to cope with the
hypercompetitive dynamics of the new competitive landscape. So what
are those "other forms of competition"? Hamel and Prahalad have been
among the few to discuss this explicitly in some detail (1994), and they
propose that competition has three sides: product-market competition,
competition to foreshorten migration paths, and competition on industry leadership. The two "new" kinds of competition are:

- *Competition for industry foresight and intellectual leadership.* This is
  competition to gain a deeper understanding than others on the
  factors (be they technology, demography, lifestyle or others) that
  could be used to transform current product-market competition
  by, for instance, creating new opportunities, new products, new
  ways of viewing customer needs, etc. This kind of competition has
  a long time-horizon compared with the others.
- *Competition to foreshorten migration paths.* In between the battle for
  intellectual leadership and the battle for market share is competition to influence the direction of industry development, that is, a
  race to accumulate the necessary competencies, to test and prove
  out alternate product and service concepts, to attract coalition
  partners with critical complementary resources, and many other
  things. This kind of competition has a middle time-horizon com-

pared with the others, leaving product-market strategy as the competition with the lowest time-horizon.

In short, Hamel and Prahalad's work offers an expanded view of competition, where the well-known product-market competition is supplemented with two other forms of competition with longer time-horizons and different contents.

Empirical Challenges

In general, there seems to be agreement that an entirely new competitive situation has arisen. This is nicely summarized by D'Aveni (1994) under the concept of "hypercompetition." Hypercompetition, according to D'Aveni, is a competitive situation where the key competitive success factor is the ability to constantly develop new products, processes, or services providing the customer with increased functionality and performance (D'Aveni, 1994). In a hypercompetitive environment, firms cannot count on a sustainable competitive advantage, but must continuously develop themselves in new directions.

The well-known Danish company LEGO has experienced this new competitive situation and can illustrate the points made in the introduction about environmental challenges facing firms. LEGO is one of the world's leading brands within the toy industry. The company's famous LEGO bricks have been played with by generations of children, and the company now has in excess of 10,000 employees worldwide, as well as annual sales of approximately $1 billion. In recent years, LEGO has been under severe pressure to change its strategic direction, which illustrates several of the points made about empirical challenges in the introduction.

On its website, LEGO makes the following statement regarding its brand:

> . . . The LEGO Company founder Ole Kirk Christiansen invented the term LEGO in 1932. Born out of the two Danish words "LEg GOdt" meaning "play well" in English. Nearly 70 years later, there are probably few children—or parents—in the world who have not at some point or another experienced the wonder of playing with LEGO products. The concept of "Play Well" continues to serve as the philosophy for all LEGO products today. A philosophy encouraging children to be open and curious. To stimulate their creativity, imagination and learning—while they're having fun . . . (*www.LEGO.com*, 2001).

Despite the strength of its brand, LEGO has run into serious problems twice over the past five years. The first time was in 1998, when LEGO lost about $50 million. The second time was in 2000, when LEGO lost about $100 million. Even for a company that has made a profit for 50 years, this is unacceptable. So what are the challenges faced by LEGO?

Innovate or Die

Statistically, children do not play as much as they used to. This apparently sad fact illustrates the need for LEGO to innovate. Of course it is not the truth of the matter—depending on how you define playing. Apparently, using computer software does not equal playing in statistical terms (even though it can be both education and great fun). Thus, the market for toys is shrinking in these years.

However amusing, this goes to illustrate the need for LEGO to rethink its products and the concept of children's play—the latter being close to the heart of the mission statement of LEGO. Over the last 15 years, the products of LEGO have slowly begun to change. First, products became prepacked in kits with one or two generic solutions, rather than "just" being bricks that can be used to build anything. Later on the idea of prepacked products was developed even further into products that did not resemble—or even use—the traditional LEGO bricks but seemed to compete with Playmobil or Barbie dolls.

Recently, the idea of LEGO MINDSTORMS and other new products that use a great deal of software as well as the Internet for LEGO communities has taken this development even further, and a new division—LEGO Direct—has been designed to deal with these kinds of new products.

This innovation has made it critical to rethink LEGO's strategy and mission statement, not to mention its organization and management. Innovation is never free; it requires a great deal of effort and change in the strategy of the firm.

Technological Challenges

In LEGO's case the challenges of technology center on the products of the firm. The Internet and all of the software for games and entertainment that has been invented over the past 15 years has taken away parts of LEGO's market. We must speak of a revolution in technological opportunities that has been taken full advantage of by firms not normally producing toys. In the introduction, I mentioned that the first Playstation has the same computing power as a Cray Supercomputer of the 1970s, which illustrates just how fast things have changed. Firms such as Sony and many others have been quick to take advantage of the new technologies from the IT revolution and capitalize their lead on an emerging market for children. Thus, technological dynamics has also created a number of new competitors for LEGO and in general increased the environmental complexity that LEGO must face.

For many other firms, including LEGO, the IT revolution also poses challenges related to administrative technologies and/or process technologies. LEGO is a firm that is very highly automated in manufacturing and has an impressive setup. Of course, this system needs to be able to react to the dynamics of the new market, which is not always possible.

New Forms of Work and Workers

The technology revolution and corresponding development in LEGO's marketplace and products also have ramifications for the way LEGO is organized and works. For instance, LEGO Direct has a small part of its workforce located in Billund, Denmark, where the main part of LEGO still is located, but the major part of the workforce is located in New York. The part of LEGO Direct that is located in Billund is stable and includes top management, whereas the emphasis in New York is temporary workers, many of whom are Internet designers. This, of course, tends to create two subcultures that are quite different. Furthermore, the stable part of LEGO has a difficult time dealing with the rest of the workforce in New York, as they tend to resemble members of Generation X rather than the traditional Danish industry workers of Billund, Denmark.

Taken together with the opportunities for new ways of working in a geographically dispersed environments offered by technology these days—for instance e-mail, intranet, video conference, and group ware systems—this creates a number of serious managerial and organizational issues for LEGO. Indeed, LEGO faces a number of new ways to work and organize work and must deal with these issues quickly. This challenge is not made any easier by the fact that most of LEGO today remains a traditional industrial company manufacturing LEGO bricks in the same ways it always has.

Competition and Strategy

LEGO must rethink its strategy and view of competition. Apart from starting to focus even more on the brand of LEGO as a means of differentiation, the competencies of the company start to become important. New markets require new ways of working and, hence, the development of new competencies for LEGO. At the same time, LEGO needs to consider how to keep something in its strategy stable. This

---

Points for reflection
- What are the current strategic challenges in the environment that your firm faces?
- Are the challenges related to the marketplace, technology, internal organization or something else?
- What are the implications of these challenges for the competencies of your firm?

could well be its mission statement and perception of the customers (children playing) rather than its current core competencies. This, in turn, calls for a reformulation of the core competencies of LEGO.

THE APPLICATION OF STRATEGIC MANAGEMENT

The Role of Strategy

In light of the discussion so far, it is fair to assert that the role of strategic management is to make sure that the organization at all times is in line with the demands of its environment. We could say that strategic management is about *balancing the customer and the competencies of the organization*, and there is, indeed, some truth in that. The customers are one of the main stakeholders in any organization, and providing value to the customers certainly should be a guiding principle in any organization's work with its competencies. However, strategic management is far from that simple. The environment is much more complex than just the customers of the organization. There are many other stakeholders to an organization. There are the shareholders—owners—of the organization, legislative bodies, financial institutions, suppliers, competitors, and many others. Thus, there are many different interests to fulfill in a complex interplay between many stakeholders and their political power over the organization.

What we can say, then, is that *the role of strategic management is to link the organization to its environment and make the proper adjustments to the organization*. This role is, in fact, even more complex than "just" dealing with the many different external stakeholders of the organization. There are other important forces at play in the environment of an organization.

Demographics, legislation, financial climate, and technological changes are major forces for any organization and too often forces that the organization can do little more about than adapt to them. These forces push the strategic management of a firm, whereas the customers and other stakeholders pull the strategic management of the firm.

Finally, there is the issue of the "style" of the firm. Firms can have quite different traditions with regard to the starting point of their strategy. Consider the following two examples of firms with quite different approaches to the balance between the market and the competencies of the firm.

The Denmark-based multinational firm Coloplast has used its internal core competencies as a firm basis for the creation of competitive advantage. Coloplast develops, manufactures, and markets products for the health and medical industry. The company headquarters are located just north of Copenhagen, and Coloplast has three manufacturing facilities in Denmark. Outside of Denmark, Coloplast has manufacturing facilities in the United States, Germany, Costa Rica, and China, as well as sales departments all over the world. More than 97% of Coloplast's products are sold outside of Denmark. Coloplast has some 3,000 employees, half of whom work in Denmark. Annual sales exceed $500 million. The company has a strong mission statement that drives the company to the aid of disabled and ill persons.

Coloplast's mission statement:

> Throughout the world we wish to be perceived as dependable providers of consumable products and services. Our customers are health care professionals and users. Our primary concern is to improve the quality of life of individuals suffering from a disabling condition.
> - We respond quickly to market needs to ensure the highest level of customer satisfaction. We strive to offer preferred product ranges based on innovation, advanced technology and cost-effectiveness.
> - All employees must be recognised for their empathy with user needs and dependability in business relations. It is our ambition to attract and retain the best human resources.
> - As individuals and as an organisation we will act responsibly and be socially and environmentally conscious.
> - We strive to be the best within our businesses, thereby achieving growth and value for the company, the employees and shareholders.

Traditionally, Coloplast has produced ostomic products for people whose intestinal outlet or urinary tract has been surgically rerouted through the abdominal wall. A key element of these bags is the adhesive that keeps the bag close to the skin of the patient. Over the years Coloplast has developed a number of different products that allow ostomy patients to live close to a normal life based on this adhesive competence that the firm masters as a core competence. This has allowed Coloplast to create new business opportunities based on the adhesive's competence. For instance, in line with the mission statement of the firm, Coloplast has created a new business within external silicone breast forms and standard breast prostheses to fit all ages, sizes, and colors of skin. Coloplast also offers a wide selection of specially designed bras and swimwear. Furthermore, perhaps less in line with the mission statement, Coloplast has used its adhesives competence to create an entire business on foot care and first aid products to name two examples. Coloplast is an example of a firm that is based on a few core competencies that can span new business opportunities while being refined and developed at the same time. But not every firm can do so.

Bang & Olufsen is a company with an entirely different tradition when it comes to core competencies. This company, which has been through a major turnaround effort since the early 1990s, has about 2,500 employees today, but at the same time one of the strongest brands in the audio and video industry. Its annual sales are in excess of $400 million. Bang & Olufsen produces audio and video products (and others as we shall see) that are based on a unique combination of technology and design. The mission statement and values are as follows.

Courage to constantly question the ordinary in search of surprising, long-lasting experiences.
   The vision is rooted in Bang & Olufsen's values.
Poetry.
- Like a piece of poetry, Bang & Olufsen's products are always open to interpretation.
- Created to stimulate curiosity, the senses, the intellect.
- Created to surprise, to astonish and to please.

Excellence.
- We strive to create quality which goes far beyond what is expected. Our products must do more than function impeccably. They must reflect an attitude to quality.

Synthesis.
- The synthesis arises out of a dialogue between technology and emotion, between professionalism and personality, between engineer and designer.
- Contrast and constructive criticism generate valid solutions. Compromise means emasculation.
- The synthesis is the coming together of diverse talents that have the courage and the skills to stand up for their convictions.

At Bang & Olufsen, the identity and mission statement is so closely related to the products of the firm that the approach to strategy seems completely different from that of Coloplast. The core competencies mentioned officially from Bang & Olufsen are also very closely related to the products of the firm; consider for instance design, integrated control of products, sound, and picture. In fact, I would argue that the key element for Bang & Olufsen is the firm's ability to implement the ideas of its designer into the products as closely as possible. Thus, the products and customers of Bang & Olufsen are to be kept unchanged, whereas competencies should be changed accordingly to the changing taste of customers and market. The word of product design is the law. If a new product requires new process technologies, they must be developed accordingly; and it is rarely the other way around!

   In summary, we see that there can be quite different traditions within strategic management depending on what is seen as the stable element of the strategy—customers or competencies.

Issues of Strategic Management

I have tried to express the duality of strategic management in terms of two sets of issues that management needs to deal with in arriving at strategy, because I believe that this is a good way to communicate what strategic management is about. Even though this does not tell us how issues should be dealt with, it is nonetheless useful.

Issues of Product-Market Strategy

Product-market strategy deals with competition on the product/market level. Important references on the questions related to business strategy include Ansoff (1965, 1990), Andrews (1960), Porter (1980, 1985), and Hofer and Schendel (1978). Important issues inspired by these publications are:

- What needs does the firm attempt to fulfill with its products?
- How can these needs be met in terms of product functionalities?
- Which products should the firm produce?
- On which markets should the firm sell its products?
- How should the company compete with its products? On low cost, on differentiation from other products, or on focusing on a few customers and their needs?
- How can the company ensure that cash generated from older, mature products get reinvested in newer and cash-demanding products to maintain a steady income to the company?
- What kinds of new products and/or markets can the company diversify into without moving away from its mission?

This definition of product-market strategy also includes issues that in some of the strategy literature is attributed to "corporate strategy" and "competitive strategy." To avoid too much confusion, I have chosen to label these as *product-market strategy* as a unifying concept.

Issues of Competence-Based Strategy

Competence-based strategy deals with competition at competence level. Important issues include:

- Which core competencies are needed to fulfill the needs of the customers?
- Which core competencies are needed to produce and sell the current portfolio of products?
- On which core competencies should the company base its competitive strength (e.g., innovation, service in sales, manufacturing at high speed, high quality)?

- What is needed to maintain the core competencies for the future?
- Which support competencies are needed to produce and sell the products of the company with the current set of core competencies?
- When should core competence areas be abolished to new areas?
- What are the risks/rewards related to the development of new core competencies?

Seminal references on competencies and competence-based strategy include Prahalad and Hamel (1990), Prahalad (1993), Hamel and Prahalad (1994), Hayes and Pisano (1996), and Eriksen (1993a).

What Are Your Issues?
The issues described here are generic. They should be formulated to reflect the realities of individual and unique firms.

Points for reflection
- What are the issues that capture what your firm needs to decide regarding product-market strategy?
- What are the issues that capture what your firm needs to decide regarding competence-based strategy?
- Why are your issues different from the generic ones?

The Basic Concepts of Strategic Management

We are now able to formulate the basic elements of strategic management as they will play themselves out in the remainder of this book. This also serves as a basic vocabulary for the book.

Mission of the Firm
The mission of the firm is a formulation of what is held as the most basic and invariant in that particular firm. The mission is, therefore, also close to a formulation of the identity of the firm in question and serves to provide a sense of identity and mission for the employees of the firm.

Vision of the Firm
The vision of the firm is a formulation of where the firm wants to be ultimately and what it wants to achieve. A vision is a clear stretch of current achievements and position and challenges the people of the firm to reach further and higher than they would have otherwise. At the same time, the vision is in line with the mission of the firm to avoid corporate schizophrenia.

Product-Market Strategy

Product-market strategy is the subset of strategic management that deals with competition at the product-market level and is concerned with selecting and marketing the right products at the right markets to give customers what they want.

Competence-Based Strategy

Competence-based strategy is the subset of strategic management that deals with competition at the competence level and is concerned with identifying, selecting, and developing the right competencies to support the current and future product-market strategy of the firm.

THE APPLICATION OF COMPETENCE-BASED STRATEGY—THE FRAMEWORK

This section discusses the application of all the theory on competence-based strategy and presents the framework for competence-based strategy.

The Balances of Competence-Based Strategy

Even those who willingly accept the rhetoric of strategic management may find it useful to clarify in managerial terms the why of competence-based strategy. All firms have to make decisions that commit the firm for extended amounts of time. For instance, the development of a new product requires that a number of decisions be made on price, function of the product, quality level, etc. Such decisions cannot be changed easily later. Furthermore, often a new product requires investment in new process technology—technology that the firm must accept to pay over several years and perhaps use for other future products. Delivery, investment, and setup times are factors that point toward the need for planning capacity building. This is also true for the expenses that usually are written off over a number of years. Strategic management, thus, is an important tool for managers to secure the coordination of future actions in advance, so that the new product has the unique selling points required by the particular market segment at which the product is aimed—or manufacturing has capacity to match demand. In this way, strategic management also becomes an important means for coordinating decisions and actions made in the functional departments of the organization.

Decisions regarding the future, however, have to be made under uncertain conditions. Uncertainty may stem from both external and internal sources and can change the prerequisites underlying a strategic plan. As opposed to action plans, the strategy should relate only to high level issues and, thus, be more robust to changes in the internal and external prerequisites of the plan. In the real world it is difficult to define a robust strategy that, on the one hand, is so clearly formulated that it can be used to coordinate actions and decisions within the firm but, on the other hand, is robust enough to secure a long life of the strategy.

Points for reflection
- Consider the current formal strategies of your organization. How long do you expect those strategies to live?
- Are the current strategies robust? Why/Why not?
- What are the prerequisites on which the strategies of your organization are based?

In short, strategic management is about:

- Balancing the customer versus the competencies of the firm.
- Selecting what should be kept the most stable.

Customer versus Competence

As noted previously, strategy can be said to be a balance between two things: customer and competence. On the one hand, we have the customers of the firm. In conjunction with competition and competitors, the customers plainly decide (with their feet and/or wallets) how much profit the firm can make this year. On the other hand, we have the competencies of the firm. It is constantly necessary to develop the competencies of the firm to be able to develop new products, new markets, and find new business opportunities just to keep up with competition in the industry. To go beyond that and innovate, the firm must stretch its imagination and competencies even further. This is where the strategic vision of the future of the industry becomes important.

Customer and competence represent two different perspectives on a company and thus the strategy of that company. Each perspective highlights particular aspects of the overall strategy and offer us particular methods of analysis and theories to use. For this reason, I have spent a great deal of energy trying to describe the product-market perspective of strategy, as well as the competence-based perspective.

Strategic management is not a choice between the two perspectives as much of the strategy debate in the 1970s and 1980s seemed to assume.

Strategic management contains both perspectives. Instead of trying to choose between short-term, bottom-line thinking and long-term, competence thinking, strategic management should really do both at the same time. As has been pointed out repeatedly in the strategy literature (Miles & Snow, 1978), the firm chooses its market and customers and, based on that, establishes the necessary competencies to service the product-markets chosen. But it does not end there. The competencies of the firm tend to evolve over time, and this is part of constraining or offering possibilities in changing the product-market strategy already chosen earlier.

Finding the Constant Factors

In light of the preceding discussion and in light of the external dynamics that most firms are faced with, I tend to formulate the most generic strategic challenge that firms are faced with as follows: What parts or activities in the firm should be viewed as the most constant over time? Is it to be the market, customers, products, distribution, manufacturing or something else? I know of no general answer to this question; each company is unique and its situation will probably even be quite different at different times.

Some firms have spent a large number of years developing a deep and unique knowledge of a particular group of customers. Consider firms such as LEGO, with a very deep understanding of how children play and interact, or Bang & Olufsen. For such firms it makes a lot of sense to maintain their customers as the most constant factor in their strategy. Go with the customers and change everything else accordingly. Other firms have used their resources to build knowledge and competencies related to certain technologies and/or competencies. Coloplast illustrates a firm that is focused on a particular technology (among other things) that the firm masters so well that it can create new business opportunities. Another example could be the Danish firm Rockwool, which makes insulation products. Their many products are based on a deep knowledge of the process technology of melting rock (as it is). Rockwool used tremendous resources to develop their knowledge of that process technology in great detail. It does not seem traditional to define a company by means of a process technology—at least not in textbook examples—but for Rockwool, the most constant factor is melting of rock.

The Role of the Competence-Based Strategy

Based on the preceding discussion, competence-based strategy can be perceived as a substrategy under the overall strategy of the firm. This substrategy must be defined in dialogue with the product-market (sub) strategy of the firm. In the rest of this section, I discuss the elements of a competence-based strategy.

In light of the turbulent external conditions that many firms face these days that make it difficult to define a robust product-market strategy, I have noticed a trend in many firms to identify their competencies as the most constant element of the overall strategy.

Points for reflection
- What are the elements of your firm that have been chosen, perhaps implicitly, to be the most constant and, hence, as a starting point for your strategy?
- Are the elements related to product-market issues or competence issues?

On the Dynamics of Competencies

The literature describes inimitable and constant competencies that need not be changed over time. It is my experience and firm belief that competencies tend to either become irrelevant or just rot away over time if they are not developed.

There are several indications in the literature and from the case examples of this book that customers tend not to focus on the same criteria for buying over time. In his seminal work on manufacturing strategy—with a firm starting point in the product-market strategy of the firm—Terry Hill has coined the terms *order winners* and *order qualifiers* (1985). The latter are the things, seen from the customer's perspective, that need to be in place for the customer to even consider (products of) the firm in question. Order winners, then, become the things that differentiate the product and make the customer place an order on that particular product and not some other product. In the vocabulary of this book, we can say that order winners are the areas in which the firm provides unique value to its customers; that value is the output of the core competencies of the firm. However, all is not well. One of the basic points of Hill's work is that order winners tend to become order qualifiers over time. At some time, ABS braking was all new and an order winner in the auto industry. Today we take ABS braking for granted, and new features have replaced ABS as order winners. Customers tend to refine their taste over time—what was value for the customers today is taken for granted tomorrow. Thus, the core competencies of the firm will simply rot away if not constantly maintained.

Furthermore, competitors will try to imitate the unique competencies and corresponding unique value provided to the customers even if this is extremely difficult. Even though my emphasis on people, values, and corporate culture indicates that this should be impossible, several things point toward the exact opposite. For one thing, technologies have never been more transparent than today. It is no longer possible for a firm or a country to base its competitive advantage solely on being "hi-tech." Basically, the same hi-tech machines and robots that we have in the West can be found in China and Korea. This points toward a diminishing importance of simple competencies and technology. This is not only the case in manufacturing. Consider, for instance, the many quite similar ERP systems that have been installed in firms all over the world. This is bad news for those who have based their competitive advantage on technology alone. But there is bad news even in the case of complex competencies, even though they are based on implicit knowledge, values, and culture to a much larger extent than simple competencies; this is not to say that they cannot be imitated. In today's labor market, people no longer stay in the same firm for years—the golden watch is now awarded after 25 months rather than years in some industries. The exchange between firms of key personnel with much of the implicit knowledge is one factor that increases the likelihood of competencies being imitated. This is supplemented with much of the work on knowledge management that takes place in many organizations. Knowledge management, in part, attempts to make knowledge explicit and, thus, less dependent on key individuals and easier to copy and imitate. Add to that the greater focus on organizational learning and development in many firms and we come to my second point here. It is becoming easier to actually imitate competencies, thereby making a constant focus on competence development critical.

A third point concerns the need for paradigm changes. Either because of technological changes or changes in the marketplace—or both—we see that the need to innovate in the marketplace and competence area is more and more common. Of course this trend is related to the idea of hypercompetition that was discussed in the introduction. The case example of LEGO, however, illustrates the point more precisely. Customers not only refine their taste, they may change taste altogether. And if this trend is not driven by technology, it is at least enabled by technology. This is more the case in some industries than in others, but this does not mean that some firms and industries are hiding in the old economy and escaping all dynamics. Consider the example of the Danish firm Crisplant. Crisplant seems firmly rooted in the old economy. It is a producer of large-scale sorting equipment for airports, postal services, and so on. Crisplant is a project company with a large workshop that works traditionally. One should think that Crisplant could hide well in a sleepy, cozy market, but this is no longer the case. Crisplant has begun to work with some new customers such as Amazon.com. These new customers from the new economy (if there is such a thing) demand reduction in lead time of 50% and cheaper prices. The new customers are used to a much more dynamic world and this demands a lot from Crisplant. I see a need more often for complete changes in the competencies of the organization rather than just competence maintenance.

Introducing Focus Competencies

In light of the discussions above, I feel it is very important to be able to focus not only on competence maintenance but also on the core competencies of tomorrow when working on competence-based strategy. Therefore, an important part of a competence-based strategy is to work with the competencies that will replace core competencies within a few years. I will propose to name those competencies *focus competencies*. I see focus competencies as the core competencies of 2-5 years depending on the firm and industry in question. In some cases, a firm can identify a focus competence that needs to be developed right away, whereas other cases point towards building a certain state of readiness regarding a competence without actually devoting too many resources to the competence just yet. The logic of this thinking is illustrated in Table 6-1.

Table 6-1 is based on the previous discussions on the dynamics of competencies. Some of the current core competencies should be maintained for the future as customers refine their taste. However, some core competencies will no longer appeal to the customers in a few years because the values that they offer are either irrelevant or taken for granted. In the latter case, the old core competencies become support competencies; in the former the old core competencies should be destroyed all together.

TABLE 6-1. From Focus Competencies to Core Competencies

	Now	Middle time horizon (e.g., 2 years)	Long time horizon (e.g., 5 years)
Focus competencies	Focus competencies that we need to develop now	Focus competencies that may become important in the long run	
Core competencies	Core competencies of today	Focus competencies of two years ago plus core competencies that should be maintained	
Support competencies	Support competencies of today	Old support competencies plus old core competencies that have lost their significance	

To make up for the changes in core competencies, a competence-based strategy needs to contain the identification of focus competencies—the core competencies of the future. Some of the focus competencies need to be developed right now (within the middle time horizon of two years), whereas others only need to be scanned and may not materialize at all (those that we believe will be necessary in the long run).

Of course, finding the focus competencies of the firm is far from an analytical activity in the sense that finding the core competencies should be. We will be looking into the future and try to foresee that future customer needs, technologies, and so on when finding focus competencies. In the case of core competencies, much more can be analyzed according to current/existing customers and products. Nonetheless, because of the inherent dynamics of competencies, a competence-based strategy must discuss the focus competencies of the firm.

Definition of Competence-Based Strategy

I can now define competence-based strategy in terms of application. Competence-based strategy is the part of the overall strategy of the firm that is concerned with integrating technology, human knowledge, values and culture in order to create and maintain a set of core competencies that create value for the customers and thereby support the product-market strategy of the firm. In this way the competence-based strategy becomes the integrating element between external market dynamics, as treated in the product-market strategy of the firm, external technological dynamics of the firm, and internal organizational learning.

In working with a competence-based strategy, I will define the following set of elements that will define the content of the competence-based strategy of the firm:

Identification of the competencies of the firm
- What is the overall list of competencies that the firm posseses? Where are those competencies organizationally?
- What are the most important competencies?
- What characterizes the most important competencies of the firm?

Analysis of the competencies of the firm/choice of focus and core competencies
- What external dynamic threats are the most important competencies?
- What are the focus and core competencies of the firm?
- What is the total competence portfolio of the firm?

Competence development
- When should which competencies be developed?
- How should competence development take place?

Each element can be formulated differently, but I believe that these issues describe what should be part of an applied competence-based strategy; they form the basis of the rest of this book.

THE ELEMENTS OF A COMPETENCE-BASED STRATEGY

What Is the Overall List of Competencies of the Firm?

The starting point for any competence-based strategy should be identification of all the competencies of the firm to provide the best possible foundation for selecting the right focus and core competencies. A total list of competencies can be long. Even in small and medium-sized enterprises, I have helped create lists of 80 to 100 competencies in a short time. Nonetheless, making such a list is important for the rest of the work on the competence-based strategy.

Brainstorming with carefully selected representatives from different departments in the firm is an excellent way of getting the first list of competencies in the firm. This can be aided by using different models as checklists to make sure that the group has considered "everything" in its brainstorm. The value chain, for instance, is one such model.

The types of competencies in Chapter 5 can be helpful in identifying the competencies of the firm. They indicate a great deal about where to look for the competencies of the firm; for example, sometimes looking across department boundaries is the most crucial.

What Are the Most Important Competencies?

The next step in formulating a competence-based strategy of the firm is to reduce the number of competencies chosen for further analysis, but without yet selecting core and focus competencies. In general terms, I propose to reduce the number of competencies to 20 to 25 important competencies.

My thinking on the choice of the 20 to 25 competencies is twofold. First, there is usually some kind of Pareto effect related to the total list of competencies, making it easy to identify a large number of competencies that are obviously *not* important to the customers. Second, if the first step fails, considering the product-market strategy of the firm in general terms usually is effective.

In practical terms, the same team that identified the total list of competencies can also work on the first reduction of the list, preferably in a second meeting.

What Characterizes the Important Competencies?

Without considering core or focus competencies explicitly, the next step is to consider the elements of each of the 20 to 25 important competencies, as well as their interplay. This is a characterization of the important competencies with respect to elements, dynamics, type, and so on and functions as an important foundation for the analysis, leading, finally, to the choice of focus and core competencies of the next stage.

In this stage, one usually needs to abandon the team from the first two stages. The characterization is more of an analytical activity. Besides, in the organization there are bound to be domain experts on the competencies in question, and they should be consulted here.

What Are the External Dynamic Threats to the Most Important Competencies?

To get a little closer to the actual choice of focus competencies and core competencies, which corresponds to focusing on approximately 10 of the 20 to 25 important competencies, one can look at the external dynamic threats of either technological, market, or another kind.

Since it has already been established that the 20 to 25 competencies chosen are important, it is now important to dig a little deeper. Evidently, the customers and/or product-market strategy is one kind of important element. However, technological changes or other changes in the environment can also help make a decision on the relative importance of a given competence.

Again I see this activity as something that can be done centrally rather than by means of brainstorming or team.

What Are the Focus and Core Competencies of the Firm?

This element is perhaps the least analytical part of arriving at a competence-based strategy. At this point, it is necessary to choose what should be the focus competencies of the firm by looking into the future and deciding on some strategic priorities of the firm as such. Basically, the same is true for choosing the core competencies of the firm. Even though that does not require looking into the future, it does require looking at the firm through the eyes of the customers.

At this point, the management of a firm needs to show leadership and make the decision. I do not believe that such a decision can be delegated to a technical planner. It is a managerial decision that needs to be taken on the best and most informed basis, but still will require a great deal of tacit knowledge, experience, and instinct.

What Is the Total Competence Portfolio of the Firm?

What can perhaps be a help to the choice of core competencies and focus competencies is the element that is concerned with formulating a total portfolio of competencies for the firm. This is certainly a big help in working with competence development, but the analysis of this stage also points backwards.

The idea of having a competence portfolio comes from the field of management of technology, but is a natural consequence of accepting that competencies, such as technology, need to be developed and changed constantly. We can say that there will be a certain life cycle for competencies in much the same manner as technologies and products have life cycles. But if that is so, then the firm will need to balance its use of resources over time, as well as the risks and possible rewards involved. This can be done for technologies and should be done for competencies as well.

Some form of iteration between this stage and the previous one can be of great assistance when trying to reduce the number of the competencies of the firm from 25 to 10. A total view of risks, rewards, and resources can sometimes help to make priorities easier. This stage concludes the analysis element of a competence-based strategy.

When Should Competencies Be Developed?

The next stage is also related to the portfolio of competencies and their characteristics. Usually by now the firm has chosen about five core competencies and five focus competencies and can start to decide when and how these competencies should be developed. This stage is thus concerned with setting objectives for the timing, content, and results of competence development.

This cannot be done without considering the role of organizational learning, as this is the main means for competence development. For one thing, learning is not the same for a simple and complex competence; there are some major differences between the learning of individuals, small groups and organizations. Furthermore, learning will be very different in the cases of maintaining an existing core competence and developing an entirely new one. This corresponds to continuous improvement versus innovation or paradigm change.

How Should Competence Development Take Place?

In light of the preceding discussion, setting objectives for competence development and choosing the means for competence development cannot be kept separate. The two last stages of formulating a competence-based strategy will, thus, tend to overlap and be iterative in nature.

In general, however, there are many different kinds of organizational learning, partly because learning must be different in different situations. It is also important to note that the means for creating learning goes beyond courses and traditional educational means. There are also IT means for learning (the whole knowledge management scene) as well as organizational and personal approaches other than courses.

Formulating a Competence-Based Strategy

I discuss identification and analysis of competencies in the same chapter because the issues of those two elements are closely related. Thus, competence development is discussed separately in Chapter 8.

Often firms have not tried to formulate a competence-based strategy before, which certainly calls for a bottom-up, employee-involving process, perhaps organized as a project related to organizational development. The project organization will, incidentally, secure that some of the stages of the process can be done centrally in the project group, whereas others can be done with a great deal of involvement.

There are many positive aspects of a bottom-up process. Since competencies are internal to the organization, it is not likely that top management will have all the knowledge about competencies; involvement will always be a good thing. Furthermore, in the case of cross-functional competencies, it is often a revelation for the shareholders of that competence to see the context that their work should be seen as a cross-functional process that yields an important output to the customer. Again, involvement is a good thing. In that light, I have formulated a few general guidelines to the the process of formulating a competence-based strategy—indeed, any strategy. As described in Drejer and Riis (2000), my thinking regarding the process is inspired by the work of Henry Mintzberg (1994), James March (1992), and others who have proposed alternatives to rational, top-down strategy formulation processes.

Strategic Thinking Before Strategic Programming

Strong evidence has been presented regarding how strategic decisions are actually made from research that seems fit to reveal process of strategic management (Starbuck, 1993). However, I argue that a contingency view of strategy theory is important. The fact that a new school of strategy has emerged, with a nonplanning perspective as one of its virtues, does not, however, imply that the school of long-range planning is outdated today, as there may be environments that are characterized by relatively stable and predictable changes. In other words, I agree with Henry Mintzberg and others that nonplanning strategy processes are needed, provided that the situation is very complex and unstable. Regarding the traditional approaches to strategy making, these generally assume and demand that decision makers be rational and analytical and use a top-down approach. These kinds of problems, that is, where means and measures are known and agreed on for the problem to be solved, is what Peter Checkland refers to as "restricted problems" (1981), and he argues that such problems can be solved by analytical approaches. However, this is not the case in crafting strategies under difficult environmental conditions of technological changes, international competition, and other effects changing industries and competition. As a normative statement, I view systems thinking as a much better approach to design of strategies under such conditions than analytical/rational planning. Peter Checkland agrees with this theory and proposes a holistic, synthesis-oriented approach to problem solving in human activity systems, where the very nature of what a problem is will be part of the problem-solving effort.

In other words, I see the purpose of a strategy process as giving managers a chance for thinking strategically before programming their competence-based strategy. Thus, during the course of the methodology, the participants are supposed to build a common picture of means and measures related to strategic integration at a given point in time. Once this is done, strategic programming may be undertaken.

Dealing with the Issues of Competence-Based Strategy

With strategic thinking as a starting point, I have reached two conclusions as to how the issues identified in this section should be resolved:

1. There are many best ways to deal with each issue.
2. Issues should be dealt with in a multiprocessual manner.

There are many best ways to deal with each issue

The vast number of contributions in the literature and the different models and schemes for dealing with similar issues in the case firms of this book suggest that there may not be one best way to deal with each issue. For one thing, firms are different—if nothing else there may be differences in "style"—and, as with the case studies, may desire different models or schemes. This conclusion is merely another restatement of my commitment to a contingency view and is not discussed further.

Issues should be dealt with in a multiprocessual manner

In the introduction I discussed Peter Checkland's notion of "unrestricted problems" in which the very definition of the problems and the measures to solve them are part of the problem-solving (Checkland, 1981). C. West Churchman (1968) discussed this as "open problems," while James March proposed applying "technology of foolishness" to discuss means and measures simultaneously. My proposal is to work with the different issues in a multiprocessual manner. For instance, instead of "finishing off" the discussion of what are focus and core competencies, it could be left "open" while the issue of competence development is discussed. In this manner, it is possible to resolve interconnected issues.

Each issue of competence-based strategy can be dealt with by means of several models, techniques, or theories. This further supports the open-ended nature of the decisions.

Participants—A Team From Lots of Different Places

Evidently, most departments in a firm will have a stake in competence-based strategy. Marketing will be focused on the product-market strategy, product development in new products, finance in the investments resulting from new strategies, and so on, but will also need to secure that the competence-based strategy supports product-market strategy. If nothing else, all departments are interested because they are carriers of core or support competencies. In my view, it is only natural that representatives from all departments of the firm should be part of the strategic thinking of formulating a competence-based strategy.

How can we ensure that the participants "speak the same language" and actually arrive at a common view? My answer is to introduce a facilitator function into the process. The facilitator function is concerned with the process going on, to be a neutral player in the process, explain the issues as well as theoretical for each issue, ask the questions related to each issue, and attempt to guide the participants on to the next issue. Thus, the process becomes a combination of an employee-involved bottom-up process and a more central top-down part that supports the former.

7

Identification and Analysis of Competencies

The first two steps in formulating a competence-based strategy, identification and analysis, are treated together in this chapter for two reasons. First, it is my experience that the decision-making process of these two steps is different, more intuitive and less tangible, than the decision-making process in the last step of competence development. Second, there is a tendency (which I find less than encouraging) that the third step is a matter for the human resource management (HRM) function of the firm alone, whereas the other two steps usually are the matter of top management. Even though I believe that this tendency should be broken, I also find that the HRM function certainly should be involved in the issues related to competence development as well as the other two issues. Nonetheless, I will treat the issues in two chapters. The third reason is that we need to develop a lot more knowledge about how to apply theories and models related to, especially, organizational learning to competence development than what goes for the identification and analysis of competencies.

ISSUES AND PROCESS OF IDENTIFICATION AND ANALYSIS

This section deals with the issues that need to be resolved to arrive at, for example, five core competencies and five focus competencies for the firm, which is the objective for the first two steps of the process of formulating a competence-based strategy, and discusses how managers should go about arriving there. The latter corresponds to a decision-making process and, of course, depends on the issues that need to resolved.

Issues of Identification and Analysis

The issues here are an elaboration of the issues proposed in Chapter 6. The basic idea with formulating issues is to free the decision-making process from its more generic content side. Organizations and managers are so different that they will resolve this list of issues in many different ways; however, in my experience, the issues are generic from firm to firm.

The first step toward being able to handle competence development as any other management activity in the firm is to break down competence development into a set of subissues. Even though such issues must be overlapping in practice, they still help to maintain an overview over the identification and analysis effort. Only a few people have discussed this issue in the literature, so this list is actually somewhat pioneering; for example, Anders Nielsen (1998), has given this issue due consideration before. This list of issues is based on my experiences in a diverse range of firms. In identifying and analyzing their competencies, firms should:

- Define what is meant by "competence" and "core competence." It is necessary to find a common understanding of what competence means for the individual firm. Since firms are different and place emphasis on different things, it is nonsense to believe that one common definition should suffice.
- Select the appropriate unit of analysis. Furthermore, organizational levels are often important in the identification process and should be selected with great care. For instance, too low a level will make it difficult to identify competencies at firm level.
- Identity a full list of competencies for the firm. Without any consideration of what is strategically important, the starting point for the process should be to try to cover all of the competencies of the firm in a total list.
- Select the 20 to 25 most important competencies from the full list. Based on strategic considerations and by applying the Pareto rule and other rules of thumb, it is usually possible to reduce 100 competencies to a more manageable number of 20 to 25. Later those should be reduced even further by means of a thorough strategic analysis.
- Mapping of competencies. To provide the foundation for further work on the firm's competencies, it is necessary to map and describe the 20 to 25 competencies.

- Selection of five core competencies and five focus competencies. This should be done by means of a detailed strategic analysis of what is important to the customers, other shareholders, and so on. Linking to product-market strategy is always a great help. It is also critical to be able to discuss how each competence is linked to the firm's product-market strategy and, hence, the customers.
- Define a portfolio of competencies. This implies deciding on the development speed, balance, and means for competence development for the selected 10 competencies.
- Test the validity of the selection. That core competencies become core rigidities has been observed all too often. It is critical to ask whether the identification of a core competence is valid or just a result of habit, power, or culture.
- Creating an organizational process for the identification and analysis effort. Finally, it is necessary to discuss who should be part of the identification and analysis team, how top management and others should be involved, and so on—in short, how to create an organizational process for identification and analysis. The latter is the subject of the next section.

Process of Identification and Analysis

In light of the cognitive difficulties discussed in Chapter 6 and the risk of micropolitics affecting the identification and analysis of competencies, the organizational process of identification and analysis becomes immensely important. In this section, I discuss three different approaches to an organizational process: top-down, bottom-up, and a dual approach.

Top-down Approach

Lewis and Gregory (1996) have proposed what they refer to as an *analytical* approach. Since this approach is clearly top down in the sense that it starts with top management and the rest of the organization is involved only after the identification is over, we shall use the approach as an example of a top-down approach. The approach consists of a series of internal (managerial) and external (customer) interviews/questionnaires followed by review workshops in order to build consensus and avoid omissions. Working at strategic business unit (SBU) level, the approach consists of four phases:

- Activity and resource analysis.
- Strategic process review.
- Competence sieves.
- Review process.

The first phase begins by analyzing the firm's activities and resources to gain an understanding of the firm's managerial perceptions of competence. Top-level activities are identified and analyzed in greater detail in terms of their importance, performance, imitability, transparency, and replicability. Furthermore, phase 1 examines tangible, intangible, and management resources related to top-level activities.

Phase 2 analyzes the firm's internal environment, reviewing business planning processes, firm goals, and the associated strategy of the firm. To further understand the type of organization being analyzed, data collection is facilitated through a business planning process and open-ended questionnaires. The next phase, phase 3, filters the data obtained from phases 1 and 2, using *competence sieves*. The filtered data form the input to a series of internal and external interviews and enable a provisional list of firm competencies to be generated. After the firm goals and strategy determined in phase 2 are compared with the provisional competence list, core and distinctive competencies can be selected. Lewis and Gregory's analytical approach (1996) has been developed and tested through a series of case studies in the aerospace industry. Output from the analytical approach, other than identification of core competencies of the SBU in question, includes the underlying activities and resources and a completed industrial mapping exercise. The latter is partly based on Porter's model (Porter, 1980).

Another example of a top-down approach to competence identification is described in Drejer (1996a). Danfoss's original work on its so-called *technology pyramid* (technologies also meaning competencies) was also a top-down initiative. The core competencies and underlying *core disciplines* of Danfoss were identified by the top managers of the firm based on internal discussions in groups of functional managers. For instance, product development managers, manufacturing managers, and so on of the ten divisions of Danfoss were asked to identify core competencies for the entire firm. In other words, a core competence must be a value to several divisions of Danfoss.

Furthermore, the groups of managers were asked to identify "core disciplines" as the development areas that, in the future, would yield new core competencies. The result—after some filtering by the top management of the firm—was a list of six core competencies and about 20 core disciplines for the firm. This provided a great focus for the firm's central department labeled the *Technology Center*, which had responsibility for developing the core disciplines and competencies. Certain measures were developed to ensure that the technology pyramid was taken into account in the business planning of each division, but the individual divisions were not supposed to develop their "own" core competencies or work with a similar "local" process.

Bottom-up Approach

The bottom-up process is different from the top-down process. Bottom up in this book means starting with the employees of the firm and with their knowledge of the competencies of the firm before any analysis of what top managers think. Even though it is "only" a process aimed at manufacturing competencies, I will present Bang & Olufsen's approach to identification and analysis of competencies as an example of a true bottom-up process.

The purpose of B&O's approach to competence-based strategy is integrate customer demands, product technologies, and process technologies, both in development projects and with business strategies. In this section, I will focus on the latter use of the process, as this use is most relevant in this context. B&O's approach is a three-stage process :

- Technology mapping
- Future objectives
- Technology strategy and communication

At the time of analysis (1996), B&O had only recently started working with the approach. In the development process, the respondent and a few other members of the staff group had read a lot of literature and visited a number of companies, including Grundfos. Furthermore, consulting firms had been invited to present their suggestions regarding B&O's needs for integration of business strategy and competence development. According to the respondent, much of this effort had been in vain: nothing had been felt to be applicable to B&O's situation and needs. B&O has, therefore, developed its own process. The first two stages are clearly defined because they have already been undertaken. Stage 3 will be undertaken after stages 1 and 2. Thus, stage 3 must be interpreted as a future plan for the approach.

Stage 1: Technology mapping

In the first stage, B&O has mapped each of its process technologies, including the ones supplied from outsiders. More than 110 individual technologies were analyzed and mapped. The mapping consists of few analyses conducted by a member of the staff group plus those who had the essential knowledge regarding the technology. Selection of who to include was of course a difficult task, but it had to be rather subjective in the first attempt to run the process.

Stage 2: Future objectives

In stage 1, a vast number of mappings are made, but how are B&O managers supposed to consider the objectives for all of the process technologies? In stage 2, two things were done. First, a description is made for each of the process technologies. This is a short, written description regarding the particular technology, its present level, and which means should be applied to improve the technology. The written statement is aimed at top managers and technology managers (from the business creation department) who are not supposed to understand the technical mappings of stage 1.

Furthermore, an overall picture of B&O's process technologies is created (Figure 7-1). The figure illustrates a technology matrix, in which internal and external productivity are the two axes. On such a matrix, all of the technologies are placed. As it is illustrated, technologies that contribute heavily to external productivity are labeled *key areas*, while technologies contributing to high internal productivity are labeled *competence areas*. According to the respondent, when the contributions both to external and internal productivity are high, one may speak of core competencies.

The matrix was used to discuss future objectives for the technologies. This is done in a group of managers assigned to follow the process. The group consists of the director of business development, the director of operations, and the managers for each of the main areas in operations: purchasing, electronics, mechanics, assembly, and the so-called customer center (which manages planning, forecasting, and contact to sales companies all over the world). Evidently, normative statements can be deduced from a matrix like the one in Figure 7-1. For instance, all key

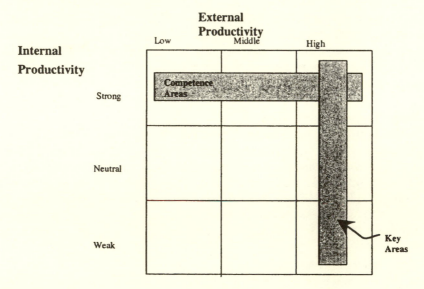

Figure 7-1. An overall picture of B&O's technologies. (Adapted from Drejer, 1996)

areas should have as high internal productivity as possible; competence areas, which have low contribution to external productivity, should perhaps be sold to others; and so on. Such guidelines were used to generate future objectives for each of the technologies, of which, it must be said, about 20 were claimed to be highly important.

Stage 3: Technology strategy and communication

At the time of analysis, B&O was finishing off its technology mapping and generation of future objectives. This had taken more than 6 months and has been a long process. Regarding the future, two things are planned: 1) communicating the results to top managers in connection to overall strategic planning, and 2) undertaking an entire technology planning process some time in the future.

Evidently, top-down and bottom-up approaches have their advantages and disadvantages. Where a bottom-up process has immense potential for motivating employees and getting access to their valuable knowledge on competencies, it also runs the risk of getting lost in detail and/or departmental rivalry. Basically, the top-down approach has the opposite risks, even though the importance of organizational micropolitics cannot be understated in a top-down process. However, the advantages/disadvantages make it natural to look at a compromise—the dual approach.

Dual Approach

Coarse (1996) suggests that competencies are underpinned by either technical or marketing capabilities, leading to two general kinds of competencies: core technical competencies (CTCs) and core marketing competencies (CMCs). To focus on CTCs, since they are more prone to be overlooked, Coarse developed two approaches to identify and analyze a firm's core competencies:

- A top-down approach in which the identified competencies are broken down into their constituent capabilities.
- A bottom-up approach in which a list of the firm's capabilities is used to identify possible competencies.

Table 7-1 illustrates the more intuitive top-down approach. The outcome from the top-down approach depends largely on the participants involved in the process. Thus, the participants should reflect the organization involved. For large diversified organizations, participants should be senior managers and business leaders to ensure that the process will identify the core competencies required to support business strategies. When focusing at a lower level, for example SBU level, participants should consist of a large variety of senior and middle

TABLE 7-1.   Top-down Part of Coarse's Dual Approach

Module	Activities	Outputs
1. Starting up the program	Create steering group and working teams Conduct start-up meetings	Agreed scope, focus, teams, responsibilities, timing, inventory categories, assessment parameters, and measurement scales
2. Compiling candidate core competencies	Formulate possible statements of core competencies representing the corporate business position	A long list of relevant promising areas of expertise based on senior executive perspective, or that of a cross section of the organization
3. Testing candidate core competencies	Apply the tests of core competence validity. • Competitive advantage • Customer-perceived value • Difficult to imitate • Market mobility	A set of valid, intuitive core competencies expressed at either the corporate level or as seen by a cross section of the company
4. Evaluating core competency position	Research external perceptions of core competence leadership, matching internal perspective to the views of observers and analysts	Agreed scope, focus, teams, responsibilities, timing, inventory categories, assessment parameters, and measurement scales
5. Constructing the inventory of capabilities	Deaggregate the core competencies into capabilities, irrespective of location in the corporation	A long list of relevant and promising areas of expertise regarded as critical to the success of the company

managers, resulting in an "organizational" top-down approach that can identify core competencies sustaining product portfolios (Coarse, 1996).

A similar procedure is followed for the bottom-up part of Lewis and Gregory's approach. An initial inventory of the firm's capabilities is formed, and each is assessed in terms of strength and performance on a 5-point scale. By examining groups of related capabilities, possible core competencies can be identified and eventually tested. Then the bottom-up approach facilitates an evaluation of the core competence position.

Coarse proposes that a top-down approach is more appropriate in large diversified firms and vice versa. However, under "certain circumstances" (which are not specified), a combination is the most appropriate approach. A dual approach: "... may identify gaps between the top-level perception of competency and the actual reality of available capability ..." (Lewis & Gregory, 1996, p. 41).

What Process Should Be Selected?

It is difficult to generalize about what process to select. The "style" of every organization is different, and some firms are more biased toward one kind of process than the others. In addition, situations can change quite suddenly; for instance, in a crisis situation there might not be time and resources to implement a bottom-up process. Thus, every firm should choose its own process based on its own situation, style, bias, and so on.

DEFINING WHAT IS MEANT BY COMPETENCE

A competence identification and analysis process needs to start by defining the competencies for the firm in question. This is a difficult step, as most competence definitions need to be able to both focus on the results of the competence (consider customer demands) and describe the internal elements of the competence (and make the competence operational). Few definitions manage to do both these things at the same time. Second, firms are different and place different emphasis on, for example, technology; therefore, a competence definition must be right for the firm in question at the time in question.

Traditionally, the multinational Danish firm Grundfos has focused on a rather technology-heavy definition of the firm's strengths or competencies. Thus, Grundfos founded and developed its "technology center" to develop process technologies in harmony with the product development of the firm. The firm even developed a so-called "technology planning" method for identifying necessary new process technologies in the firm based on product development projects. Thus, a fitting definition of "competence" for Grundfos would have been to define competencies as process technologies.

In the last few years, however, Grundfos has become under increased competitive pressure from the Far East. This has led to a number of managerial reconceptions, one of which is that Grundfos needs to focus on fast and efficient product development. This kind of competence is clearly outside the bounds of the process technology definition of competencies, indicating that a broader definition of competencies is right for Grundfos at this time.

The Grundfos example illustrates the usefulness of the operational definition and typology discussed in Chapter 5: The three different types of competencies place different emphasis on technology and, hence, on organization, culture, and people. For some firms, it might be a good idea to discuss what kind of competencies the firm has and, hence, what emphasis should be placed on technology. This may prove to be an excellent starting point for a proper definition of competencies.

Furthermore, there seems to be a trade-off in defining competencies. On the one hand, definitions must be practical, intuitive, and understandable for managers. Thus, definitions need to be sufficiently broad to capture many different competencies within the firm. On the other hand, however, definitions need to be sufficiently operational to describe competencies in at least some detail, thereby rendering competence analysis possible. In some cases, more than one definition may, in fact, be needed. In practice, extensive definition testing is needed to stimulate discussion and motivation for the competence identification and analysis.

Points for reflection
- Does your firm have its own definition of core competencies? Should it have one?
- Why do you think it is necessary to make a specially adapted definition for your firm or other firms?

SELECTING THE APPROPRIATE SCOPE OF ANALYSIS

There has been much debate over whether core competencies should be defined at the corporate level only or whether a core competence can be located at a division or function of the firm. For instance, is Toyota's production system (one of) its core competence or does this competence, in fact, consist of several core competencies residing in, for instance, quality management, production planning, inventory control, and many other places? It seems only natural that a core competence may reside at any level and that it is a matter of convenience that defines the level of the competence. Returning to the Toyota example, it would probably make life somewhat easier for the firm's management, if competencies were not defined as the entire production system but at a lower level. On the other hand, defining the competence at too low a level compromises overview. Prahalad and Hamel have noted that a firm probably only has 6-10 core competencies, since this number makes it possible to focus on the competencies while still maintaining the necessary details.

A problem related to the discussion of competence definitions is the problem of selecting the right unit of analysis. Traditionally, scope of analysis has been at company, strategic business unit, department, or team level (Lewis & Gregory, 1996). To illustrate the problems related to scope of analysis selection, we may think of the following examples of a competence:

- A production plant
- A production group or workshop

- The whole industrial enterprise
- A logistic supply chain.

Toyota's production system (Womack et al., 1990) has an entirely different organizational level than a production group or workshop, and the selected scope of analysis will constrain the findings of an identification and analysis process, if the level is defined too low. However, it is not useful the divide the Toyota production system as consisting of several subcompetencies; every element of the system needs to be present for the competence to function, as many attempts to implement Japanese quality control methods, just-in-time, and so on, in the West has proved. On the other hand, the competencies tend to be increasingly complex, with a higher level/scope of analysis making the process unmanageable.

As discussed previously, Bang & Olufsen attempted to develop a process technology plan a few years back with the explicit objective to identify the core competencies of the operations department to clarify these for the product development function of the firm. The objective was to "market core competencies to the product design team of the firm" and as such the process presumably worked fine. A number of process technologies were identified and developed according to formulated objectives.

What the process did not and could not do was to identify the core competencies of Bang & Olufsen as such. Later, the firm's management found that the core competence of Bang & Olufsen is the ability to produce truly innovative product concepts from its design team in such a manner that the eventual products are close to the initial idea. A result of this identification and analysis is that the basic idea of the process technology plan is no longer valid; marketing competencies to the designers is not relevant with such a core competence.

Competence identification and analysis can become "unmanageably complex" (Lewis & Gregory, 1996), and it is recommended that the scope of the analysis be discussed and defined beforehand. Knowing the type(s) of competencies to be identified can help clarify the boundaries of the identification and analysis process. Large corporations consisting of several strategic business units and/or divisions will tend to focus on the overall level of competencies, as these competencies are shared among divisions. However, it is also necessary to focus on the division level, that is, to break down the overall competencies into manageable subcompetencies in order to reach a manageable kind of competence. Still, it is critical to maintain the overview of the competence discussion by means of the scope debate. Also large corporations tend to have enough resources to identify existing and potential competencies, so these can be taken into consideration in the analysis process. Smaller firms, on the other hand, have fewer resources and must focus on present competencies. So far, scope of analysis has been discussed at firm or division level. However, network competencies represent competencies that exist across the company, its customers, suppliers, and other companies. In today's economy, these kinds of competencies are becoming increasingly relevant and for some firms it may be critical to broaden the scope of analysis to include this kind of competencies.

Points for reflection
- What scope would you choose for analysis in your firm? Why?
- What are the implications of this choice for the competencies that you will identify?

IDENTIFICATION OF COMPETENCIES

The next step in the identification and analysis process is to generate a full list of competencies. To this date, several practical models for assiting in this proces have been proposed by theorists, practitioners, and consultants. I would like to separate the identification of competencies in general and *core* competencies, as they are entirely different. It seems evident that most firms cannot deal with a large number of *core* competencies. However, an identification of competencies in general is likely to yield a fairly large number. At Bang & Olufsen, more than 110 process competencies were identified. Rockwool identified more than 80 competencies at a brainstorming session that I attended. The identification of competencies in general must precede the identification of core competencies, as the former will create a pool of competencies from which to discuss core competencies. In the words of Prahalad and Hamel: ". . . A company that compiles a list of 20 to 30 capabilities (as the result of a competence identification process) has probably not produced a list of core competencies. Still, it is probably a good discipline to generate a list of this sort and to see the aggregate capabilities as building blocks. . . ." (1990, p. 21). The step from general list to core competencies can be made by discussing competencies in relation to the firm's customers and product-market strategies as means for separating noncore from core competencies.

There is not a lot to be said about the process of generating a list of competencies. It can be done in brainstorming sessions of different kinds. More important are the actors of the identification process. Representatives from several departments in the firm selected on the basis of their ability to think strategically and work together as a team get the best results.

This section reviews a number of models for identifying competencies. These models have all appeared in recent literature and each can help a firm to identify its competence pool. The models reviewed are hierarchical models, structural models, and knowledge models.

Hierarchical Models

Hierarchical models attempt to view competencies as part of a hierarchical relationship, where the products of the firm usually are the top level of the relationship and competencies are the bottom level.

Prahalad and Hamel (1990) were the first to analyze the diversified corporation in a competence context, by comparing a diversified corporation with a tree: ". . . the trunk and majors limbs are core products, the smaller branches are business units, the leaves, flowers and fruit are end-products. The root system that provides nourishment, sustenance and stability is the core competence. . ." (Prahalad & Hamel, 1990, p. 24). This hierarchical approach (Figure 7-2) has similarities to other contributions to the field. For instance, Giget uses a tree structure to visualize the integration of technical capabilities into products: ". . . with the roots representing technologies, the trunk the firm's technological and industrial potential, the branches representing sectors and sub-sectors of valorisation, and the fruit representing products. . ." (1988, p. 35).

Giget's way of thinking, in turn, is inspired by the way Japanese corporations used to illustrate how their products/markets were cre-

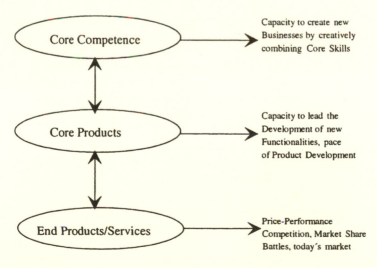

Figure 7-2. Prahalad and Hamel's model. (Adapted from Prahalad & Hamel, 1990)

ated by internal capabilities, the so-called bonsai tree view of the firms (Dussage et al., 1991).

Based on this way of thinking about competencies and their relationship to end-products, it should come as no surprise that competencies in general should provide potential access to a variety of markets and enable the firm to compete in diversified businesses. This is, however, not a characteristic that will separate noncore competencies from core competencies.

Hierarchical approaches have been empirically tested (see Knott et al., 1996, or Lewis and Gregory, 1996), and a number of difficulties have been found. For instance, difficulties arose because of the blurring between skills and competencies. It was frequently difficult to distinguish between competencies and skills. Furthermore, the core product and competence concepts are also difficult to separate, especially in smaller firms. Finally, it was difficult in general to use the hierarchical model on smaller units (SMEs or a business unit).

Despite the difficulties associated with a hierarchical approach, it still constitutes the foundation for much of the present-day competence thinking. The approach creates a critical link to the products of the firm and thereby enables the identification process to discuss competencies in light of the customers. This ability becomes critical when identifying core competencies. Furthermore, a strong link to the customers is also a means to avoid validity problems in the identification and analysis process. It is obvious that many of the identified problems of hierarchical models deal with what these models do *not* take into account—what is inside identified competencies.

Structural Models

Other models are based on a more practical approach to competence-thinking, models that focus on what is "inside" the competencies rather than on their output in terms of relationships to product-markets and so on. I have already discussed such models and even proposed one when discussing the definition of competencies in the introduction of this book and in Chapter 5. Riis and Drejer (2000) and Drejer (1996b) view competencies as a system consisting of human beings, technology, organization, and culture. In different kinds of competencies, these general elements weigh differently in the overall system. For instance, in a simple competence, technology is likely to be extremely important, whereas in more complex competencies, such as Toyota's lean production system, technology is less important. According to Leonard-Barton (see Chapter 5), such definitions lack operational content and should be supplemented with other definitions (Leonard-Barton, 1995).

Knott views competencies as functioning systems within the organization. In other words, competence is an attribute of an organization that is affected by a number of factors in both the external and internal environment. Many of the same elements, however, are believed to be part of a competence (Figure 7-3). Individuals, formal systems and social systems carry a certain resemblance to human beings, organization, and culture; and even technology seems to be part of the formal system of Knott et al. (1996). At least, there is a technical system within the formal system.

The internal models represent a valuable supplement to the hierarchical models. Where the latter focused on product-markets, the internal models provides a foundation for discussing the elements and characteristics of individual competencies in their own right. Both aspects are needed in a competence identification and analysis process.

Knowledge Models

Complex competencies consisting of a complex integration of several technologies, many individuals, a complex organization, and a strong culture seem to be what Western firms need to base their competitive advantage on now and in the future (Drejer & Riis, 2001). This model is needed because core competencies of firms must be difficult to imitate to provide some sustainability of the competitive advantage of firms (Prahalad & Hamel, 1990; Barney, 1991). This approach may sound acceptable, but it has one important implication that should not be forgotten. Knowledge of individuals and the organization become more

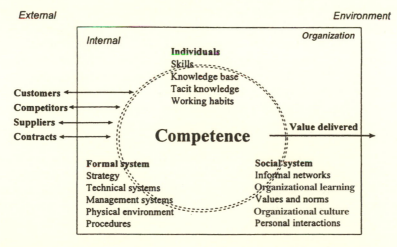

Figure 7-3. The systems approach. (Adapted from Knott et al., 1996)

critical in the case of complex competencies. Thus, some would say that we need to discuss competencies seen in a knowledge perspective.

Nielsen (1998) proposes to view competencies in terms of knowledge. Nielsen's starting-point is that: ". . . It has been chosen to use knowledge as the central building block as knowledge is conceived to be independent of the medium carrying the knowledge. As such knowledge might reside in and be reproduced in organizational processes or forms of collaboration, in hardware, e.g., equipment as well as in software, procedures and organizational routines and heuristics. Technology can also be seen as having a very close connection to knowledge. . ." (p. 161).

Specifically, Nielsen views a competence as consisting of three different kinds of knowledge: specific knowledge, integrative knowledge and deployment knowledge (see Chapter 3).

Even though my structural model of competence does not divide knowledge about competence into knowledge about each of its elements—technology, people, organization, and culture—there is some similarity between Nielsen's views and the internal models discussed previously. For instance, specific knowledge is knowledge about technology, as well as something else. Furthermore, knowledge about people, organization, and culture will be included in integrative knowledge. Thus, Anders P. Nielsen's view is different from the preceding view, where a core competence is seen as a system of technology, people, organization, and culture, but the two views are not mutually exclusive. By viewing a competence as a system of three different kinds of knowledge, it is made clear that to develop a competence, learning must be the prime tool.

Max Boisot and others also discuss competencies in terms of knowledge and offer a valuable supplement to Nielsen's work by discussing the dynamic development of competencies based on the characteristics of the knowledge related to competencies (Boisot, 1995; Boisot et al., 1996). Boisot does not distinguish between different forms of knowledge as does Nielsen; rather, he discusses all knowledge related to a competence as one and the same. The starting-point for Boisot is that competence imitability and value are two very different things. The more imitable a competence, the less diffused and codified it is; typically, only a few persons work with the competence in a very tacit manner. However, to be valuable, knowledge about the competence needs to be disseminated and used by many individuals in the organization. Hence, knowledge must then be codified for everyone to gain access to it. But, the more codified the knowledge, the easier for competitors to gain access to the knowledge and, thus, the less protected the competence. This apparent paradox is visualized in Figure 7-4 by means of the codification-diffusion curve in Boisot's so-called C-space.

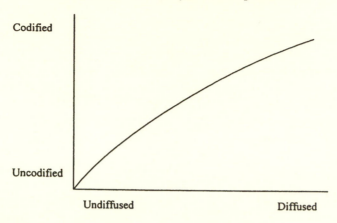

Figure 7-4. The C-space and the codification-diffusion curve. (Adapted from Boisot, 1995)

In Boisot's own words: ". . . An effective technology strategy . . . [competence strategy] . . . is one that maximizes the long-term value that can be extracted from technology assets. Maximum value, however, is only achievable in the least stable region of the C-space—the Northwest region—where, by dint of its degree of codification, knowledge is both at its most useful and at its most diffusable. . . ." (Boisot, 1995, p. 112).

Boisot and others apply the thinking behind the C-space to the process of identifying competencies at a synthetic fiber manufacturer. Boisot (1995) argues that core competencies of a technical nature consist predominantly of tacit knowledge and firms processes and thus can be represented in the C-space. As argued previously, core competencies should be difficult to imitate, which locates them in the Southwest corner of the C-space (Figure 7-5).

Thus, the C-space can be helpful in identifying core competencies by looking at their characteristics in regard to the knowledge involved. The C-space is also useful in analyzing how competencies change over time and must eventually be abandoned. Learning processes and technological dynamics will cause a competence to move along the codification-diffusion curve over time. This is an important aspect of competence development in general and, indeed, a critical characteristic of identified competencies.

Boisot (1995) discusses an entire process of competence identification. A core competence is involves: ". . . an organizational integration of technological and related assets into uniquely valuable configurations that gradually come to acquire strength and stability . . ." (Boisot, 1995, p. 124). The process of identification consists of scoring the technologies, processes, and interrelated activities in terms of the degree of

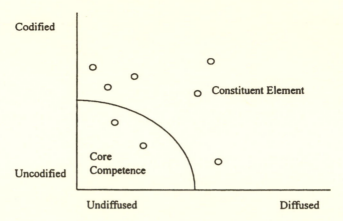

Figure 7-5. Core competencies located in the C-space. (Adapted from Boisot, 1995)

codification and diffusion. The linkages are also scored in this manner, and all scores are mapped into the C-space. Those elements that lie in or near the uncodified-undiffused region, representing the highly embedded tacit knowledge of the firm and a situation where competitors would have difficulty duplicating such knowledge, constitute core competencies. Here I focus on C-space as a means for characterizing competencies in regard to their knowledge content.

Points for reflection
- What type of model fits your company and situation? Why?
- Can you generate a list of 100 competencies? Why/why not?

SELECTING 20 TO 25 IMPORTANT COMPETENCIES

The next stage in formulating a competence-based strategy is to reduce the list of 80 to 100 competencies to a manageable 20 to 25. These competencies should be analyzed and mapped in detail before the final selection of approximately five core competencies and five focus competencies. How this selection is carried out is up to the individual firm.

Selection of Important Competencies

The step from a set of competencies to a list of the firm's 5 to 10 *core* competencies is not straightforward. Even if the competencies have been identified properly, analyzed thoroughly, and linked successfully to customer demands, it is still a *managerial decision* to select the core competencies of the firm because uncertainties are still high as to what the customers are assumed to want (the real customers may want something else) and so on. Thus, the mapping and modeling of different factors still create uncertainties that must be considered. The decision is a managerial decision for two reasons. First, it is presumably necessary to have a certain amount of overview over the firms, its customers, and its products to decide on its competencies. Such an overview can be found in many different places, of course, but top management should most certainly be one of them. The other reason is that the decision is, in essence, a matter of setting priorities for the entire firm, which should be the role of top management. The selection of core competencies also represents a selection of what is not core competencies and guidelines for where to focus efforts and investments.

Despite all of the models for mapping and analysis, core competencies must still be selected via a top management decision. The analyses and mappings discussed in this chapter can be a help for (some) top managers, but some difficult decisions are necessary.

Linking Customer Demands to Competencies

The first approach to customer demands takes the product program and the associated customer services as the point of departure. The process begins by identifying what the customers appreciate and what it takes to win an order (thus including the competitive situation). The product and its services are then broken down into parts or functions, until it is possible to connect a specific part, or sets of parts, to a number of competencies. Several methods follow this approach, detailed here is the quality function deployment (QFD) method (Figure 7-6) (Hauser & Clausing, 1988).

To fill out the quality house illustrated in Figure 7-6, it is necessary to:

1. Discuss a division of products into types fit for analysis.
2. Discuss—in the order that seems most fit for the present purpose— the following set of questions:
   a. Who have demands to the product in question? Who are users and who have additional demands?
   b. What are the demands to the product in question?
   c. How important is each demand on a scale from 1 to 10?
   d. What are the design features of the product in question?
   e. How are design features and demands related? How well are they related on a scale from 1 to 10? Why?

Typically, this process will be done by a team of persons from marketing, R&D, and production.

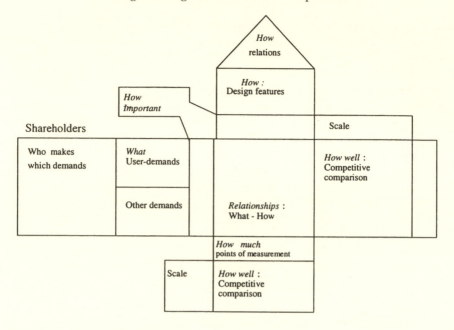

Figure 7-6. The quality function deployment approach.

Figure 7-7 shows an empirical example of how this approach has been used in practice. Empirical models tend to be much simpler and easier to use than, for instance, QFD models from the literature. Traditionally, this kind of approach—which is that of Coloplast that I have discussed earlier—is designed to connect competencies in production processes and product technologies with the properties of the product that customers appreciate. It has been useful to assign priorities to engineering design, for example, where to build in quality, at which level. However, the approach has not been used to identify some of the more complex competencies associated with delivery.

From Figure 7-7, it is evident that Coloplast attempts to link customer demands to competencies and evaluate the relative importance of each of the competencies. By doing so, it is possible to evaluate and select the most interesting technologies: core competencies.

Regarding technology and/or core competencies, Grundfos advocates a view of technology that includes product, process, and administrative elements. Furthermore, the softer sides of technology are also emphasized. For example, one of the core competencies of the corporation is claimed to be that of managing an entire product development process. Image and reputation are also defined as part of the technology concept.

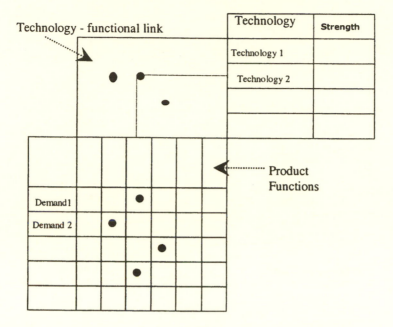

Figure 7-7. Coloplast's technology mapping scheme. (Adapted from Drejer, 1996)

In stage 1 of the process, representatives of the product management department of Grundfos define and evaluate the consumer demands to the product in question and assign weights to the set of demands. In the procedure for stage 1 it is advised that weights are differentiated as much as possible on a scale from 1 (low) to 7 (high). The scheme to be used in stage 1 is illustrated in Figure 7-8. Furthermore, the fulfillment profile of Grundfos and competitor products is evaluated (lower part of Figure 7-8).

Stage 2 deals with technology mapping and is undertaken by product and process developers from the technology center, often in cooperation with blue-collar workers or others with relevant expertise. A scheme is then filled out by systematically looking at the components in the product in light of the manufacturing process to be applied, much like the QFD model. Manufacturing processes are divided into mass reducing, mass increasing, and mass containing. To each of these categories, a number of specific processes are applied, which are not discussed here.

MAPPING OF SELECTED COMPETENCIES

After the competencies have been identified, it is necessary to describe them in more detail. Apart from the more general models dis-

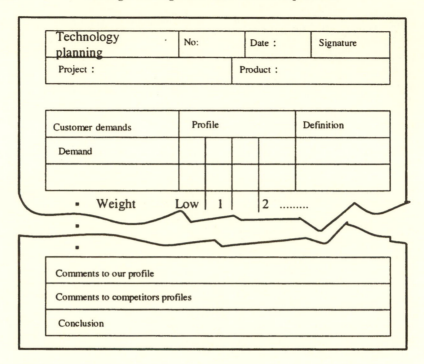

Figure 7-8. Scheme for stage 1 of Grundfos's approach to linking customer demands and competencies.

cussed previously, for example, the systems model and other models, little is written about the mapping of competencies. I offer two models developed in case firms for the purpose of mapping competencies. The models emphasize that each individual firm probably needs to develop its own mapping models for its own purposes, but the models here can be used for inspiration.

Mapping of Competencies at Coloplast

The firm Coloplast divides the actual competence mapping into two steps: an overall identification via the value chain and a mapping of individual competencies.

Step 1: Use of Technology
In step 1, how the competitors of the company use technology to create product offerings is compared with how Coloplast uses technology. This step involves analyzing and discussing Porter's value chain:

marketing, manufacturing, procurement, development, finance, and management.

Step 2: Individual Competence Mapping
In the next step, the competencies of Coloplast are described in writting, but with no specific model for the mapping. Bang and Olufsen, however, offer a specific model.

Mapping of Competencies at Bang & Olufsen

The mapping at B&O consists of a few analyses conducted by a member of the staff group plus those who have the essential knowledge regarding the technology. Selection of whom to include was a difficult and somewhat subjective task. The mappings addressed these questions:

1. Is the competence mainstream? If so, it is used on almost the entire flow of components at B&O.
2. What is the technological development for the next five to seven years? This question is mapped by selecting a point on a 1 to 10 scale to rate how fast the technology will develop.
3. What is the knowledge on the competence? Here a brainstorming clarifies all possible issues regarding the competence. Then four to five are selected as the most important, and the level of knowledge present, as well as desired, is mapped by means of the 1 to 10 scale.
4. What is the performance of the competence? Next the actual performance of the competence is analyzed in terms of what activities are important and how desired performance was. Again four to five competences are selected as core activities.
5. How was the management of the process? This implies how well the process is managed in terms of dealing with outside and inside issues. Again a few core issues are selected and evaluated.

For presentation of this knowledge, the following mapping model has been developed (Figure 7-9).

TEST OF VALIDITY

If the selection of core competencies is still a managerial decision in essence, then the issue of the validity of the decision process becomes important, and this issue has received some attention in the literature recently. Snyder and Ebeling (1992) refer to identifying "real" compe-

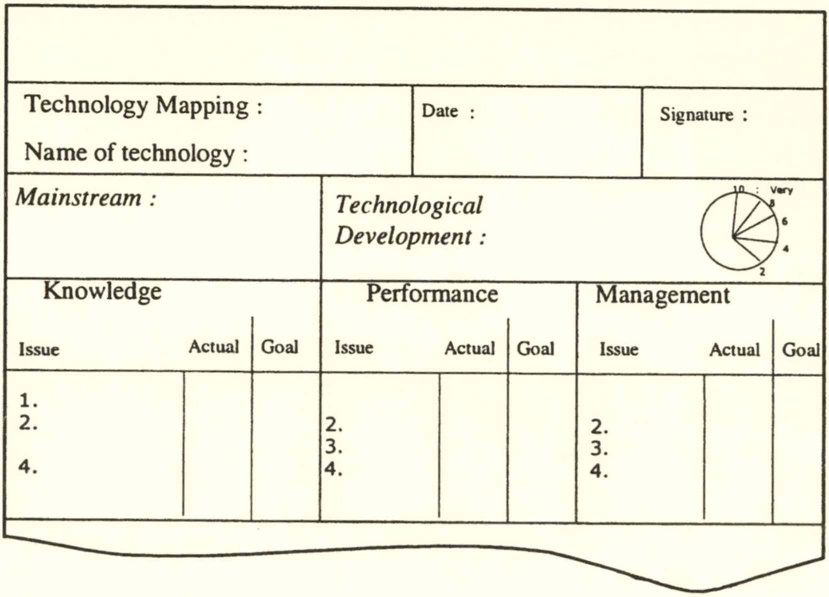

Technology Mapping : Name of technology :	Date :	Signature :

Mainstream :	Technological Development :	

Knowledge			Performance			Management		
Issue	Actual	Goal	Issue	Actual	Goal	Issue	Actual	Goal
1. 2. 4.			2. 3. 4.			2. 3. 4.		

Figure 7-9. Technology mapping scheme for B&O. (Adapted from Drejer, 1996)

tencies. Lewis and Gregory (1996) refer to identifying "valid" competencies. Others refer to "truly existing" competencies or "correctly"
identifying competencies (Hamel & Prahalad, 1994; Boisot, 1995). What-
ever the terminology, the issue of validity has received a great deal of
attention because identifing the *real* core competencies offers a number
of advantages:

- Reduced risk of poor investment decisions in competence building
  and development activities
- Alignment of competencies with business strategy enabling the
  firm to sustain change
- Focus on effective competence protection activities

Just as the identification and selection process is not straightforward,
however, the risk of distortions—of identifying competencies to be core,
when they in fact are not—is great. There are several reasons why this
is the case. Some of the most obvious reasons are interdepartmental
rivalry, struggle for competence recognition, and the existence of pet
projects within any firm. Since the competence selection process is a
matter of setting priorities for the firm, some managers may feel threat-
ened to—or see opportunities in—engage in political games to secure

that their department or function is not made second priority. Careers are made and destroyed in the setting of priorities in any case; and in the competence identification and analysis process, some managers may find a way to affect the setting of priorities by "marketing" themselves and the competencies of their department. There will, thus, be a struggle for competence recognition during the identification and analysis process. Finally, there is the matter of pet projects. In any ongoing organization, there will be a number of development efforts—"projects" of different kinds—going on at any moment in time. Evidently, these projects will not be independent of the managers who have launched them, invested in them, and hope to reap the career benefits of their outcome. Once again, this leads to a struggle for competence recognition, in this case of future competencies.

Competencies place great cognitive demands on managers. Despite their importance, competencies are difficult to grasp even for the most experienced and open-minded manager. Competencies consist of tacit and intangible elements (such as knowledge and skills) and represent rather "abstract" concepts (Gallon et al., 1995). Considering how managers in general process information and approach problem solving, Lewis and Gregory (1996) have identified five key factors affecting managers' perception of competencies:

- Organizational culture
- Perceived benefits of competence
- Coupling to markets
- External (customer) opinion
- Organizational micropolitics.

The last factor, organizational micropolitics, affects and is affected by the other four. For instance, the culture of the organization will affect micropolitics in the competence identification and analysis process. Just think of the "games" played in a highly competitive organization as opposed to an organization with great emphasis on cooperation.

One might ask what the risks are of identifying the wrong competencies as core competencies. Leonard-Barton (1995) has given part of the answer to that question, as she has introduced the concept of "core rigidities" to denote competencies that are no longer *core*, perhaps because customer demands have changed, but are still identified as being core. Typically, this can happen as the result of organizational micropolitics, for instance, if the department or function responsible for what was once a core competence still holds power over the rest of the organization. Evidently, core rigidities have the opposite effects of core competencies: risk of poor investment decisions, less tolerance for change, and ineffective competence protection. What can be done to avoid core rigidities and secure the validity of the process?

- The more input from customers, competitors, and others, the better. Properly acquired and considered, such input can help to clarify assumptions about customer demands, core competencies, and so on. Furthermore, the process of obtaining input is an opportunity to test some of the hypotheses.
- It is also important to be aware of the existence of bias throughout the competence identification and analysis process. Awareness may take several forms, "reality check" via market input being one. Other ideas include the use of an external—and thus independent—facilitator to guide the process and point out when decisions seem to be biased.

Points for reflection
- What are the five largest risks against the identification and analysis process?
- What steps have been taken to minimize those risks?
- What are the implications of these risks for the competencies of your firm?

FORMULATING THE PORTFOLIO OF COMPETENCIES

The last step of the identification/analysis exercise is to formulate a portfolio of the chosen core competencies and focus competencies to get a first impression of the competence development involved. A large amount of literature is available from the MoT field, and I have chosen some to illustrate the formulation of a portfolio.

The portfolio formulation involves:

- Analysis of the dynamics/need for development of the strategically important competencies of the firm—core competencies and focus competencies
- Analysis of the need for developing these competencies with focus on risk and rewards.
- Overall analysis of the resources available and needed for achieving the desired competence development.

The steps are iterative, not linear. Too many competencies selected as important in the first step will inevitably lead to the need for too many resources needed, which in turn will make it necessary to return to the selection step.

Analysis of the Dynamics of the Selected Competencies

We now have selected approximately ten competencies. We need a more detailed analysis of these competencies with respect to competence development. Based on the MoT literature, I propose the following list of items for analysis:

- *Reward:* How is the importance related to the product(s) of the firm?
- *Other competencies:* Is the technology in some way part of the competencies of the firm; that is, is it part of larger systems of technology, people, organization, and culture within the firm?
- *Risk:* How large is the external technological dynamics of the competence and the risk of being shifted to another technology?
- *Resources:* How difficult is it to maintain and even further develop the competence?
- *People:* How is the competence related to the human resources of the firm?
- *Style:* Are certain competencies closely related to the identity and style of the firm?

There may be many other priorities, of course, but this list shows that it is possible to use the thinking outlined in Chapter 5—the external technological dynamics and market dynamics—to deduce the need for competence development for selected competencies. That the priority of resources is added should come as no surprise, as competencies do not evolve by themselves. Furthermore, the list of priorities includes some issues related to human resources: the right people need to be available in the firm to handle technology and competencies. The latter is important, because technology can be competitively important, not only directly as part of the core product of the firm but also less directly as part of the competencies that produce the product of the firm. We may perceive the core competencies of the firm as part of the extended product of the firm, for example, excellent logistics, customized product development, service. If this argument is accepted, then it should be remembered that technology is a part of all aspects of the product(s) of the firm from the physical core product to the less tangible parts of the product. It is not enough to rely solely on the analyses introduced previously on the relationship between technology and the product, as these are only concerned with the physical product.

Analysis of the Need for Competence Development

After having selected the 10 to 20 important competencies for the firm, the need for competence development must be assessed and analyzed. This is not an easy task either, and it is closely related to the next step of the final analysis—the planning of the efforts for competence development. The latter is important for two reasons: resources and the likelihood of achieving results. However, the main vehicle for the analysis of the need for competence development is the competence portfolio. See Figures 7-10 and 7-11 for an illustration of portfolio models that may be used in the analysis of the need for competence development.

The idea of a portfolio of competencies points us toward the first important issue in the analysis of the need for competence development—the need for having a balanced portfolio of competence. A balanced portfolio of competence is important for several reasons. First, according to A.D. Little's investment principle for technology (Bhalla, 1987), a balanced portfolio of technologies (but also of competencies)

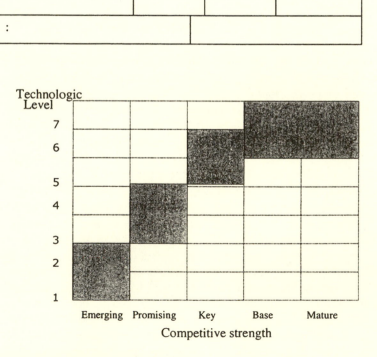

Figure 7-10. Grundfos's portfolio model.

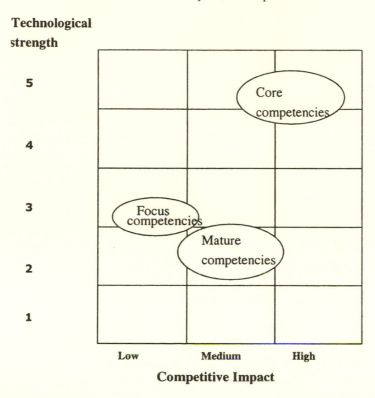

Figure 7-11. Competence portfolio with respect to balance, time, and resources.

will, per se, secure that the necessary resources are kept constant at all times. This is desirable at least for planning reasons and for accountants because a "young" portfolio consisting of a set of emerging competencies would require much more resources to develop than an aging portfolio. A balanced portfolio would at all times contain a mix of aging, emerging, and key competencies. Second, a balanced portfolio would correspondingly secure the largest possible competitive impact from the competencies because focus competencies alone, or mature core competencies alone, have a smaller competitive impact than a mix of focus competencies, core competencies (that are being developed further), and mature core competencies (that are being maintained). The key here is to have core competencies in their competitive prime; but to have that at all times, it is also necessary to maintain a few focus technologies (that are becoming core competencies) and a few aging core competencies (that not too long ago were core competencies).

The third reason is directed inside the firm. Just as it is important to have a balanced portfolio of technologies for competitive issues related to products, the balance is also important for competencies. It is necessary to have a sufficient amount of knowledge regarding, say, new administrative technologies, such as an Enterprise Reserve Planning (ERP) system, before the technology is implemented into the daily operations of the firm.

Grundfos's portfolio is focused on the third reason for maintaining a balanced portfolio. The portfolio does not list competitive impact of competencies on its Y-axis, as portfolios traditionally do. Rather, the Y-axis is concerned with the level of knowledge about competencies at Grundfos. This is measured on a scale from 1 (meaning that only one or a few people have even heard about the competence) through 5 (where the competencies are available to use in operational work) to 7 (where the use of the competence is a routine matter for Grundfos).

In summary, the portfolio of competencies can give some clues as to the need for competence development by hinting at (1) the external competitive impact of the entire portfolio and (2) the internal impact of the entire portfolio. There are at least two critical issues that are not taken into account by the competence portfolio considerations: time horizons and resources.

- *Time horizons:* As discussed in Chapter 5, technological dynamics and market dynamics are important factors in competence-based strategy. The individual firm is subject to an external "force" of developing technologies because competitors, universities, and firms in other industries struggle to develop each technology. Therefore, the speed with which the technologies of the competencies of the firm evolve must be taken into account. The same is true for market dynamics. This will provide a clue to the number of years, months, decades, etc. that is available for doing competence development. The smaller the window of opportunity for bringing a new competence to market, the larger the need for quick and precise competence development.
- *Resources:* The resources needed for the necessary competence development, individually and in an overall view, is the second important issue to be considered. As no firm has an unlimited budget for competence development, it is necessary to limit not only the number of core competencies and focus competencies but also the development of those competencies.

Three important issues are involved in step 2, analyzing the need for competence development: (1) maintaining a balanced portfolio to be as competitive as possible, (2) develop competencies in the right time as chosen based on technological dynamics and/or internal needs, and (3) making an "optimal" choice between the many possible competence development projects so that the resources are utilized as well as possible. Figure 7-11 illustrates an alternative competence portfolio from the firm Coloplast, where all three issues are illustrated.

The portfolio in Figure 7-11 illustrates the competitive impact of competencies on customers on the X-axis and the performance relative to competitors on the Y-axis. A balanced portfolio will be somewhere along the path from the lower-left corner of the portfolio to the upper-right corner. Furthermore, by drawing individual competencies in circles, where the diameter of the circle illustrates the internal knowledge of the competence (basically the Y-axis in Grundfos's portfolio), the issues of internal "balance" is covered in Coloplast's portfolio. Even further, arrows from each circle—or balloon as they are called—can be used to indicate the speed of competence dynamics and/or the objectives for developing each competence in the portfolio. Resources for competence development are discussed separately.

Overall Analysis of Resources

As mentioned previously, the resources of individual technology development projects can be estimated and/or discussed in the context of a number of other issues related to a competence development project (e.g., choice of external partners). Thus, the discussions on resources cannot be kept completely separate from those in this section.

In an analysis of the need for competence development, however, resources for individual "projects" and the overall resources must be included. Looking at Coloplast's portfolio model in Figure 7-11, it could be tempting to set as objective that all the competence—or "balloons"— were moved to the upper-right corner within 2 years; however, this will be impossible to achieve. If it is not made impossible by lack of technological maturity because of some of the technologies involved, then it will be impossible because even Coloplast does not have an unlimited budget for competence and technology development.

Thus, the final step involves attempting to optimize the use of the limited resources available for competence development, looking at the possible effects of individual projects compared with the possible costs and risks. In the "real world," this choice will be dependent on the decision maker, the firm, and the style of the two. Typically, competence development with large potential impact is also the competence development with the largest potential risks and costs and vice versa. Thus, the risk evasiveness of decision makers will be clearly visible in the choices made. Apart from that—or perhaps because of that—I can offer little more to potential decision makers in this step other than noting that the step must be taken and that the decision must be made.

8

Competence Development

Let me be honest with you—there is a lot we do not know about competence development. Too much, in fact. For one thing, the realization that competencies need to be developed is actually quite new in the literature and needs to be explored thoroughly. At the same time, companies all over the world embrace the idea of competencies and competence development and develop interesting solutions to the problems that we theoretical people have—albeit not always consistent or perfect. Thus, this chapter is based on my empirical observations as well as theoretical considerations, perhaps a little more than I could have wanted. But this is a first step in a long process of coming to terms with the idea of competence development.

Hence, this chapter is concerned with the formulation of a framework for understanding the development and change of the competencies of firms. Today, there is near universal agreement that the competitiveness of firms rests on the (core) competencies that firms possess; however, little attention has been devoted to the notion of competence development. I will argue that there is a need for management practice of competence development. I will also argue that organizational learning theory is a key to understanding competence development and based on this, I propose a model for competence development. The model is discussed and illustrated by means of a case study.

COMPETENCE DEVELOPMENT SHOULD BE MANAGERIAL

Today, there seems to be near total agreement on the assertion that the notion of "core competencies" is paramount to explaining competitiveness of the firm. Since Prahalad and Hamel's seminal paper on the subject (1990) there has been a surge of interest in competencies and competence-based strategy followed by a stream of conferences, books and, now, an international association for competence-based strategy (Sanchez, 1995). The literature on core competencies and competence-based strategy has many virtues, but being specific with regard to the structural characteristics of competencies is not one of them. In a previous publication, Drejer and Riis (2000) argued that most competence definitions in the literature are based on functional characteristics; that is, what are the effects caused by a competence? This is effective for those who are mainly interested in the strategic implications of a competence, as an effect could be value delivered to customers, and hence the creation of competitive advantage. In other words, if our game is competitive strategy alone, these are the kinds of definitions you would want to look for; however, this only explains part of the truth about competencies.

Competence Is One Among Other Concepts

Incidentally, "competencies" is merely the latest—but perhaps greatest—of a number of concepts aimed at explaining the competitiveness of firms, that is, why some firms achieve better performance than others with similar functional characteristics in terms of, for instance, product-market strategy, and so on. This issue has been discussed for as long as we have had the notion of strategic management in the vocabulary. From Penrose's idea of the firm as a collection of resources (Penrose, 1957) and its later comeback as the resource-based view of the firm (e.g., Wernerfelt, 1984; Barney, 1991) to the classic SWOT analysis, generally attributed to Kenneth Andrews (1971), researchers have attempted to explain to managers what internal, structural issues of the firm needed attention in the process of strategic management (Drejer, 1996a). Please note that I also include "soft" aspects such as human knowledge and corporate culture in the structural issues of strategic management (as do Penrose, Andrews, and others). The term *structural* comes from systems theory, not organizational theory. Obviously, history did not stop with Penrose and the resource-based view of the firm. Evolution spun the work on "critical capabilities" (e.g., Aaker, 1989) with theories perhaps better suited to account for the role of human beings, tacit knowledge, and other "soft" aspects of the internal structure of a firm. This has been our explanation of the evolution of a new conception in strategic management (Drejer, 1996a). Finally the notion of *core competencies* (Prahalad & Hamel, 1990) was introduced. Some of the literature on core competencies clearly builds on and extends previous work on resources and capabilities, whereas other parts of the literature on core competencies ignore the existence of any theories before 1990.

I believe that one should build on previous contributions to theories in this field and feel that the notion of competence seems to be a natural starting point for a discussion mainly because it is intuitively closely connected to the notion of organizational learning. As you shall see, the latter is close to the heart of my work (see also Drejer & Riis, 2000). You will find references to the *resource-based view of the firm*, *critical capabilities*, *management of technology*, and other areas of research where relevant.

Competence Has Been Defined Only from a Functional Viewpoint

Normally, core competencies are defined in terms of their functional characteristics, for instance, that they offer superior value to the customers of the firm, but what about the structural characteristics of competencies? The how? What are the elements of a competence and its relations? These are some of the questions of this section. I have defined a competence as consisting of four elements and their relations: technology, people, organizational structure, and organizational culture (Drejer & Riis, 2000), thereby making it possible to discuss different types of competencies ranging from simple (one technology and few people) to complex (cross-functional processes with a large number of people and technologies). This will make it possible to start considering *how competencies should be developed over time*, and it is the purpose of this chapter to present a framework for research on competence development. First, let me establish why this is necessary.

Competencies Need to Evolve Dynamically

It is usually assumed that core competencies should be impossible to imitate. Hamel and Prahalad (1994), for example, even include this as a demand for a competence to be considered "core"—most important—in their work. When it is assumed that competencies cannot be imitated, then it is natural to conclude that their development, and eventual replacement, is not an issue for research and/or management attention. Apart from being rational in an economical world (e.g., investors will be more phrone to invest in a firm with unshakeable, inimitable core competencies than a firm admitting that it must develop new competencies every three to five years) this also seems to be based on a belief that there is one recipe for success in business. The latter is best exemplified by *In Search of Excellence* (Peters & Watermann, 1982) with its advice on how to achieve business success. The eventual fate of *In search of . . .* and its "excellent" firms warns us away from taking such an approach (Shapiro, 1996; Drejer & Riis, 2000).

Seldom is the internal functioning of competencies discussed in detail. In many cases, the "competencies" that authors identify to be "key" for a firm's success are, at best, at metalevel, for example, innovativeness, high speed product development, and their likes. In fact, many of the existing books on competence-based strategy never go beyond such meta-competencies. Such competencies are hard to get a firm grasp of. This raises the question of ex-post versus ex-ante strategies. Maybe some of the research on competencies has had an ex-post focus, meaning that a number of competencies have been identified as important *after* their value has become evident to everyone—and not before the competencies, perhaps, were identified, developed and exploited. If this is so, then it is fair to ask whether competence-based strategy is a tool for managers to use for ex-ante strategy formulation, or a tool for researchers to use for ex-post strategy explanation.

Rarely is the link between competencies and their underlying technologies discussed in any great detail, apart from being part of the definition of a competence (with any luck) (e.g., Hamel & Prahalad, 1994). Thus, theories on competencies do not include answers to the important issue of what happens when inherent technologies change according to their well-known S-curve life cycle. The dynamics of technological changes, however, is well known from the management of technology literature (e.g., Tushman & Anderson, 1990), and it seems clear from this research, and empirical cases to support it, that technological change can be "competence-destroying" as well as company-destroying (Christensen, 1998; Downes & Mui, 1998). Since the latter in some instances is well-known from research, the former should be part of the work on competencies. Therefore, it is somewhat strange that the dynamics of competencies caused by external changes of technologies has yet to be covered in research on competencies (Drejer & Riis, 2000).

Another reason for dynamics of core competencies is changes in the product-market strategy of the firm (Drejer, 1996b). Here it seems to be assumed that competencies somehow are not affected by changes in the product-market strategy of the firm. Sometimes the firm is illustrated as a tree with product-market combinations as branches and leaves firmly attached to the main part of the tree which equals the firm's combined set of competencies (Dussage et al., 1991; Prahalad, 1993). Such an image excludes the possibility of unrelated diversification and/or basic changes in the products of the firm. Yet in the real world this is also an option on the agenda of managers, if for no other reason than because of technological changes altering the market of the firm.

In some industries, this tends to happen quite often even though everyone is equally surprised every time. Consider, for instance, computers. The change from mainframe computers to laptop PCs demanded such a change in internal competencies that it took established firms like IBM years to catch up with newcomers in the industry—a pattern that was repeated (Christensen, 1998). Technological changes altering the market is just one example of the need for dynamic competencies in order to keep up strategically.

ISSUES AND PROCESS OF COMPETENCE DEVELOPMENT

Before we get to the detailed discussion of competence development, let us ponder the issues and process of competence development.

Issues

The starting point for the activity in a competence-based strategy that is concerned with competence development is a list of core competencies and focus competencies selected and/or approved by top management. This list is in line with the overall strategic direction of the firm and the strategic decisions and options of top management. Perhaps there has even been serious consideration given to the issue of resources and timing of competence development, so that the list of competencies selected for development comes in the form of a portfolio. This is what I proposed in the last chapter. Should this have escaped the attention of top management and/or the project team responsible for the competence-based strategy, my suggestion is simply to make the formulation of the portfolio the first issue of competence development.

What is it, then, that we can expect to gain from the activity of competence development? If the starting point is achieved then I would expect it possible to deal with, at least, two issues:

- When should which competencies be developed?
- How should competence development take place?
- What means for competence development should be chosen?

In this chapter I cannot deal with those issues as directly as in Chapter 7. The need for formulating what competence development really is and how it is to be achieved is too great for that. Thus, this chapter is mainly concerned with the formulation of a framework for competence development.

Why Is Competence Development Located at the HRM Department?

It is my experience that the activity of competence development rarely is a top management responsibility, whereas the identification and analysis of competencies—that is, the choice of core competencies and focus competencies—are usually top management privilege. In all of the cases that I have experienced or read about, competence development is "outsourced" to the human resources (HR) department or its equivalent. Why is that? Should top management not be as concerned with the timely development of core competencies as with the choice of them?

The answer in part lies in the overall responsibilities of top management in relation to the total strategy process (see Figure 1-3, p. 13). This figure depicts a typical proposal of a strategy process. Actually, there are both planned (and rational) processes and emergent processes, but let us just use the one in Figure 1-3, which seems fairly rational. Nonetheless, in both processes, we can see that the issue of "resources" or "competencies" or "strengths" is merely a part of the overall process. Top management also must analyze the environment, formulate vision and mission, find strategic options, evaluate these options, and many other things. No wonder that certain parts of the overall strategy process are sometimes out-sourced to certain parts of the organization.

Furthermore, who is more fit to take responsibility for competence development than the HR department? Actually, I would argue that the HR department (at least the departments I have seen over the years) can make more of competence development than any other department. This is because the HR department can make the connection from the kind of competencies that we are discussing in this book—organizational competencies—to individuals and their individual competencies. In that way, competence development can become truly operational in a way that we could not even have imagined. Core competencies should not just be a "fluffy" concept that top managers talk about—it should be operational and part of everyday life in the organization. The HR department can do just that by taking the given starting point—a limited number of chosen (organizational) core competencies and focus competencies—and translate that into focused and operational action within education, training, organizational development, and so on.

Points for reflection
- Do you agree that competence development should be the responsibility of the HR department in your firm?
- Is that because of a certain managerial style or situation?
- What role should top management play?

The HR Plan Is the Means for Creating Competence Development

How can the HR department make the connection between organizational competencies and individual competencies alone? Is a competence not defined as a system of human beings, technology, culture, and organization? Shouldn't all of these elements be manipulated to create competence development?

A few years ago I was contemplating the idea of having firms make four equally important plans derived from the list of chosen core competencies and focus competencies—an average technology plan, an HR plan, a culture development plan, and an organizational structure development plan. This I believe is "overkill." First of all, as it is the human beings and their development that change the culture of the firm, I find it hard to see how a "culture development plan" can be different from an HR plan. Second, technology has its own logic and development patterns, which is why many firms have a technology plan and technology department. This is logical because technology development requires a great deal of resources and time. Even so, the technology plan and technology development need to be synchronized with the HR plan. The 1980s taught us this lesson. Technology cannot be brought to function well if the employees of the firm are not trained and ready for the new technology—or, in other words, technology is part of competencies and not isolated entities. Thus it is natural to conclude that part of competence development actually is dealt with in the technology plan and that the portfolio of core competencies and focus competencies should also be an important input to technology planning in firms where this is essential. Of course, knowledge-intensive firms may not need to focus so extensively on technology, in which case we are back to the HR plan. At any rate, the HR plan should be developed with emphasis on integrating it with technology development. The latter is another important input to the HR plan.

So far we have cancelled the "culture development plan" (what a shame—nice concept) and dealt with the technology plan (that is, input to the HR plan and besides the responsibility of someone else). But what about the plan for the organizational structure? A few years ago, quite a few managers spent a great deal of time reorganizing the boxes and lines of their formal organizational chart every time some problem occurred. I am not sure that this is still the case. On the one hand, the structure of the organization can be an enormous boundary for the competencies of the firm. Remember, competencies often work across traditional functional departments toward the customer. On the other hand, there is often not a lot one can do to influence the formal structure. Top management rarely sees the structure in a competence light and reshuffles the deck without considering the effects on competencies anyway. That indicates that the organizational structure should be considered in the HR plan as something given from the outside and little else. In this case, the "organization structure plan" is left for top management and does not influence competence development more than as a mere input to the HR plan.

Recently I have begun to see a little hope. Several organizations have begun to contemplate using their core competencies as the starting point for the organizational structure. This probably implies leaving a functional organization behind and replacing it with a process organization, but if that is what the customers benefit from, why should that suffer because of some old-fashioned idea of functional organization? If firms started to organize based on their core competencies, once again we could eliminate the "organization structure plan." It would then be derived from the HR plan and chosen competencies of the firm.

Points for reflection
- How should competence development be planned in your firm?
- Is that because of a certain managerial style or situation?
- How do you propose to secure the link to the overall strategy of the firm?

COMPETENCE DEVELOPMENT

I have now argued that an HR plan is what needs to be formulated and carried out in order to secure competence development in a firm. This leaves us with the question of what should be in the HR plan. To answer this, I need to discuss some definitions.

From Organizational to Individual Competence

Sport is a great place to find inspiration when it comes to competencies of the kind that I am talking about.

Let us contemplate football. Football is a team sport where 11 players work together to accomplish victory over another 11 players. So the teams is the sum of its players? Well, yes. Let me present a few definitions that may make you understand how we go from data and information to individual competence and to organizational competence since any team is—more or less—the sum of its players.

A word of caution before I proceed. The debate on knowledge, wisdom, competence (and data and information) has been going on for more than 2,000 years, probably dating back to Aristotle (Drejer & Henriksen, 1999). Therefore, there are probably as many perceptions of what is information, knowledge, and competence as there are authors within that field. However, my definitions fit within the framework of this book—as good a reason as any to choose between conflicting definitions, in my view.

Data are discrete, objective facts about events. In an organizational context, data are most usefully described as structured records of transactions, for example, when a supplier delivers a number of components to the inventory, that transaction can partly be described by data—when the delivery was made, the order number, the inventory number of the component in question, the amount delivered, and so on. The data, however, cannot tell us why the supplier made the delivery at that time, how important the delivery was, and so on. In and of themselves, such facts tell us nothing about the performance of the supplier, whether the delivery was important to our firm, or why our firm should continue to work with the supplier in question.

Information is, in the words of Peter Drucker, data endowed with relevance and purpose. This suggests that data alone have little relevance or purpose. I define information as a message, usually in the form of a document or another form of communication (audible or visual). The message has a sender and a receiver. Information is meant to change the way the receiver perceives something, to have an impact on her judgment and/or behavior. Thus, the message must inform what of its data makes a difference. Based on this definition, we can say that it is, strictly speaking, the receiver, not the sender, who decides whether the message she gets is really information (or just meaningless junk data). Data, then, become information when its creator adds meaning to it. Generally speaking, we can transform data into information by adding value in various ways. Davenport and Prusak propose the following generic methods (1999):

- *Contextualization*—to define the purpose for which the data was collected.
- *Categorization*—to define the unit of analysis or key components of the data.
- *Calculation*—analysis of data by mathematical or statistical methods.
- *Correction*—removal of errors from the data.
- *Condensation*—the data are summarized in a more concise form.

Note that while IT can help to add these values and transform data into information in several ways, it can rarely help with context, to name but one important value added that seems exclusive to humans. Furthermore, humans must usually help with categorization, calculation, and condensation. Thus, information should not be confused with the technology delivering it. IT is not information; it is a technology to deliver information and little more. Having a telephone does not guarantee or even encourage brilliant conversations, nor does owning a state-of-the-art DVD player make sure that you watch anything but B-movies on killer aliens going on killer sprees. A problem for managers these days is that having more information technology does not necessarily improve the state of information.

Knowledge is more than information. Most of us have an intuitive sense that knowledge is broader, deeper, and richer than data and information. Some even talk about a knowledgeable individual to denote someone with a thorough, informed, and reliable grasp of a subject, someone both educated and intelligent. I tend to agree. I see knowledge as framed and contextualized information that provides a framework for evaluation and incorporating new information. The important idea here is the interpretation of information in the mind of the knowing person—knowledge is for human beings only, not for IT at all. If information is to become knowledge, human beings must do all the work through, for example:

- *Comparison*—deciding how information about this situation compares with other situations that we have known.
- *Consequences*—deciding what implications the information has for decisions and actions.
- *Connecting*—deciding how this bit of information relates to other information.
- *Conversation*—finding out what other people think about this information.

It is clear that knowledge is not neat or simple. It is fluid as well as formally structured; it can exist beyond completely logical terms and is a part of human beings. Knowledge assets are hard to pin down. Furthermore, you can have a lot of knowledge without being able to apply that knowledge; thus, being knowledgeable is not the same as being capable of something.

Individual competence is the result of being capable; that is, you cannot, per definition, be capable just because you are knowledgeable—something more is needed. Davenport and Pruzak (1999) have called this "knowledge in action," but it is much more than that. Consider, for instance, the young M.Sc., who joins her first firm. She may be very knowledgeable but that does not mean that she will be a capable employee from day one. There is too much that she needs besides knowledge and information. Three things strike me as important: context, organizational possibility, and experience. *Context* implies that there is a lot that is unique when we talk about one particular firm—an extra dimension of context that can be said to be (corporate) cultural and that cannot be accessed from the outside, and, hence, not taught in school. This includes norms, values, and micropolitics of the firm; and it takes a while before you come to grips with this extra dimension of context. Furthermore, in an organization, employees are not always allowed to exercise their capabilities. Our employees know much more than our firm understands how to use or want them to use. Thus, in my world, *possibilities for action* are an important part of individual competence. The final aspect of individual competence is *experience*. Experience is the kind of knowledge that results from comparing results of your behavior with planned results and deciding what to do next time by means of reflecting. It is exclusively related to action in the organizational context and cannot be taught in school. Thus, I see experience as a special kind of knowledge that is only interesting when seen as part of individual competence. By adding more and more of this special kind of knowledge, along with other forms of knowledge, a person will become more and more capable, given that the learning taking place is not false and actually leads to better action and better performance.

In summary, individual competence means applying knowledge and experience into action in a qualified manner. Qualified refers to the result of the application that can lead to more or less desirable outcomes. As individuals, we sometimes define what "desirable" means ourselves; in organization this is usually given/defined by others. Thus, data and information are merely steps on the way toward knowledge and experience and, hence, individual competence. Where does this lead organizational competencies?

Organizational competence (from a bottom-up perspective) takes as its starting point that most activities in firms (1) are done in groups or teams and not by individuals, and (2) are done under strong influence by technological means, culture and values, and the formal organizational structure. On the outset, this is not the same definition of competence that we have reached in this book (it is defined top down, for one thing), but let us see if I can make the two definitions meet. From the bottom-up perspective of this section, I would define organizational competence as the ability of a team of individuals to apply their own and shared knowledge and experiences into action in a qualified manner.

In light of these definitions, I can now define the HR plan on competence as developing the individual competencies in the organization in such a manner that organizational competencies are supported by individual ones.

Taking Team Effects into Consideration

In sports teams, I would ask, does this definition imply that a team is just the sum of its players? Not necessarily. A few years ago, the English club Wimbledon had a team called "the Crazy Gang." Among its members was Vinnie Jones, now a movie star in films such as "Snatch" and "Lock, Stock, and Two Smoking Barrels." In terms of talent and market value, this team was among the least competent in the English Premier League. Nonetheless, "the Crazy Gang" got results and never finished last. Obviously, the team was more than the sum of its individual members. Now, we have Chelsea Football Club, located in almost the same region of London and even (until this year 2001) employing one of the key players of "the Crazy Gang," Dennis Wise, for several years. Chelsea has 30 players of greater talent and market value than those of "the Crazy Gang" and should be able to present three teams capable of beating Wimbledon. But they just cannot seem to make it to the top. Despite investing large amounts of money in players every year (they paid more than $10 million for Dane Jesper Grønkjær in the 2000/2001 season), Chelsea has not won the Premier League in more than 20 years. I am tempted to say that the Chelsea team is less competent than the sum of its individual members. We see this all the time in sports. The key is not (just) to find the individuals who are the most competent; the key is to make the individuals you have work together as a team. In terms of this book, I would say that the culture, technology, and organizational structure of Chelsea/Wimbledon play an important role in how their teams perform. For instance, a former Norwegian national coach tried to change the culture of Wimbledon FC a couple of years ago (away from "the Crazy Gang" to a more professional attitude) with less than encouraging results.

Thus, contrary to the (fairly) neat definitions from data to individual and organizational (or just group) competence, it seems obvious that there is more to the competence of an organization than simply the sum of the competence of its individuals. Of course, we knew that already, having defined competencies in this book as systems of human beings (with individual competence), technology, structure, and culture. Now, we have found that the same truth applies when starting bottom up.

Thus, the HR plan should take into account synergistic effects as well as individual competencies. How can that be done? I have found three approaches, each with advantages and disadvantages (Drejer, 2001):

- Top-down approach
- Bottom-up approach
- Dual approach

Top-Down Approach: Mapping of Intellectual Capital
In recent years the notion of intellectual capital has begun to rise in management circles, among both researchers of management and

practioners of it. A stream of articles, conferences, seminars, and lately books (Stewart, 1997; Edvinsson & Malone, 1997; Kaplan & Norton, 1996) show that "intellectual capital" is a star among management fads and buzz-words these days. Much of the work is based on the notion that intellectual capital should be accounted for just like physical capital.

How would an accountant react to a new competitive landscape in which knowledge was more important than technology and physical assets? The accountant would react to being in a new (kind of) landscape by checking whether his instruments were still sufficient to make adequate measurements in the new competitive landscape. According to quite a few people, accountants have had to realize that their traditional instruments (the balance sheet and the income statement) no longer can explain which companies are/will be successful and which will not. Consider for instance the example of IBM versus Microsoft (Stewart, 1997). Which company would you invest your life's savings in? IBM's total sales are 15 times greater those of Microsoft; however, Microsoft is the more valuable company. As of November 1996 IBM's total market capitalization was about $70 billion, whereas Microsoft's was $85 billion. Furthermore, the assets underlying that capital are entirely different. In the beginning of 1996, IBM owned (net of depreciation) about $17 billion worth of property, plant, and equipment. Microsoft's net total assets equalled just $930 *million*! In other words, apart from the obvious fact that the accountants would not be able to predict which company would be more worthy of your life's savings—no more than I can—this example shows us that Microsoft is a company built on an entirely different model than IBM. We can say that Microsoft is a knowledge-based company—a company based on knowledge rather than assets. It is precisely this type of company that prospers in the new competitive landscape, and it is also this type of company that accountants find it hard to deal with by their traditional measures.

Accountants cannot count the value of knowledge! The reason for this is quite obvious. Consider this quotation from David Wilson, CPA at partner at Ernst & Young: ". . . It has been 500 years since Paciolo published his seminal work on accounting and we have seen virtually no innovation in the practice of accounting—just more rules—none of which has changed the framework of measurement. . ." (Stewart, 1997, p. 58). The balance sheet took its present form in 1868, the income statement dates back before World War II. Thus, naturally this traditional scheme will not work in a new competitive situation and landscape. The accountant, thus, looks at the new competitive landscape with horror, because his basic tools no longer are adequate to do their job.

Luckily, a lot of work has been done in the field of mapping intellectual capital. Every organization houses valuable intellectual materials in the form of assets and resources, tacit and explicit perspectives and capabilities, data, information, knowledge, and maybe wisdom. However, we cannot manage intellectual capital if we cannot locate it in places in the company that are strategically important. The question is: where to look? Stewart offers a couple of ideas. Intellectual capital can be divided into three forms: human capital, structural capital, and customer capital.

- Human capital is the capabilities of individuals in the firm required to provide solutions to customers. Human capital is the source of innovation and renewal and seems a natural part of intellectual capital. However, human capital would amount to very little if there were no knowledge flow. This is where structural capital comes into play.
- Structural capital is the organizational capabilities of the organization to meet market requirements. It is what is required to share and transport knowledge (for example, information systems, laboratories, competitive and market intelligence, knowledge of market channels, and management focus). Structural capital turns individual know-how into the property of a group.
- Customer capital is the value of the organization's relationships with its customers—the likelihood that our customers will keep doing business with us—and can be broadened to include all relationships (e.g., with suppliers) and thus be called relational capital.

The three kinds of intellectual capital defined above are what some use to measure intellectual capital (Stewart, 1997). Others place more emphasis on, for example, innovation and change focus and provide measurements for this (Edvinsson & Malone, 1997), or business processes (Edvinsson & Malone, 1997), or some other aspect of the firm's internal functioning. Whichever is chosen—perhaps even because of a fit between the company's situation and the mapping scheme—the basic idea of mapping intellectual capital is the same. A number of indicators are usually provided to measure each kind of intellectual capital.

I will not go into detail with indicators for intellectual capital here. The issue requires much more space than I have within this context and, incidentally, much more consideration than any discussion in a short section can provide. The reader should study Stewart (1997) or Edvinsson and Malone (1997) for a discussion of indicators for different kinds of firms.

The purpose of this approach is not to create the kind of HR plan that I have been discussing here, but to map and measure the value of the firm's competencies on an aggregate level. Sometimes this takes the form of a knowledge account, where individual competence areas are mapped (based on a predefined, centrally decided list) and aggregated (to corporate level). This almost certainly does not take into account synergistic effects of any kind.

Bottom-up Approach: Mapping of Individual Competencies
The opposite approach to the top-down approach is to decentralize the mapping of individual competence to the employees themselves. Ideally, why not let the employees define the set of competence areas that they believe are vital to their current job (and would like to get measured on) as well as define the set of additional competence areas that the employees feel they have. This should be as realistic as possible. Each employee would have her own personal competence profile. Of course, this would lead to a high degree of diversity, but perhaps that is a small price to pay.

If we continue this line of thought, employees could also appraise their own level of competence within each of the chosen areas and deduce the need for training, education, and competence development. In the real world, I would like to see some kind of control over what employees appraise and so on, perhaps as part of the annual appraisal interview that has become so fashionable in European firms in the last few years.

The advantage of the bottom-up approach is that it is realistic and, for top management or the HR department, manageable in terms of resources. Besides, it corresponds to what I have seen in many firms as the standard operating procedure anyway: much too often employees are left to take care of their own competence development. They must update their CV themselves; make their own career plan; determine whether their current job functions support that career plan; find competence gaps; find opportunities for training, education, or competence development; and convince their boss that they should have the opportunities for developing their individual competencies. Much too often decisions from the manager are based not on competence considerations but on budgetary ones. This is to say that I do believe that employees in general are quite capable of handling their own individual competence development and that a bottom-up approach does not seem such a bad idea to me.

Nonetheless, there are several disadvantages of a bottom-up process. For one thing, a true bottom-up process will tend to neglect group competencies and synergistic effects. In my experience, individuals tend not to emphasize their roles in groups when mapping individual competence unless this has been emphasized strongly by management. And then the process cannot be said to be truly bottom up. Thus, most core competencies will be neglected in a bottom-up process as they are related to groups—perhaps even cross-functional and informal groups—of individuals.

Second, a bottom-up process is difficult to manage or coordinate, so how can top management or the HR department create a corporate HR plan for competence development, let alone manage the resources for competence development centrally? This seems to me to be the greatest disadvantage of a bottom-up process. Finally, it will be difficult, if not impossible, to aggregate individual competence profiles into a shared, coherent picture of the competencies in the organization. Hence, measuring the value of competence, or intellectual capital, will be impossible.

Dual Approach: Managing the Mapping of Individual Competencies

Just as before, rescue comes with the dual approach. Unless our purpose is to measure intellectual capital at corporate level only (in which case the top-down approach seems fine) or measure individual competencies only (in which case the bottom-up approach is the right choice). In other words, the dual approach is appropriate when you want to create a link between core competencies and focus competencies and individual competence as well as manage competence development in the organization according to that link. This calls for a combination of top-down elements and bottom-up elements.

The top-down part can take on many forms. Of course, it should be based on the identification and analysis of competencies stages that have led to the choice of a limited number of core competencies and focus competencies. These competencies and plans for their development should guide competence development in the organization. But how can this be linked to individual competence? Please note that I did not write "broken down into individual competence." In my view an intermediate concept is needed to create the link from individuals (and their many competencies and qualifications) and competencies at the organizational level.

Based both on the world of sports and on experiences from innovative firms, I find that the concept of formal organizational roles can serve as a link between organizational and individual competence. A football (soccer) team is more than just 11 individuals, but most coaches can use the notion of roles to describe in more detail what each individual should be able to do and how each individual should work together with the rest of the team. For instance, the notion of a libero is very different from that of a sweeper. One is proactive and part of the attack strategy of the team, whereas the other is reactive and constrained to defensive work. The same goes for many other roles in football. Thus, roles can be used to describe much more than just individual competence. Furthermore, roles can ensure that the team still functions, even if a given person is injured. Perhaps it is possible to find someone else to play the same role. The same line of argument can be completed when we talk of organizations outside the world of football. I have been part of several processes where firms defined their core competencies (and focus competencies) in the form of roles, that is, "selected the team for that game." The roles, then, could be described in terms of a set of individual competencies (chosen from a centrally decided list of "all" relevant competencies in the firm) and assigned to persons in the organization (together with relevant managers and the persons themselves).

In this way it is possible to focus on the development of the persons who are part of a chosen few competencies and, hence, on the relevant competence development at the organizational level. The analysis and formulation of competence profile and competence development for persons with roles to play in core competencies can be supported by the HR department that can make sure that the entire team and shared learning of the team is emphasized (along with individual career plans and so on). This, of course, should be supplemented with as much bottom-up activity as possible, for example, that individuals still have the opportunity to make their own (predefined) competence profile, are part of the assignment of roles, are allowed to change roles according to their own wishes, and can give feedback and come up with ideas for the roles and relevant competencies of the firm. This is also true for those employees who are not linked to core or focus competencies. This group can go through a more bottom-up process, but should probably use predefined roles and competencies to formulate their own competence profile as well, although evidently under less influence by the HR department.

In my view, the HR department can also make additional analyses regarding the chosen core competencies and focus competencies and use these as additional input to the decision-making process of competence development. Such analyses could include the influence of technology and structure, thereby creating the important links to technology planning and decisions on the organizational structure of the firm. Furthermore, the HR department can make aggregation and analyses on that level, perhaps even leading to an estimate of the value of intellectual capital.

For my purposes, the dual approach has all of the advantages. It creates the link between core competencies and individual competencies, it is manageable, and it focuses competence development at organizational level without sacrificing individual competence development.

In short, this is a natural part of the process of a competence-based strategy. There are several disadvantages. First, the dual approach is demanding in terms of resources. Second, the dual approach will not be valuable if top management does not take active part in the process by choosing core competencies and focus competencies and use the results of the dual approach in their strategic decisions. On the other hand, as the HR department needs to take responsibility for this part of the dual approach, a separation of responsibilities cannot be avoided. This call for a strategic role for the HR department in many firms in order for competence-based strategy to be successful.

Points for reflection
- Does your firm need a dual approach? Why?/Why not?
- Is your firm normal in this respect?
- How should the approach to competence development planning be integrated with the overall strategy of the firm?

A FRAMEWORK FOR UNDERSTANDING COMPETENCE DEVELOPMENT

I have now argued that competence development should be part of management practice in many industries and laid the foundation for discussing the phenomenon further. To do this I have made a number of assumptions that enable me to propose and discuss a preliminary model for competence development.

The Natural Links between Organizational Learning and Competencies

It is interesting to see how organizational learning theory, especially when focusing on the process of learning, places as much emphasis on the human element as I do in the definition of competencies from Chapter 5. There seems to be a quite natural link between the two areas of research there. Furthermore, it is most intriguing to see how the three types of competence seem to be mirrored in the work on organizational learning. With this in mind, it seems natural to continue to be inspired by organizational learning theory in this section on competence development.

We tend to focus on complex competencies in this section because developing complex competencies must be assumed to be the most difficult to manage, that is, a "worst case" for competence development.

Developing a Competence

We now must decide how a team of human beings (using technology for some end) improve their performance in terms of the output of the competence of which they are part. That is, how does a group of individuals become more and more *competent*?

I will assume that this happens via a process of learning to do things "better and better"—"better" meaning closer to the objectives for the output of the competence, which in turn is generally defined as a function of the demands of the customer. In slightly different words, the better the group of people are at fulfilling the demands of the customer (be it internal or external to firm), the more *competent* the competence that the group of people constitute along with technology and other elements. I realize that I am dealing with two different uses of "competence/competent" here, but as you shall see this enables me to superimpose well-known models for individual competence development to the development of competencies at firm level.

I have assumed that the development of a competence to function better and better (become more competent) must be a function of the learning of the individuals (elements) of the system. Of course, new technologies, new organizational forms, new norms and values, etc. may well emerge in the process of developing the competence, but if these are not linked to part of the individuals' learning, then there will be no competence development. Consider, for instance, the many times firms have used IT implementation to formally program procedures and practices long overdue for change, all because the individuals of the firm were not involved in "implementation" of the new IT system and not allowed to learn and change their practices *before* the technology was rolled in.

If the learning of a group of individuals is the key to understanding how a competence develops and becomes more competent, then it is tempting to take a look at some of the well-known models of how individuals learn and become increasingly competent. For instance, could it be possible to use the well-known Dreyfus and Dreyfus (1986) model for a person's learning, where a person starts off as a novice, becomes an advanced beginner, proficient, competent (!), and finally expert? In our research, we will assume this is the case and maintain all of the categories except for the last two. To avoid a third instance of *competent* being used, we would prefer to label the last two categories *expert* and *world class*, respectively.

It must also be assumed that the group of people will have a level of knowledge that evolves in the same manner as that of an individual along the categories. Most notably, at novice level the group will mainly use explicit rules and forms of knowledge, whereas at world-class level the group will use implicit and tacit rules and forms of knowledge. It is necessary to assume that the knowledge of the group somehow is uniform, that is, that the group will be, more or less, at the same level at the same time. At least, there will be a majority of persons at the same level at any given time and it is this majority that decides the group's level of competence.

This discussion enables us to propose the first basic model for competence development (Figure 8-1). Please note that I have yet to solve the issue of how to actually measure how a group of people (as part of a competence) is at this or that level of competence. This remains to be resolved.

Metaphor: The Competence Levels of a Football Team

To get some indication as to whether we are on the right track, I will shortly discuss the metaphor of a football team to illustrate and elaborate the model in Figure 8-2. Starting from the bottom of the model, children's football teams, when they are small and novices, tend to be organized so that all the players follow the ball at all times, including goalkeepers. In other words, the basic rules and how to play the game are what a coach for a team of novices must focus on. When the team advances to advanced beginners, the players know the basic rules and most are eager to improve. Training can now focus on technical details and performance of the individual player. Later, as the team becomes proficient, focus will be on rehearsing combinations and "procedures" for how the game is to be played. This could, for instance, be a young team at division 4 level, where everyone is eager to practice offside traps and so on. When the team advances, what happens becomes more

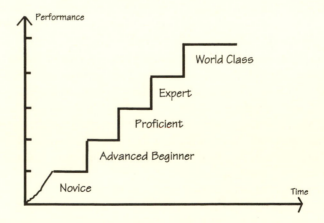

Figure 8-1. The levels of competence development.

implicit. Suddenly players know each other so well that they do not need to make formal arrangements and plans for making the offside trap work, they just "know" what to do and when. The team is on its way to becoming expert and world class, the latter, of course, stemming from years and years of practice at expert level. Far from all "expert teams," that is, national champions, make it into Champions League in their first attempt.

It seems as if the competence levels of a football team can be fitted into the general model, so the model may well be descriptive for some groups of individuals. What about (organizational) competencies in firms? This is another issue for future research. Another interesting point now is how to move from one stage to another—the process of competence development.

Points for reflection
- Do you recognize the levels of competence development in your firm?
- If not, what are the differences?
- Can the model be applied to understand and plan competence development in your firm?

MEANS FOR COMPETENCE DEVELOPMENT—LEARNING

In this section, I discuss the issue of organizational learning as a starting point for formulating a framework that will enable us to understand competence development and the choice of means for competence development in organizations.

Perspectives on Organizational Learning

Obviously, there are many different perspectives on organizational learning and many different contributions to the vast field, some of which do not even adhere to the term *organizational learning*. Claus Neergaard has developed a model that identifies four major types of learning, each representing a specific perspective (Neergaard, 1994).

The individual behavior perspective deals with informal learning processes of an individual. It captures information about human behavior, for instance, how individuals react in given situations and under specific conditions, as well as the personal interactions among people. Attention is focused on the informal, unconscious behavior of a single organizational member and the interpersonal interactions among a number of members of an organization (Argyris, 1992).

The decision support perspective focuses on formal, individual learning processes in organizations. The main interest is how an individual decision maker learns in connection with problem-solving situations. This includes the use of information technology and decision models to support decision making. The perspective is mainly used to study and understand how individual learning is influenced by available information technology and its institutionalized knowledge (Duncan & Weiss, 1979).

The management systems and organizational structure perspective concentrates on collective learning processes as guided by formal organizational structure and by management systems through formal planning and control processes, operating procedures, and reward systems (Riis, 1978; Cyert & March, 1963). The allocation of responsibility and authority and the structure of divisions, departments, and sections also regulate organizational learning processes.

The corporate culture perspective represents what an organization knows, which is neither codified nor formalized in systems (Schein, 1985). The focus is on social, informal relations, collective habits, behavioral patterns, and attitudes existing in an organization. Corporate culture is seen as emerging from collective learning processes and guides and shapes collective and individual behavior.

Apart from a fairly efficient way of ordering the many different contributions to an expanding and vast field, it should be noted that these four perspectives are just that—perspectives. Thus, they are not necessarily mutually exclusive with regard to specific literature. Even though the opposite is sometimes true, much literature tends to combine two or more of the perspectives. Nonetheless, it is possible to order the field of learning into these four perspectives (Figure 8-2).

The Process of Learning

Unfortunately, Neergaard's perspectives on organizational learning does little to help us understand the process of developing competence as a result of learning. It is this process that we are interested in; competence *development* is the key term. Luckily, others have been interested in the process of learning something to improve one's competence.

Today, it is widely accepted that learning takes places as a result of critical reflection on personal experiences (Marsick & Watkins, 1990), rather than as a result of formal training in dull theories. In the U.S. tradition, this is usually assigned to the efforts of John Dewey (1938), the first American to write on the subject. Dewey felt that education must address the notion of reflective thought. Reflective thought begins with an ambiguous situation that in some way represents a dilemma for

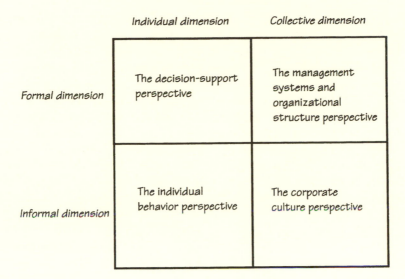

Figure 8-2. An overview of perspectives on learning.

an individual. From this "felt difficulty," the individual locates and defines the problem. The third step is a consideration of solutions with analysis of their many angles. This leads to an observation and experimentation and, finally, to a decision to act or not act on these possible solutions. It seems obvious that Dewey's notion of reflective thought is similar to the way we normally perceive the general scientific method (when applied to everyday problems).

Several models have been proposed to illustrate the process of learning as a result of reflective thought. Dewey's thinking shaped the work of several other theorists, for example, Argyris and Schön's idea about action science (1978, 1998), which is also based on Kurt Levin's approach to uniting theory and practice in an action research approach. Usually facilitated by an outside consultant, action research has been used to create organizational development, that is, to improve the way organizations function (Marsich & Watkins, 1990; Burke, 1992). Argyris & Schön are, like many others with them, bent on improving practice. They believe that no one ever sets out to deliberately create error, but despite our best efforts errors frequently occur. They propose that this is caused by a gap between the formulation of plans and their implementation (1978). This gap is the difference between our espoused theories and theories-in-use, that is, the difference between "what we think we do" and "what we actually do." One reason for frequent errors in organizational life, then, is caused by not digging deeply enough into the basic assumptions guiding our actions, something that Argyris and

Schön are the first to admit is tricky, as basic assumptions are normally taken for granted. Thus, they propose to call learning with change of basic assumptions "double-loop learning" and learning without changing assumptions "single-loop learning" (Argyris & Schön, 1978).

Perhaps the best-known perspective on learning from experience is that of Kolb (1984). Drawing on a number of different sources, among others Levin, Dewey, and Argyris and Schön (Marsick & Watkins, 1990), Kolb suggests that people comprehend and transform their experiences differently. Some comprehend through concrete experience and others through abstract conceptualization. Some transform through reflective observation and others through active experimentation. These two dimensions interact resulting in a typology of learning styles and an experiental learning cycle that goes from experiencing to observing to conceptualizing to experiementing and back to experiencing.

Kolb's learning cycle, albeit developed to explain the learning of an individual, has often been used to explain group learning. The model asserts that to have actually learned something, one must go through a full cycle of the model, turning actions (and their results) into experiences, complete reflection on these experiences (what can be learned here), develop and plan for new actions, decide on a course of action, and change (if feasible) one's actions according to the solutions decided upon.

In recent years, a number of additional notions have been formulated that may also shed light on the process of learning. Marsick and Watkins (1990) emphasize informal and incidental learning as a contrast to formal learning. Both are seen as learning taking place outside formally structured, institutionally sponsored, classroom-defined activities. Informal learning is experiential and noninstitutional, whereas incidental learning is unintentional and a by-product of other activities. The point of Marsick and Watkins is that the major part of learning of individuals and organizations is either informal or incidental, and formal learning is the minor part. Furthermore, Polyani has discussed the "object" of learning—knowledge—and proposed that all knowledge is tacit and impossible to express explicitly (Polyani, 1983), making what is expressed mere data or, perhaps, information. This is often misunderstood as in the case of Nonaka (1990), who proposes that there are several forms of knowledge, most notably explicit and tacit knowledge. Sadly, some prominent authors do not even seem to bother with the potential difficulties in expressing knowledge in explicit terms. Nonaka accuses Peter Senge (1990a) of not bothering with this issue (Nonaka & Takeguchi, 1995) and with some justification (Drejer & Henriksen, 1999). Nonetheless, the notion of tacit knowledge emphasizes even more strongly the informal aspects of learning (Spender, 1996).

Different Types of Learning and of Competencies

It seems as if some of the thinking about the process of learning has been directed at the individual level, whereas other thinking is more directed toward the group and/or organizational level. But what is the connection? Marsick and Watkins manage in a most elegant manner to connect many of the preceding concepts and ideas plus a few others in a set of three windows for three types of learning (Marsick & Watkins, 1990).

The starting point is that of individual learning, the area where we feel most comfortable when applying the thinking of people like Dewey and Kolb. Here Marsick and Watkins use the so-called Johari window, developed by Joseph Lufts and Harry Ingram, as their starting point (Marsick & Watkins, 1990). The basic assumption of the Johari window is that individuals learn by being open to others (Figure 8-3).

Through feedback, individuals learn how others see them and through self-disclosure they open themselves to the potential of more intimate relationships and also subject more of their perceptions of themselves to public reflection. In this process, others may help shape and affirm their self-understanding. The four quadrants of the model represent the open area (which is known by the individual and openly

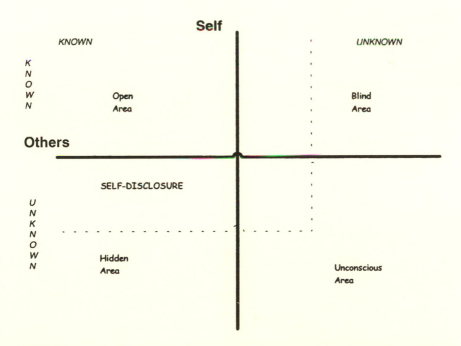

Figure 8-3. The Johari window: a model for understanding individual learning.

shared by others), the blind area (which others may observe, but the individual is unaware of), the unconscious area (the part of the individual which is not known by the individual or others), and the hidden area (which is the part of ourselves that we choose to keep to ourselves—including our secrets and dreams).

Using the Johari window, growth of an individual can be seen as a process of learning about oneself and the feedback of others, reflecting on what has been learned, and making changes based on feedback and self-disclosure. The latter can easily be seen in relation to the learning process discussed previously and illustrated by Kolb's model.

It is easier to grasp the notion of individual learning since we have all experienced it. It may be more difficult to think of group learning, but most people can probably recall instances where a group acted as one entity. In groups, individuals think and learn differently as a result of their interaction with others. Groups learn when they monitor the effectiveness of the process of group interaction, while at the same time focusing on accomplishing the task. As illustrated in the modified Johari window for group learning, groups also confront potential dysfunctions through processes of feedback and disclosure (Figure 8-4).

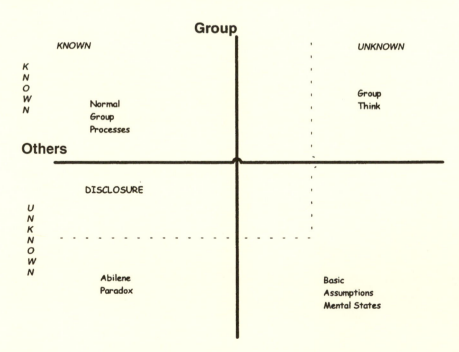

Figure 8-4. Adaptation of the Johari window: a model for understanding group learning.

The upper-left quadrant, when all is reasonably well, represents normal group processes visible to all. The upper-right quadrant includes what is known to the individuals, but not acknowledged and dealt with by the group. An example of the latter is that of "group think," where the pressure to conform to group norms is so great that individuals form strong common values and bonds that do not allow them to subject areas to a thorough hearing or a true critical test. The lower-right quadrant represents the unconscious states at the group and individual level. Unconscious states pull the attention of the group member away from the task and include fight, flight, pairing, and dependency. Finally, the lower-left quadrant includes situations where all group members agree on something privately, but as individuals do not own up to this when in the group. An example of this is the "Abilene paradox" (Marsick & Watkins, 1990), in which everyone knows that they are about to embark on a dangerous process/journey (trip to Abilene) but are unwilling to express the truth because of the perceived risks.

Finally, we have the case of organizational learning. Many organizational theorists distinguish between the way in which individuals go about their own learning and the way in which a larger collective unit learns to function in an environment. In both cases, individuals are involved. However, when organizations learn, individuals become agents who in some way influence the way others in the organization think, act, and learn. This opens up for the power-interpretation of organizational life and or learning that we have discussed earlier, but also for the less controversial work on corporate culture as a process of organizational learning.

Once again using the Johari window as starting point, Marsick and Watkins (1990) examine organizational learning in terms of the interaction between what is known to the organization and what is known by others in the environment. This makes it possible to position some of the concepts clearly related to organizational learning rather than individual learning (Figure 8-5).

The productive work state, represented by the upper-left quadrant, where something is known both to an organization and the environment, is depicted as an open system. Central to this concept is the assumption/idea that a learning organization is productive, but it is also open to learning from internal and external feedback from its environment. Double-loop learning permits internal feedback, whereas reframing encourages disclosure. But there is also the organization's blind side as described by Argyris and Schön's concept of dysfunctional theories-in-use (in the upper-right quadrant) and the organization's hidden side (the lower-left quadrant) where mistakes and defects are hidden from the environment. Finally, there is the collective uncon-

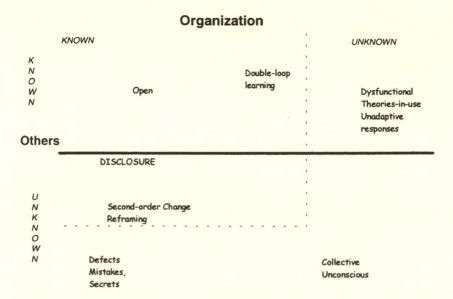

Figure 8-5. Adaptation of the Johari window: a model for understanding organizational learning. (Marsick & Watkins, 1990)

sciousness of the organization (lower-right quadrant), which may include the embedded values of the organization's culture and subcultures and unstated interpretations of the organization's experiences (myths and legends).

COMPETENCE DEVELOPMENT PROCESSES

I am a firm believer in a situational—contingency—approach to management in general and competence development in particular. Such a situational approach would naturally suggest that there are differences between the individual stages in terms of at least two things. One issue is the starting point for developing the competence further, and the other issue is the means for creating the organizational learning of the persons involved to develop that competence. I explore these differences next.

Metaphor: The Development Process of a Football Team

The assertion that the starting point for developing a competence will differ from stage to stage can be translated to the notion that different forms of coaches are needed for different kinds of teams. This is, for instance, institutionalized in the coach-education of Dansk Boldspil Union, the national Danish football association, and probably practiced in many clubs. Imagine, for instance, that Sir Alex Fergusson, manager of the mighty Manchester United, coached Man U's youth teams. It is quite unlikely that Sir Alex, famous for his temper, would be as successful in developing the competence of such a team as he obviously has been in developing the Premiership team. This may be because the children's team has a different starting point. For one thing, the children will be differently motivated and have completely different social interactions. Second, the children will still need to learn a lot of basics in hard training before they can start focusing on, for example, opponents, individual specialties, and mutual understanding between players. Thus, metaphorically, the starting point at different competence levels is different.

What about the means for creating the organizational learning that, in turn, develops the competence that the football teams create together? We have already hinted that the novice children's team needs to train hard on learning the basics of football to become an advanced beginners team. And the novice team can probably find time for little else, whereas the world-class team does not need to focus so much on basic skills. Instead, the world-class team might focus on rehearsing new combinations, new free-kick combinations, and so on. Most important, they can rehearse in living under the pressure of being a world-class team. The coach of Aalborg Boldklub (AaB), the local club of Aalborg that won the national premiership title of Denmark in 1998, Peter Rudbæk, uses videotaping of individual players to improve combinations in defense and attack, as well as many other advanced methods of training. However, for Peter Rudbæk the most important task of AaB now is to change into a team that consistently wins championships and participates in international football. This can only be learned through experience and quite informal means. Perhaps this is typical of the process of going from expert to world class.

Regarding the first issue—the starting point for learning at each stage—I propose that there must be quite different starting points in each stage, especially if the novice stage is compared directly to the world-class stage.

The Development from One Stage to the Next

Obviously, no one can tell exactly how to move through the entire cycle of competence development. The list of possible means for creating, supporting, and facilitating the necessary organizational learning is much too long. The list of contingencies (e.g., type of competence, environmental dynamics, product of the firm, style of the firm, national culture) is probably even longer, and far too much in the process can never be expected to be made explicit. From the world of football, the example of Liverpool FC comes to mind. In the club's heyday in the early 1980s, it was hailed for its efforts in learning and continuous development. However, in the late 1980s something went wrong and despite everything that was known in Liverpool, the club has not been able to recover to its former glory even though it appears as if the well-known recipe, as well as a few new ones, has been tried since. Thus, it seems difficult to explain and recreate competence development.

Notwithstanding these difficulties, I feel that it is possible to contribute to both sides of a discussion of competence development. The first contribution is on the issue of organizational learning, where well-known models may be used to create and generate further understanding. The other contribution is on the issue of change.

CASE EXAMPLE OF COMPETENCE DEVELOPMENT

Methodology and Case Company

There has been a lot of (renewed) talk about action research in recent years. Stemming from the traditional literature on organizational development and learning, the concept has come back in fashion as a means of bringing researchers even closer to their fields of study than is possible by means of survey and even case studies.

To me, action research means two things. First, it is a possibility for the university researcher to contribute closely to an actual learning process in a company on a subject close to his/her field of research. Second, it is a chance for the company managers to "become researchers into their own practice," as Argyris and Schön (1996) would have put it. In other words, I see an action research project as a joint research project with two success criteria: (1) it should work in the company, and (2) it should yield experiences and learning that are of interest to other companies and/or managers with an interest in the issue of research.

In this section, I report the results from an action research project aimed at competence development in a medium-sized Danish company. The company is privately owned by the family of its founder and designs, sells, and purchases socks with different motifs such as Barbie, Disney characters, and so on sold in malls, supermarkets, and stores all over Scandinavia. The actual manufacturing is done by suppliers located in the Far East. The company is basically a project-based company, since socks are designed to coincide with a large number of occasions throughout the year. Apart from seasonal variations, occasions could be the release of another Disney film, Christmas, Father's Day and so on. As a result, the company executes several large and many small projects every year, where new products are designed, specified, ordered by purchasing, and marketed. Obviously, this is a complex, cross-functional competence that involves collaboration in all of the departments in the company, which is organized in a traditional functional organization.

In practical terms, the cooperation has taken place within the boundaries of a formal project at the case company with the purpose of developing the company's cross-functional core competence in developing, marketing, and producing new products (the product development or innovation process). The project has been ongoing for 2 1/2 years. The two internal managers from the case company have been project managers and responsible for the project. As an integral part of the management of the project, a so-called process group was initiated with participation by myself and the internal project managers. The purpose of the group was to reflect, experiment and initiate experiments to improve the competence development process in the company.

For reasons of validation, minutes were kept of the meetings and discussions. Furthermore, detailed analyses were carried out related to the experiments undertaken. Finally, the external researcher carried out independent interviews with the involved employees on several occasions throughout the project.

The First Phase: Cleaning Up

In the spring of 1999, I was approached by a medium-sized, order-producing Danish firm, where top management has recognized that a number of problems needed to be solved. Problems included difficulties in finishing off product development in time for sales, a high work load in development, duplication of work, lack of traceability of decisions, and so on. With the input of employees, an analysis quickly revealed that the problems were not being created by lack of individual skills. Rather, the problems seemed to be created by the system by which order handling happened, a "system" that had never been formally defined or planned. The systems had merely emerged as the company had grown. Based on the company's merits and our general feel for the entire competence development process, we would tend to locate the firm as a proficient firm in the model. After the analysis, by means of the so-called "problem-matrix" (see Riis, 1990), the employees of the firm were made to realize that the problems were systemic rather than individual. Five areas of attention were identified and turned into development projects in the firm. A mere five months later, four of the projects were completed with great results; for instance, a planning method for coordinating sales and design had been put in place. And for the first time, everyone felt that efforts were well coordinated. I view this as an example of progressing from the proficient stage to the expert stage.

Step Two: Expanding the Project into an Overall Effort

The firm in question, however, still plans to grow rather rapidly and, furthermore, the first successes have made top management as well as employees realize that much more can be done. In fact, the fifth project of the first development has expanded into a large company-wide project of order handling, information system design, and some large strategic implications. In planning for the next set of projects, top management now realizes that they are faced with a completely different task than in the spring of 1999. This time several more projects need to be defined and coordinated, resources need to be much larger—and dispersed in the right order—and the time-horizon needs to be larger, much larger, than 5 months. Furthermore, it is evident that the technological solutions on the IT side that are currently being dreamed up need to be integrated with the organizational development of the firm. I will assert that this development could well be an example of progressing from expert to world class or maybe "just" of progressing to expert from proficient.

Interpretation: Two Phase Shifts in a Competence Development Effort

An interpretation of the case example would be that we have witnessed the shift from one stage of the model to another, as well as the beginning of another shift. We label the first shift a "cleaning up" learning effort where the main ingredients were analysis of existing practices and processes, as well as a reengineering effort aimed at designing improved processes. This could be undertaken rather quickly and by fairly simple means. The next phase, however, quickly proved more tricky and was planned to take much longer and use more resources. The effort is now one year underway and has not proved any easier than expected. I shall interpret this as a result of another kind of effort needed for the next shift, which we will label *holistic solution*, with both organizational and technological means (Figure 8-6).

The case example tells us a little more about the learning process of competence development. I assert that the first part of the case consisted of at least one full cycle of Kolb's learning cycle, with the dialogue

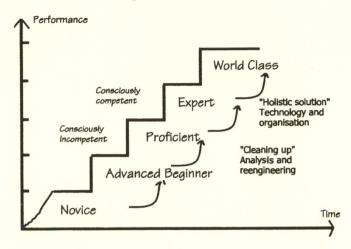

Figure 8-6. Illustration of the case of organizational learning of competence.

focused on making problem-matrices the means for creating reflection on the experienced problems. Later in the case solutions were generated and put into action. Now the firm needs to go through another Kolb cycle of learning. However, the case also shows that the next shift will have to be much different from the first. Several learning cycles will probably be needed to travel the next step of the way.

SUMMARY AND CONCLUSIONS

In this part of this book, I have moved from a structural definition of competencies as systems of technology, human beings, organization and culture toward a model for explaining competence development. Based on my definition of competencies, I have also proposed a typology of three different kinds of competencies: simple, moderately complex, and complex competencies.

The means for making the part of the journey related to competence development has been a discussion of the existing theory on organizational learning. In this course of our journey, I have found that there are many striking parallels in competence theory and organizational learning theory. For one thing, theory on organizational learning strongly emphasizes the human element (albeit there is a distinct tradition for focusing on organizational and technological elements as well). Furthermore, organizational learning seems to be divided into work on individual, group, and organizational learning.

The last type fits nicely with the types of competencies I have proposed.

In light of these parallels, I have found it natural to base our work on competence development firmly on concepts from organizational learning. With this basis, this chapter contains a proposed model for competence development and a discussion of this model.

Bibliography

Aaker, D. A., "Managing Assets and Skills: The Key to a Sustainable Competitive Advantage," *California Management Review* 17, Winter Issue 1989, 47–50.

Abegglen, J. C., & Stalk, G., Jr., *Kaisha—the Japanese Corporation*. New York: Basic Books, 1985.

Abernathy, W. J., *The Productivity Dilemma*. Baltimore: Johns Hopkins University Press, 1978.

Abernathy, W. J., & Clark, K.B., "Innovation—Mapping the Winds of Creative Destruction," *Research Policy* 14, 1985, 3–22.

Abernathy, W. J., Clark, K. B., & Kantrow, A. M., "The New Industrial Competition," in *Survival Strategies for American Industry*, A. M. Kantrow (ed.). New York: John Wiley & Sons, 1983.

Ackoff, R. L., *A Concept of Corporate Planning*. New York: John Wiley & Sons, 1970.

Adler, P. S., "Technology Strategy: A Guide to the Literature," *Research in Technological Innovation, Management, and Policy* 4, 1989, 19–78.

Amit, R., & Schoemaker, P. J. H., "Strategic Assets and Organisational Rent," *Strategic Management Journal* 14, 1993, 33–46.

Andersen, D., *Mission Management* (in Danish). Copenhagen: Børsens Forlag, 1995.

Anderson, P., & Tushman, M. L., "Technological Discontinuities and Dominant Designs—a Cyclical Model of Technological Change," *Administrative Science Quarterly*, 35, 1990, 604–633.

Andreasen, M. M., "Production and Product Development Integration," in *Production, Learning and Competence*. A. Drejer (ed.). Aalborg University Press, 1999.

Andrews, K. R. *The Concept of Corporate Strategy*. London: Richard D. Irwing Inc., 1967.

Ansoff, H. I., *Corporate Strategy—an Analytical Approach to Business Policy for Growth and Expansion*. New York: McGraw-Hill, 1965.

Ansoff, H. I. "Critique of Henry Mintzberg's 'The Design School,' " *Strategic Management Journal* 12, 1991, 449–461.

Ansoff, H. I., & Hayes, R. L., *From Strategic Planning to Strategic Management*. New York: John Wiley and Sons, 1976.

Ansoff, H. I. & Stewart, J. M., "Strategies for a Technology-Based Business," *Harvard Business Review*, November-December, 1967.

Ansoff, H. I., & McDonell, E., *Implanting Strategic Management*. Englewood Cliffs, NJ: Prentice-Hall, 1990.

Argyris, C., & Schon, D. A., *Organizational Learning. A Theory of Action Perspective*. Reading, MA: Addison-Wesley, 1978.

———, *Organizational Learning II*. Reading, MA: Addison-Wesley, 1998.

Bakka, J. F., & Fivelsdahl, H., *Organizational Theory* (in Danish). Copenhagen: Handelshøjskolens Forlag, 1985.

Barney, J. B., "Firm Resources and Sustained Competitive Advantage," *Journal of Management* 17, 1991, 12–26.

Bates, D. L., & Dillard, J. E., "Generating Strategic Thinking Through Multi-Level Teams," *Long Range Planning* 19, October 1993, 117–128.

Bayus, B.L., "Are Product Life Cycles Really Getting Shorter?", *Journal of Production and Inventory Management* 7, 1994, 300–308.

Bessant, J., & Haywood, B., "Islands, Archipelagos and Continents—Progress on the Road to Computer-integrated Manufacturing," *Research Policy* 17, 1988, 73–92.

Bettis, R. A., & Hitt, M. A., "The New Competitive Landscape," *Strategic Management Journal* 16, Summer 1995, 7–19.

Betz, F., *Managing Technology: Competing Through New Ventures, Innovation, and Corporate Research*. Englewood Cliffs, NJ: Prentice-Hall, 1989

Bhalla, S. K., *The Effective Management of Technology*. Batelle Press, 1987.

Bogner, W. C., & Thomas, H., "Core Competence and Competitive Advantage," in *Competence-based Competition*, G. Hamel & A. Heene (eds.). New York: John Wiley and Sons, 1994.

Boisot, M., *Information and Organizations*. New York: Harper Collins, 1987.

Boisot, M., *Information Space: A Framework for Learning in Organizations*. London: Routledge, 1995.

Bowonder, B. & Miyake, T., "Japanese Technological Innovation Strategy: Recent Trends," *Technology Analysis and Strategic Management* 1, 1992, 9–18.

Burgelman, R. A., & Rosenbloom, R. S., "Technology Strategy: An Evolutionary Process Perspective," *Research on Technological Innovation, Management and Policy* 4, 1989, 51–61.

Burgelman, R. A., & Sayles, L. R., *Inside Corporate Innovation*. New York: The Free Press, 1986.

Burke, W. W., *Organization Development*. Reading, MA: Addison-Wesley, 1992.

Campbell, A., & Goold, M., *Many Best Ways to Make Strategy*. Cambridge, U.K.: Blackwell Publishers, 1995.

Campbell, A., & Tawady, K. (eds.). *Mission & Business Philosophy*. London: Heinemann Publishing, 1990.

Campbell, A., & Yeung, S., "Creating a Sense of Mission," *Long Range Planning*, August 1991a, 9–20.

Campbell, A., & Yeung, S., "Mission, Vision and Strategic Intent," *Long Range Planning* 19, August 1991b, 99–112.

Campbell, D. T., "Variation, Selection and Retention in Sociocultural Evolution," *General Systems* 16, 1969, 69–85.

Champy, J., *Reengineering Management*. New York: The Free Press, 1995.

Checkland, P., *Systems Thinking, Systems Practice*. New York: John Wiley and Sons, 1981.

Checkland, P., "From Optimizing to Learning: A Development of Systems Thinking for the 1990s," *Journal of the Operational Research Society* 36, 1985, 11–22.

Chester, A. N., "Aligning Technology with Business Strategy," *Research Technology Management* 23, January-February 1994, 17–28.

Christensen, S., & Kreiner, K., *Project Management in Loosely Coupled Systems* (in Danish). Copenhagen: Jurist-og Økonomforbundets Forlag, 1991.

Christensen, J. C., *Innovator's Dilemma*. Cambridge, MA: Harvard Business School Press, 1998.

Churchman, C. W., *Challenge to Reason*. London: McGraw-Hill, 1968.

Churchman, C. W., *The Design of Inquiring Systems*. New York: Basic Books, 1971.

Clark, K. B., "What Strategy Can Do for Technology," *Harvard Business Review*, November-December, 1989, 93–117.

Clark, K. B., & Fujimoto, T., "Reducing the Time to Market: the Case of the World Automotive Industry," In *Managing Innovation*, J. Henry & D. Walker (eds.). Beverly Hills: Sage Publications, 1991.

Cleveland, G., Schroeder, R. G., & Anderson, J. C., "A Theory of Production Competence," *Decision Sciences* 20, 1989, 655–668.

Cohan, P. S., *The Technology Leaders*. San Francisco: Jossey-Bass, 1997.

Cohen, W. M., & Levinthal, D. A., "Absorptive Capacity: A New Perspective for Learning and Innovation," *Administrative Science Quarterly* 25, 1990, 128–152.

Collins, J. C., & Lazier, W. C., "Vision—The Greatest Companies Started with the Founders' Core Vision," *European Management Review* 2, Spring 1993, 103–120.

Connor, K. R., "A Historical Comparison of Research-Based Theory and Five Schools of Thought within Industrial Organization Economics: Do We Have a New Theory of The Firm?" *Journal Management* 17, 1991, 121–154.

Cooper, R., & Kaplan, R. S., "Measure Costs Right: Make the Right Decisions," *Harvard Business Review*, September-October, 1988, 96–113.

Cooper, R. G., & Kleinsmidt, E. L., "New Products: What Separates Winners from Losers?," in *Managing Innovation*, J. Henry & D. Walker (eds.). Beverly Hills: Sage, 1991.

Corbet, C., & Wassenhove, L. V., "Trade-Offs? What Trade-Offs: Competence and Competitiveness in Manufacturing Strategy," *California Management Review*, Summer 1993.

Coupland, D., *Generation X*. New York: St. Martin's Press, 1995.

Cyert, R. M., & March, J. G., *A Behavioural Theory of the Firm*. Cambridge, U.K.: Blackwell, 1963.

Daft, R., *Organization Theory and Design*. New York: West Publishing Company, 1998.

Dalsgaard, L., & Bendix, J., *Netværksorganisering*. Copenhagen: Børsens Forlag, 1996.

D'Aveni, R. A., *Hypercompetition—Managing the Dynamics of Strategic Maneuvering*. New York: The Free Press, 1994.

Davenport, T. H., *Process Innovation—Reengineering Work Through Information Technology*. Cambridge, MA: Harvard Business School Press, 1993.

Davenport, T. H., & Prusak, L., *Working Knowledge*. Cambridge, MA: Harvard Business School Press, 1999.

Davenport, T. H., & Short, J. E., "The New Industrial Engineering: Information Technology and Business Process Redesign," *Sloan Management Review* Summer 1990, 93–106.

Delapierre, M., "Technology Bunching and Industrial Strategies," in *Innovation and Management*, Urabe et al. (eds.). Amsterdam: Walter de Gruyter, 1988.

Dewey, J., *Experience and Education*. New York: Collier Books, 1938.

DiBello, L., & Spender, J. C., "Constructive Learning—A New Approach to Deploying Technological Systems into the Workplace," *International Journal of Technology Management* 11, 1996, 747–758.

Downes, L., & Mui, C., *Unleashing the Killer App—Digital Strategies for Market Dominance*. Cambridge, MA: Harvard Business School Press, 1998.

Drejer, A., Integration of Business Strategy and Competence Development, Ph.D. Thesis, Department of Production, Aalborg University, 1996a.

Drejer, A., "Frameworks for the Management of Technology: Towards a Contingent Approach," *Technology Analysis & Strategic Management* 8, 1996b, 9–28.

Drejer, A., "The Discipline of Management of Technology," *The International Journal of Technovation* 17, 1997, 253–265.

Drejer, A., *The Innovative Firm* (in Danish). Copenhagen: Børsens Forlag, 2001.

Drejer, A., Henriksen, L. B., & Christensen, J. B., *Små Virksomheders Strategiske Udvikling*. Aalborg Universitet, 1999.

Drejer, A., & Kofoed, L. (eds.), *Management of Technology: At the Crossroads*. Aalborg University, Center for Technology Management, 1998.

Drejer, A., & Riis, J.O., *Competence-Based Strategy* (in Danish). Copenhagen: Børsens Forlag, 2000.

Dreyfus, H., & Dreyfus, S., *Mind over Machine: the Power of Human Intuition and Expertise in the Era of the Computer*. New York: Free Press, 1986.

Drucker, P. F., *The Practice of Management*. New York: Harper and Row, 1958.

Drucker, P. F., *Management*. New York: Butterworth-Heinemann, 1973.

Drucker, P. F., *Innovation and Entrepreneurship*. New York: Harper & Row, 1985.

Drucker, P. F., "The Emerging Theory of Manufacturing," *Harvard Business Review*, May-June 1990, 104–194.

Drucker, P. F., "The Theory of the Business," *Harvard Business Review*, September-October, 1994, 13–97.

Duncan, R., & Weiss, A., "Organisational Learning: Implications for Organisation Design," in Barry M. Staw, *Research in Organisational Behaviour*, JAI Press, 1979.

Dussage, P., Hart, S., & Ramanatsoa, B., *Strategic Technology Management*. New York: John Wiley and Sons, 1991.

Edvinsson, L., & Malone, T., *Intellectual Capital*. New York: HarperCollins, 1997.

Eriksen, B., *The Resource-Based View of the Firm: Towards an Integrated Framework of Strategy*. Odense University, 1993a.

Eriksen, B., *Firm Resources and Capabilities: a Renewed Focus for Strategic Management?* Odense University, 1993b.

Eriksen, B., & Mikkelsen, J., *Competitive Advantage and the Concept of Core Competence*. Odense University, 1993.

Ford, D., "Develop Your Technology Strategy," *Long Range Planning* 21, 1988, 79–100.

Foss, N. J., *Two Economic Strategy Theories* (in Danish). Copenhagen Business School, 1993.

Foster, R. N., *Innovation—the Attacker's Advantage*. New York: Summit Books, 1986

Freeman, C., *The Economics of Industrial Innovation*. Pinter, 1982.

Frick, J., & Riis, J. O., "Activity Chains: A Method for Identifying and Evaluating Key-Areas of Integration in SMEs," *Proceedings of CIM Europe*, Portugal, May, 1990, 377–382.

Frohman, A. L., "Putting Technology Into Strategic Planning," *California Management Review*, Winter, 1985, 19–28.

Fry, J. N., & Killing, P. J., *Strategic Analysis and Action*. Englewood Cliffs, NJ: Prentice Hall, 1995.

Galbraith, J. D., *Designing Complex Organizations*. Reading, MA: Addison-Wesley, 1973.

Galbraith, J. D., *Organisation Design*. Reading, MA: Addison-Wesley, 1979.

Galbraith, J. D., *Network Organisations*. Reading, MA: Addison-Wesley, 1995.

Garvin, D. A., "Building a Learning Organization," *Harvard Business Review*, July-August, 1993, 87–100.

Gaynor, G. H., *Achieving the Competitive Edge Through Integrated Technology Management*. New York: McGraw-Hill, 1991.

Giget, M., "The Bonsai Trees of Japanese Industry," *Futures*, April 1988.

Gilbert, M., & Gordon-Hayes, M., "Understanding the Process of Knowledge Transfer to Achieve Successful Technological Innovation," *Technovation* 16, 1996, 301–312.

Goold, M., & Quinn, J. J., *Strategic Control: Milestones for Long-term Performance*. London: The Economist Books, 1992.

Grant, R. M., "The Resource-based Theory of Competitive Advantage: Implications for Strategy Formulation," *California Management Review*, Spring 1991, 46–64.

Grant, E. B., & Gregory, M. J., "Tacit Knowledge, the Life Cycle and International Manufacturing Transfer," *Technology Analysis and Strategic Management* 9, 1997, 149–161.

Greiner, L., "Development and Transition in an Organisation's Growth," *Harvard Business Review*, July-August, 1972, 19–37.

Halal, W. E., *The Infinite Resource*. San Francisco: Jossey Bass, 1998.

Hall, R., "Complex Systems, Complex Learning and Competencies." Paper presented at the 3rd International Workshop on Competence-based Strategy, November 16–18, Ghent, Belgium, 1995.

Hamel, G., & Prahalad, C. K., *Competing for the Future*. Cambridge, MA: Harvard Business School Press, 1994.

Hamel, G., & Prahalad, C. K., "Strategy as Stretch and Leverage," *Harvard Business Review* 2, 1993, 75–84.

Hammer, M., "Reengineering Work : Don't Automate, Obliterate," *Harvard Business Review*, July-August 1993, 73–94.

Hammer, M., & Champy, J., *Reengineering the Corporation: a Manifesto for Business Revolution*. New York: Nicolas Brealy Publishing, 1993.

Hammer, M., & Stanton, D., *The Reengineering Handbook*. New York: Nicolas Brealy Publishing, 1995.

Handy, C., *The Age of Unreason*. London: Arrow, 1995.

Harrington, H. J., *Business Process Improvement*. McGraw-Hill, 1991.

Haspeslaugh, P., Portfolio Planning Methods and the Strategic Management Process in Diversified Industrial Companies, Ph.D. Thesis, Harvard Business School, 1983.

Hauser, J. R., & Clausing, D., "The House of Quality," *Harvard Business Review* May-June, 1988.

Hax, A. C., & Majluf, N. S., *The Strategy Concept and Process: A Pragmatic Approach*. Englewood Cliffs, NJ: Prentice Hall, 1991.

Hayes, R. H., Pisano, G. P., Upton, D. M., *Strategic Operations—Competing through Capabilities*. New York: The Free Press, 1996.

Hayes, R. H., & Wheelwright, S. C., "The Dynamics of Process-Product Life Cycles," *Harvard Business Review*, March-April 1979, 127–136.

Hein, L., & Andreasen, M. M., *Integrated Product Development* (in Danish). Copenhagen: Jernets Arbejdsgiverforening, 1985.

Hill, T., *Manufacturing Strategy*. London: Macmillan, 1985.

Hitt, M. A., & Ireland, R. D., "Corporate Distinctive Competence: Strategy, Industry, and Performance," *Strategic Management Journal* 6, 1985, 9–20.

Hofer, C. W., & Schendel, D., *Strategy Formulation—Analytical Concepts*. New York: West Publishing Company, 1978.

Hofstede, G., *Culture's Consequences: International Differences in Work-Related Values*. Beverly Hills, CA: Sage Publishers, 1981.

Howels, J., "Tacit Knowledge, Innovation, and Technology Transfer," *Technology Analysis & Strategic Management* 8, 1996, 91–106.

Hull, Kristensen P., *Denmark—an Experimental Laboratory of Industrial Organization*. Copenhagen: Handelshøjskolen i København, 1996.

Hunt, V. D., *Process Mapping*. New York: John Wiley and Sons, 1996.

Hviid, J., & Sant, K., *Business Process Reengineering*. Copenhagen: Børsen Bøger, 1994.

Irwin, R. A., & Michaels III, E. G., "Core Skills: Doing the Right Things Right," *The McKinsey Quarterly* 19, summer, 1989, 19–28.

Jantsch, F., *Technology Forecasting*. Englewood Cliffs, NJ: Prentice Hall, 1967.

Johnson, P., & Kaplan, R. S., *Measures for Manufacturing Performance*. Cambridge, MA: Harvard Business School Press, 1987.

Jones, O., & Smith, D., "Strategic Technology Management in a Mid-corporate Firm: The Case of Otter Controls," *Journal of Management Studies* 34, 1997, 511–536.

Kantrow, A. M., *Survival Strategies for American Industry*. New York: John Wiley and Sons, 1983.

Kaplan, R. S., & Norton, D. P., *The Balanced Scorecard—Translating Strategy to Action*. Cambridge, MA: Harvard Business School Press, 1996.

Keldmann, T., "The Environmental Part of the Product Concept," The International Conference on Engineering Design, ICED'95, Prague, August 22–24, 1995.

Kiernan, F., *Get Innovative or Get Dead*. London: Arrow, 1995.

Kim, D. J., & Kogut, B., "Technology Platforms and Diversification," *Organizational Science* 3, 1996, 283–301.

Knott, P. A. Pearson, & Taylor, R., "A New Approach to Competence Analysis," *International Journal of Technology Management* 11, 1996, 117–128.

Kogut, B., & Zander, U., "Knowledge of the Firm, Combinative Capabilities, and the Replication of Technology," *Organization Science* 3, 1992, 383–397.

Kogut, B., & Zander, U., "Knowledge and the Speed of the Transfer and Imitation of Organizational Capabilities," *Organization Science* 6, 1995, 76–92.

Kolb, D., *Experimental Learning*. Englewood Cliffs, NJ: Prentice Hall, 1984.

Kotler, P., *Marketing Management*. Englewood Cliffs, NJ: Prentice Hall, 1999.

Kotter, J., *Leading Change*. Cambridge, MA: Harvard Business School Press, 1997.

Lambright, W. H., & Rahm, D. (eds.), *Technology and US Competitiveness*. Westport, CT: Greenwood Press, 1992.

Lawrence, P. R., & Lorsh, J. W., "Organization and Environment—Managing Differentiation and Integration," *Administrative Science Quarterly* 13, 1967, 13–26.

Leavitt, H. J., "Applied Organizational Change in Industry: Structural, Technological and Humanistic Approaches," in *Handbook of Organizations*, J. March (editor). New York: Rand McNally, 1965.

Lei, D., Hitt, M. A., & Bettis, R., "Dynamic Core Competences through Meta-Learning and Strategic Context," *Journal of Management* 22, 1966, 549–569.

Leonard-Barton, D., *Wellsprings of Knowledge*. Cambridge, MA: Harvard Business School Press, 1995.

Levin, M., "Technology Transfer as a Learning and Development Process," *Technovation* 8, 1993, 17–30.

Levit, T., "Marketing Myopia," *Harvard Business Review*. July-August, 1960, 45–60.

Lewis, M., & Gregory, M., "Developing and Applying a Process Approach to Competence Analysis," in R. Sanchez, A. Henee, & H. Thomas, *Dynamics of Competence-based Competition*. Amsterdam: Pergamon, 1996.

Lorange, P., *Strategy Implementation*. Englewood Cliffs, NJ: Prentice Hall, 1986.

Lorange, P., *Corporate Planning—an Executive Viewpoint*. Englewood Cliffs, NJ: Prentice Hall, 1980.

Loveridge, R., & Pitt, M., *The Strategic Management of Technological Innovation*. New York: John Wiley and Sons, 1990.

Maack, P., *Technology Development in the Industrial Firm* (in Danish). Copenhagen: Driftteknisk Institut, DTH, 1974.

Marsick, V. J., & Watkins, K. E., *Informal and Incidental Learning in the Workplace* London: Routledge, 1990.

Martin, J., *Cypercorp*. London: Amacon, 1996.

Miles, R. E., & Snow, C. C., *Organizational Strategy, Structure, and Process*. New York: McGraw-Hill, 1978.

Mintzberg, H., *The Nature of Managerial Work*. New York: Harper & Row, 1973.

Mintzberg, H., "Patterns in Strategy Formulation," *Management Science* 9, 1978, 13–20.

Mintzberg, H., *Structure in Five—Designing Effective Organizations*. Englewood Cliffs, NJ: Prentice-Hall, 1983.

Mintzberg, H., *The Rise and Fall of Strategic Planning*. New York: The Free Press, 1994.

Mintzberg, H., *Strategy Safari*. New York: The Free Press, 1999.

Mintzberg, H., & Quinn, J. B., *The Strategy Process—Concepts, Contexts, Cases*. Englewood Cliffs, NJ: Prentice Hall, 1991.

Monger, R. F., *Mastering Technology: a Management Framework for Getting Results*. New York: The Free Press, 1988.

Morgan, G., *Imaginization—the Art of Creative Management*. Beverly Hills, CA: Sage, 1997.

Moss Kanter, R., *The Challenge of Organizational Change*. Cambridge, MA: Harvard Business School Press, 1992.

National Research Council, *Management of Technology: The Hidden Advantage*. New York: National Academy Press, 1987, 15.

Neergaard, C., Creating a Learning Organisation, Ph.D. Thesis, Aalborg University, Department of Production, 1994.

Neergaard, C., van Haueen, F., & Kastberg, B., *Den Lærende Organisation i Praksis*. Copenhagen: Industriens Forlag, 1997.

Nevis, E. C., DiBella, A. J., & Gould, J. M., "Understanding Organizations as Learning Systems," *Sloan Management Review*, Winter 1995, 73–85.

Nielsen, A. P., *Competence Development Through Commercialisation*, IPS Programme, Technical University of Denmark, 1998.

Nonaka, I., "The Knowledge-Creating Company," *Harvard Business Review*, November-December, 1991, 96–104.

Nonaka, I., & Takeuchi, H., *The Knowledge Creating Company—How Japanese Companies Create the Dynamics of Innovation*. Oxford, U.K.: Oxford University Press, 1995.

Noori, H., *Managing the Dynamics of New Technology*. Englewood Cliffs, NJ: Prentice Hall, 1990.

Norman, J., & Ramirez, P. F., "From Value-Chain to Value Constellation," *Harvard Business Review*, July-August, 1993, 85–96.

Olsen, F., "Strategic Survailance Systems" (in Danish), in *Strategy and Management*. Copenhagen: Systime, 1993.

Pearce II, J. A., "The Company Mission as a Strategic Tool," in *Mission & Business Philosophy*, A. Campbell & K. Tawady (eds.). Amsterdam: Heinemann, 1990.

Pedler, M., Burgoyne, J., & Boydell, T., *The Learning Company*. New York: McGraw-Hill, 1991.

Penrose, E., *The Theory of the Growth of the Firm*. New York: John Wiley and Sons, 1957.

Peters, T., *Liberation Management*. London: Macmillan, 1992.

Peters, T. J., & Watermann, R. H., Jr., *In Search of Excellence*. New York: Harper and Row, 1982.

Polyani, M., *The Tacit Dimension*. London: Routledge, 1967.

Porter, M. E., *Competitive Strategy*. New York: The Free Press, 1980.

Porter, M. E., *Competitive Advantage*. New York: The Free Press, 1985.

Porter, M. E., "From Competitive Advantage to Corporate Strategy," *Harvard Business Review*, May-June, 1987, 19–38.

Porter, M. E., "Towards a Dynamic Theory of Strategy," *Strategic Management Journal* 12, 1991, 95–117.

Porter, A. L., et al., *Forecasting and Management of Technology*. John Wiley and Sons, 1991.

Power, M., "Modernism, Postmodernism and Organization," in J. Hassard & D. Pym (eds.), *The Theory and Philosophy of Organizations: Critical Issues and New Perspectives*. London: Routledge, 1990.

Prahalad, C. K., "The Role of Core Competencies in the Corporation," *Research-Technology Management*, November-December, 1993, 40–47.

Prahalad, C. K., & Hamel, G., "The Core Competencies of the Corporation," *Harvard Business Review*, May-June, 1990, 97–148.

Printz, L., *A Strategic Development Model*, Aarhus Business School, 1998.

Quinn, J. B., *Intelligent Enterprise*. New York: The Free Press, 1992.

Rappaport, A., "CFO's and Strategists: Forging a Common Framework," *Harvard Business Review*, May-June, 1992, 17–28.

Rigby, D. K., "How to Manage the Management Tools," *Planning Review* 19, 1993, 8–15.

Riis, J. O., *Design of Management Systems—an Analytical Framework*. Copenhagen: Akademisk Forlag, 1978.

Riis, J. O., "Situational Production Management: A Practical Theory for the Development and Application of Production Management," *Production Planning & Control* 5, 1994, 3–18.

Roberts, E. K., *Generating Effective Corporate Innovation*. New York: The Free Press, 1981.

Rogers, E., *Diffusion of Innovations*. New York: The Free Press, 1962.

Rosenkopf, L., & Tushman, M. L., "The Co-evolution of Technology and Organisation," in Joel et al. (eds.), *Evolutionary Dynamics of Organisations*. Oxford, U.K.: Oxford University Press, 1994, 403–424.

Roth, A. V., Griffi, G. A., & Seal, G. M., "Operating Strategies for the 1990s: Elements Comprising World-Class Manufacturing," in *Manufacturing Strategy*, C. Voss (ed.). London: Chapman & Hall, 1992.

Roussel, P. A., Saad, K. N., & Erickson, T. J., *Third Generation R&D—Managing the Link to Corporate Strategy*. Arthur D. Little, 1994.

Sanchez, R., "Managing Articulated Knowledge in Competence-Based Competition." Paper presented at the 3rd International Workshop on Competence-based Strategy, November 16–18, Ghent, Belgium, 1995.

Sanchez, R., "Strategic Flexibility in Product Competition," *Strategic Management Journal* 16, 1995, 9–30.

Sanchez, R., Heene, A., & Thomas, H., "Towards the Theory and Practice of Competence-Based Competition," in R. Sanchez, A. Heene, & H. Thomas (eds.), *Dynamics of Competence-Based Competition—Theory and Practice in the New Strategic Management*. London: Elsevier Science Ltd., 1996.

Savage, C. M., *Fifth Generation Management*. New York: Digital Press, 1990.

Schein, E. H., *Organizational Culture and Leadership*. San Francisco: Jossey-Bass, 1985.

Senge, P. M., *The Fifth Discipline*. Centrum Business, 1990a.

Senge, P. M., "The Leader's New Work: Building Learning Organisations," *Sloan Management Review* 10, 1990b, 83–98.

Shapiro, E., *Fad Surfing in the Boardroom*. Addison-Wesley, 1996.

Shenbar, A. J., "A New Conceptual Framework for Modern Project Management," Proceedings of the Fourth International Conference on Management of Technology, Miami, 1994.

Solberg, S. L., & Danielsen, A. A. (eds.), *Technology Management—Marketing-Oriented Use of New Technology*. Tano, 1992.

Spender, J. C., "Making Knowledge the Basis of a Dynamic Theory of the Firm," *Strategic Management Journal* 17, 1996, 45–62.

Stacy, R., *Strategic Management and Organizational Dynamics*. Englewood Cliffs, NJ: Prentice Hall, 1993.

Starbuck, W. H., "Strategizing in the Real World," *International Journal of Technology Management* 8, 1993, 117–136.

Steele, L. W., *Managing Technology—The Strategic View*. New York: McGraw-Hill, 1989.

Sterne, D., "Core Competencies: The Key to Corporate Advantage," *International Business* 3, 1989, 111–120.

Stewart, T. A., *Intellectual Capital—the New Wealth of Organizations*. London: Nicholas Brealey Publishing, 1997.

Sun, H., *Patterns of Organisational and Technological Development with Strategic Considerations*. Aalborg: Aalborg University, 1994.

Teece, D. J., Pisano, G., & Shuen, A., "Firm Capabilities, Resources, and the Concept of Strategy," CCC Working Paper No. 90-8, 1990.

Thomas, H., Heene, A., & Sanchez, R., "Towards the Theory and Practice of Competence-Based Competition," in H. Thomas, A. Heene, & R. Sanchez (eds.), *Dynamics of Competence-Based Competition*. Amsterdam: Elsevier Pergamon Press, 1997.

Thompson, J. D., *Organizations in Action*. New York: McGraw-Hill, 1967.

Tichy, N. M., Fombrun, C. J., & Devanna, M. A., "Strategic Human Resource Management," *Sloan Management Review* 23, 1982, 19–30.

Tidd, J., Bessant, J., & Pavitt, K., *Managing Innovation*. New York: John Wiley and Sons, 1997.

Tushman, M. L., & Anderson, P., "Technological Discontinuities and Organisational Environments," *Administrative Science Quarterly* 35, 1990, 1–8.

Tushman, M. L., & Rosenkopf, L., "Organizational Determinants of Technological Change," in *Research in Organizational Behaviour*, B. Staw & L. Cummings (eds.). 1986, 311–347.

Twiss, B., & Goodridge, M., *Managing Technology for Competitive Advantage*. London: Pitman Publishers, 1989.

Ulhøi, J. P., & Madsen, H., "Strategic Considerations in Technology Management," *Journal of Technology Analysis and Strategic Management* 17, 1993, 19–30.

Venkatesan, R., "Strategic Sourcing : To Make or Not to Make," *Harvard Business Review*, November-December, 1992, 39–42.

Voss, C. A., "Success and Failure in Advanced Manufacturing Technology," *International Journal of Technology Management* 11, 1988, 73–82.

Watkins, K. E., & Marsick, V. J., *Sculpting the Learning Organisation*. San Francisco: Jossey-Bass, 1993.

Watson, G. H., *Strategic Benchmarking*. New York: John Wiley and Sons, 1993.

Wernerfelt, B., "A Resource-based View of the Firm," *Strategic Management Journal* 5, 1984, 19–30.

Wick, C., & Leon, W., *The Learning Edge: How Smart Managers and Smart Companies Stay Ahead*. New York: McGraw-Hill, 1993.

Winter, S., "Knowledge and competence as strategic assets," in D. J. Teece (ed.), *The Competitive Challenge*. London: Ballinger, 1987, 159–184.

Womack, J. P., & Jones, D. T., "From Lean Production to the Lean Enterprise," *Harvard Business Review*, March-April 1994, 71–88.

Womack, J. P., Jones, D. T., & Ross, D., *The Machine That Changed the World*. New York: Von Nostrand Reinhold, 1992.

Yavitz, B., & Newmann, W. H., *Strategy in Action*. New York: The Free Press, 1982.

Yoshibara, H., "Towards a Comprehensive Concept of Strategic Adaptive Behavior of Firms," in *From Strategic Planning to Strategic Management*, H. I. Ansoff & R. Hayes (eds.). New York: John Wiley and Sons, 1976.

Zeleny, M., "High Technology Management," *Human Systems Management* 6, 1986, 109–120.

Index

ABOUT THE AUTHOR

ANDERS DREJER is Associate Professor of Industrial Management Systems in the Department of Production, Aalborg University. Dr. Drejer has published papers in several international journals including *Technovation, Technology Analysis & Strategic Management, The Learning Organization* and *International Journal of Technology Management,* and has co-authored several books. Dr. Drejer currently is a part of the Danish National Competence Center for Industrial Production and participates in a number of Danish and international research programs on Management of Technology and Competence Development.